THE NATURE OF HUMAN SOCIETY

TOWARDS A PAX AFRICANA

THE NATURE OF HUMAN SOCIETY SERIES

Editors: JULIAN PITT-RIVERS *and* ERNEST GELLNER

TOWARDS A PAX AFRICANA

A Study of Ideology and Ambition

Ali A. Mazrui

Professor of Political Science,
Makerere University College,
Kampala, Uganda

WEIDENFELD AND NICOLSON
5 WINSLEY STREET LONDON WI

To Muna

Printed in Great Britain
by Ebenezer Baylis and Son, Ltd.
The Trinity Press, Worcester and London

CONTENTS

CONTENTS

ACKNOWLEDGMENTS

A number of colleagues in Africa, Britain and the United States have helped me with suggestions and stimulation in this analysis. But special thanks must go to Mr John Plamenatz and Dame Margery Perham, my tutors at Oxford, to Professors Colin Leys and Donald Rothchild, former colleagues at Makerere University College, to Professors Aristide Zolberg and David Greenstone of the University of Chicago, and to Mr Yash P. Ghai of the University College, Dar-es-Salaam. I am also very grateful to Professor Ernest Gellner of the London School of Economics for reading the completed manuscript and making a number of very valuable suggestions.

This study was started when I was at Nuffield College, Oxford. It was completed when I was a guest of the African Studies Center, University of California, Los Angeles. To both these centres of learning I express my gratitude. Special thanks are also due to the Rockefeller Foundation which financed my visit to UCLA.

I am indebted also to Mrs Ailene Benson of UCLA for her patience and sense of personal involvement as she typed the manuscript.

In my wife I found a dedicated research assistant and critic. In my moments of indolence she also served as a loving conscience.

Responsibility for any faults in the book is, of course, entirely mine.

ALI A. MAZRUI

INTRODUCTION

In general terms we are concerned in this book with basic political ideas in contemporary Africa and with the vocabulary in which those ideas are expressed.

But what are 'ideas'? We do not propose to limit ourselves to notions which are *articulated* in spoken or written words. We define 'ideas' to include attitudes and behavioural assumptions which are not verbally expressed but seem nevertheless to be either *felt* or tacitly taken for granted. A major premise of our analysis is that the language in which nationalism is expressed is not an adequate guide to the real ideas which motivate it. In their relations with each other and with the rest of the world Africans often have to use English or French, but these languages as used by nationalists do not adequately reveal the range of ideological assumptions made by those nationalists. In this book we have therefore tried to interpret African political thought not merely on the basis of what African leaders say, but also on the evidence of general behaviour and emotional orientation in specific situations. In one chapter we have drawn from African attitudes to the European Economic Community, in another from aspects of the Congo scene, in yet another from the experience of military insubordination in East Africa. Specific events or situations such as these sometimes reveal more about the reality of African ideological orientation than might be discerned from an elaborate theoretical tract by an African leader.

Yet our concern is not merely with describing the core of nationalistic thought in Africa. We will also attempt to analyse the various implications of individual ideas. To lay bare the implications of a line of thought is, in part, to explore the degree of plausibility it commands. Our analysis will therefore often be evaluative as well as descriptive.

Most of the ideas we shall discuss will have international implications. In an important sense nationalism presupposes internationality. It postulates a relationship with some other nation or groups of nations. National consciousness when deeply felt includes an awareness of other nationalities. It is because of this factor that central concepts in African political thought have tended to have a diplomatic depth which antedates the formal diplomatic activity we associate with sovereign status.

A concept which is perhaps particularly vital for an understanding of African modes of reasoning in politics is the almost platitudinous idea of self-government. There is a sense in which many of the ideological stands taken by African leaders are either derived from the notion of self-government or are disguised 'replicas' of the same idea. But perhaps the most crucial aspect of the ethic of self-government in Africa lies in *the African's ambition to be his own policeman.* The following question has often been asked in the last few years: 'Now that the Imperial Order is coming to an end, who is going to keep the peace in Africa?'

The story of the crisis of the Congo since 1960 has, in a sense, been one of continuous attempt to find an answer to the question. In East Africa the question reared its head when a revolution in Zanzibar was followed by army mutinies on the mainland in January 1964. The problem is also implicit in the relationship of potential conflict between countries like Ethiopia and Somalia, Ghana and Togo and the Congo and some of her neighbours.

In November 1965 yet another type of situation raised the same question. This was the situation which was created when Ian Smith unilaterally declared Rhodesia's independence. An Africa capable of being her own policeman would have been capable of dealing with Ian Smith. Yet one of the agonizing features of the Rhodesian crisis for African nationalists was their own sense of military inadequacy.

It is considerations such as these which make Africa's freedom itself sometimes depend on an African capacity for self-pacification. This is what the concept of *Pax Africana* is all about. As a distinct African aspiration the idea of *Pax Africana* will receive special attention in Chapter 12 of this book. But, in a sense, all major African ambitions are related to it or tacitly take it for granted. Just as the notion of self-government is central to African political thought, the concept of *Pax Africana* is in turn central to the ambition of self-government in the continent.

The *self* in 'self-government' goes on to raise the issue of identity. And the problem of identity at the diplomatic level in turn poses a number of other questions. What is an African? Why the mystique of attachment to a continent? How does it affect African behaviour in international politics after independence? 'Interference in the Congo' – is there a difference between Negro interference, Arab interference and the use of white mercenaries in that country? How relative is the quality of being an African?

In the context of African nationalistic sensibilities the problem of identity is intimately related to the moral notion of human dignity. The relationship is perhaps something of a paradox. After all, when a man seeks his own identity, he is seeking those qualities which distinguish him from other men. But when he is concerned with asserting his *human* dignity, he is referring to those qualities which he *shares* with other men. Nevertheless, dignity and identity remain wedded together at the centre of African nationalistic thought.

This factor, too, has repercussions in international politics. Both dignity and identity provide some of the psychological motivation behind the quest for nonalignment by African states. And the two longings affect African conceptions of the purposes of the United Nations and the justification for its existence.

There are indeed points of contact between the assumptions of African diplomatic behaviour and the traditional norms of Western international conduct. There are also areas of dissonance between the language of nationalism which accompanied a colony to independence and the idiom of diplomatic discourse which is sometimes demanded of sovereign status. The points of contact referred to will be implicit in much of the discussion in the two analytical Sections of our study. The idiomatic dissonance is what disguises the freshness which sometimes characterizes African diplomatic attitudes.

A major ambition of this book is therefore to reveal the essential ideological reality which lies behind that idiomatic disguise.

Section I

IDEOLOGY AND IDENTITY

ON THE IDIOM OF
SELF-DETERMINATION

WHAT is diplomatic thought?

In this book we define diplomatic thought to be those ideas which form the basis of evaluating international events and of response to those events. Diplomatic thought does indeed include the finer points of formal diplomatic discourse and verbal etiquette, but of greater significance are the ideas which condition people's perspectives on global events.

In an important sense it is indeed true that African 'diplomacy' started with independence. Sovereign statehood became the point of African entry into international politics. But in another sense African nationalism has always had a diplomatic dimension. If that nationalism was not exactly inter-state, it was certainly inter-continental from an early stage. Pan-Africanism as an allegiance to the African continent was born out of Pan-Negroism as a commitment to the Negro race. And the sectors of the Negro race which were brought together in this way included the English-speaking Negroes of British Africa, the British West Indies and the United States.[1]

What loosened the ties between Africans and Afro-Americans was the emergence of 'independence' as the paramount slogan of the *African* sector. For as long as the slogan was 'Negro dignity' this was indeed a shared cause. But independence was a feasible proposition only for the colonized Negroes. And the Negroes of North America were not colonized in this sense.[2]

But what gave rise to that cry of 'independence' in Africa? How native to Africa was the ethic of self-government which this cry came to encompass?[3] Here we ought to distinguish between borrowing new ideas from the West and merely borrowing a new idiom with which to express primeval aspirations. There is a

3

tendency among political analysts to equate a previous absence of a special name for a phenomenon with an absence of the phenomenon itself. For example, an absence of a special word in an African language for 'opposition', as distinct from 'enemy', might be taken to mean that such a distinction was alien to the African society concerned.[4] What this chapter proposes to evaluate more closely is in part this relationship between *words* and *ideas*. But the essential point of reference will be the ethic of *'self-determination'* in the African context, and its general implications for language and ideology.

We might begin by conceding that the range of ideas in a given society can, to some extent, be measured by the yardstick of the society's range of vocabulary. What should be noted is that there is no 'one-to-one correlation' between words and ideas. The question might be asked: 'Which comes first – the idea or the word?' And one answer is that new words are coined only *after* the ideas they are supposed to designate have been already thought of. The idea of, shall we say, an 'agnostic' in religion must have occurred to at least the man who coined the word before the word itself was coined. If, then, words *follow* ideas, and do not coincide with them, one must allow for a theoretical time-gap between the birth of an idea and the emergence of a *single* word for it.

Was the idea of *self-determination* imported into Africa? We know that there were, in fact, pockets of resistance to the European intrusion among different tribal communities from the outset. The tribes who resisted the colonial scramble demonstrated their objection to being ruled by foreigners from distant European lands. This would suggest that the love of freedom among such people owed nothing to European influence but was, in fact, offended by the European incursion. Was not a belief in 'self-determination' then implicit in the behaviour of these early tribal resisters to European expansion?

There is enough evidence to show that a love of *self-government* at any rate is as native to Africa as 'the love of rhythm'. What was new when resistance was being expressed in English was at best the neo-Wilsonian idiom which much later came to be used.

And yet, true as this is, it is not a complete picture. The principle of self-determination could have been imported into

4

Africa even if the love of freedom was already native to the continent. This is because the principle of self-determination is, of course, more than a mere recognition that men love freedom of choice. It is an assertion that they are entitled to it. One might love something and still feel that one was not entitled to it. The love of freedom could be indigenous to Africa while the right to freedom was alien. It is conceivable, for example, for a traditional African community to have believed that everyone loved freedom but that only those who could defend it were entitled to it.

Another way in which the colonial experience might have modified African notions of 'self-government' hinges on the word 'self'. As Keith Hancock put it once: 'Self-government assumes the presence of a "self" which exists as a social fact and can be translated into a political fact. . . . All three territories of East Africa, to cite one example, contain many tribal "selves" and three racial "selves" . . .'[5]

When we talk of 'self-government' the question then arises as to which 'self'. And when we discuss 'foreign rule' the question arises as to what is a 'foreigner'. To take the Uganda area as an example, the Baganda in pre-colonial days would not have regarded themselves as 'self-governing' if a vital part of their affairs was in the dominating control of someone from Lango like Obote. Similar considerations apply to other groups in the area. Self-government for the Banyoro before colonial rule was surely government by the Banyoro.

But as a result of the colonial experience the meaning of the word 'self' has expanded. Not all Banyoro would now regard themselves as being under 'foreign rule' merely because the Government of Uganda does not consist of Banyoro. The whole notion of what is a 'foreigner' has now shrunk – and many who were once foreigners are now compatriots.

In short, although the idea of 'self-government' among the Banyoro must have antedated the colonial experience, that experience has re-defined for them not only the nature of 'government' but also the boundaries of the 'self'.

In the next chapter we shall examine more closely the various senses of 'self-government' which have affected African politics. But here suffice it to distinguish between 'self-government' as government by democratic institutions and 'self-government' as government manifestly belonging to the same ethnic group as the ruled. In 1954 James Coleman asserted that the nationalist movements in Africa were 'activated by the Western ideas of democracy . . . and self-determination'.[6] What was the relative importance of 'democracy' on the one hand and 'self-determination' on the other as sources of inspiration for African nationalism?

The sense of 'democracy' which was influential in British colonies was, as might be expected, the Anglo-Saxon version of the liberal ethic. This ethic is basically oriented towards *individual* freedom. The principle of self-determination, on the other hand, is usually oriented towards the freedom of a *group*. Both nationalism and tribalism are emotions of attachment to groups. But we hope to demonstrate in this chapter first, that nationalism in British Africa derived its original inspiration from an ethic of *individualism*, and second, that it was to *tribalism* that the principle of self-determination more meaningfully applied.

Given our general hypothesis about the role of the English language in opening up new areas of thought, it is not surprising that the initial Western philosophical influence on Africans should have come from an ethic of individualistic liberalism. Leading British philosophers have seldom concerned themselves in depth with issues like the definition of a 'nation', or the reality of a 'collective soul', or the concept of 'fatherland'. In some ways it is ironic that this should be so. Carlton J. H. Hayes has argued in the following terms:

> By the seventeenth and early eighteenth centuries, national patriotism was developed more generally and more acutely in England than in any other country – more so than in France or Spain or Sweden, and much more so than in Italy or Germany or eastern Europe. Indeed, we may affirm that modern nationalism, as we know it today, has its original seat in England.[7]

Hans Kohn has argued in similar terms in his book on the origins of nationalism.[8]

And yet neither Kohn nor Hayes sufficiently differentiated between national consciousness and nationalism itself. We may define 'national consciousness' here as a sense of shared national identity. We may define 'nationalism' as a more defensive or more assertive degree of that consciousness. In the course of time England became less 'nationalistic' precisely because it had a more highly developed 'national consciousness'. England did

6

indeed have her moments of militant nationalism – but she came to take her nationhood so much for granted that her philosophers spent relatively little time on it. And so when Hans Kohn comes round to paying special attention to *nineteenth*-century nationalism he finds himself choosing John Stuart Mill as the 'prophet' of British nationalism.[9] In the company of Mazzini, Treitschke, Michelet and Dostoevsky, John Stuart Mill is hardly a striking example of a 'people's prophet'. Kohn might have done better if he had looked for a British politician to symbolize British patriotism. British political philosophers were simply not adequately preoccupied with the 'fatherland'.

American political thought has had more of the nationalistic component than is found in British thought – but American thought has had more of the opposite tradition of individualism as well. In any case, the adoption by the United States of an *ethnically assimilative* form of federalism shifted philosophical analysis away from issues like 'the essence of nationality' to issues like state-rights and the civil rights of *individuals*. In the United States, as in England, 'the nation' as a 'spiritual' entity came to be taken substantially for granted – and instead of meditating about nationhood, the most towering political thinkers in both countries concerned themselves with problems of devising suitable institutions to realize certain individualistic or regional values at home.[10]

Of the philosophies which were available in the original to English-speaking Africans, this Anglo-Saxon liberalism inevitably constituted the bulk. The result was that the rhetoric of African nationalism in British Africa was not, in fact, filled with repetitions of the term 'self-determination', as might be expected. What were more common in the language of nationalism were terms like 'individual freedom', 'democracy' and 'one man, one vote'.

Another reason why African nationalism was expressed in terms of institutional liberalism rather than those of 'nationality' arose out of the British conception of eligibility for independent existence. The principle of 'national self-determination' implied that whoever was 'nationally distinct' and wanted a separate existence was entitled to it. But British colonial reasoning asserted that independence was not automatically a right of those who were nationally distinct. It was more a right of those who were capable of maintaining liberal democratic institutions and of safeguarding individual freedom.

In 1952 Azikiwe reminded his countrymen of this British view. He said:

Thanks to the growth of political consciousness in this country our people are becoming acquainted with the practice of parliamentary democracy. This has been used as a criterion to determine the political maturity of any people under the rule of others and we can be no exception. As a matter of fact, it is a declared policy of Britain that no colony can be considered ready for self-government until it has made parliamentary democracy a political reality.[11]

Azikiwe at that time did not object to this criterion of eligibility for independence. He merely urged his countrymen to make possible 'a full-fledged two-party system in operation'.[12] The Anglo-Saxon basis of evaluating political maturity kept on affecting Azikiwe's own line of reasoning.

And as late as 1959 this sort of approach to problems of decolonization continued to be discernible in the idiom of British colonial policy. In April 1959 Alan Lennox Boyd, speaking for the government in the House of Commons, was defining British intentions in a colony in the following familiar terms:

The responsibility of Her Majesty's Government is to all the inhabitants of Kenya. . . . It would be a betrayal of that responsibility if we were to abandon our ultimate authority prematurely. . . . First, there must be in the territory as a whole a sufficient understanding of parliamentary institutions, and sufficient sense of responsibility in public affairs to hold out a reasonable prospect that parliamentary institutions, representative of the people, will produce responsible government. . . . Self-government, I think we would all agree, is but a mockery if it is purchased at the expense of personal freedom.[13]

In the context of such values capacity for self-government was, in effect, capacity for Anglo-Saxon liberalism. And the right to such government rested on that liberal capacity, and not on national distinctiveness.

A third reason why the term 'self-determination' was not more in evidence in the earlier days of African nationalism concerned the relative lack of national identity in the individual African territories. The principle of self-determination had too often assumed an old-established 'nation' currently under foreign rule. But Thomas Hodgkin has reminded us that:

There is no African Mazzini; no Gandhi or Sun Yat-Sen. This is not surprising. African nationalism differs from the nationalisms of India and China in that Africa exists as an idea only, projected into the future, not as an historic fact. There has been no single comprehensive civilisation, no common background of written culture, to which nationalists could refer.[14]

Demands for self-determination in Europe and, to a lesser extent, in Asia had often rested on cultural distinctiveness. It is precisely because of this that when the same principle of self-determination was referred to Africa, it was more to the Ashanti than to the Gold Coast that it appeared to be theoretically applicable. We can almost say that the impact of the West on Africa for the rest of this century has not been in the direction of making 'self-determination' possible – but has, on the contrary, tended towards making ethnically meaningful self-determination impractical.

It was in this century that an English-speaking statesman, Woodrow Wilson, came at last to capture the leadership in enunciating the ethic of self-determination. Commenting on that ethic Sir W. Ivor Jennings once said: 'On the surface it seemed reasonable: let the people decide. It was in fact ridiculous because the people cannot decide until somebody decides who are the people.'[15]

This is what would have made the principle more meaningful in pre-colonial Africa than it was in the Europe of Wilson's time. In pre-colonial Africa deciding who 'the people' were in each instance was easier because social organization was less complicated. Each society was organized in relatively small and culturally homogeneous groups – and quite often each group was a people. But Europe had got past that stage when it started to organize itself into large dynastic empires and then into large territorial states. As a Commission of the League of Nations observed in 1921:

To concede to minorities either of language, or religion, or to any fractions of a population, the right of withdrawing from the community to which they belong because it is their wish or their good pleasure, would be to ... uphold a theory incompatible with the very idea of the State as a territorial entity.[16]

The principle of self-determination as enunciated in Europe after World War I could easily amount to a 'Back to Tribalism'

9

clarion call. National self-determination in Europe was, in other words, a nostalgic call for a return to primeval *tribal* self-determination, at least in the sense of trying to make the units of political organization coincide with narrow ethnic identity.

A similar nostalgia has come to hit parts of Africa as a result of the Western impact. As a Prime Minister of the Republic of the Congo (Leopoldville) put it in 1961: 'The Congo is not a people. It is a collection of large ethnic groups and each of them is a people.'[17]

To whom then was self-determination to apply? We are reminded once again of Ivor Jennings' observation that 'the people cannot decide until somebody decides who are the people'.[18]

Yet if the Congo was not a people but a collection of peoples who then were the 'Congolese'? One safe answer is that Congolese are natives of that territorial entity which bears the name of 'the Congo'. This is what brings us to the relevance of *boundaries* in the issue of self-determination. In 1920 a Committee of Jurists appointed by the Council of the League of Nations reported that national self-determination was not recognized by positive international law. It said: 'In the absence of express provisions in international treaties, the right of disposing of national territory is essentially an attribute of the sovereignty of every State.'[19]

It is precisely this identification of sovereignty with territorial boundaries which made self-determination so difficult a precept to apply in the Europe of territorial States and in the Africa of the independent Republic of the Congo. In pre-colonial Africa, on the other hand, it was still possible in some regions for a small clan dissatisfied with the parent tribe to move physically and establish itself elsewhere. This might be called *nomadic self-determination*. Edmund Burke's definition of 'a country' would have found ready supporters in the Africa of such mobility. Burke had asserted:

> Our country is not a thing of mere physical locality. It consists in a great measure in the ancient order into which we are born. We may have the same geographical situation, but another country, as we may have the same country in another soil. The place that determines our duty to our country is a social, civil relation.[20]

In situations which allow for nomadic self-determination this assertion would not be devoid of sense. But in Europe self-determination had come to mean not merely determining what was going to happen to the *self*, but also determining what was going to happen to the *territory* on which the self was now resident.

A special case of nomadic self-determination was involved in the 'Back to Africa' movements of Negroes in the New World. One such movement was the unsuccessful but ideologically influential one which was led by Marcus Garvey. The Negroes in the New World were a people who had been exported to the Americas by the most blatant of all denials of freedom of choice – outright enslavement. But the dilemma as between migrating back to Africa or remaining in the United States was at times based on a meaningful set of alternatives, especially in those recurrent periods when Liberia actively tried to recruit immigrants from the United States. It would therefore be true to say that the Negroes who did return to their ancestral soil had in the main exercised some kind of nomadic self-determination.

But what about the freedom of choice of those native Africans on whom the Negro repatriates from America now descended? Was this a case in which a loose nomadic sense of self-determination exercised by Negroes from the New World came into conflict with the rights of indigenous Africans? Two hundred years or more had passed since the Negroes now returning were originally enslaved and exported. Were they still 'natives of Africa' returning home? Or were they now a new breed of invaders *denying* self-determination to others?

Rupert Emerson has no doubt about the answer in regard to the analogous case of Zionism and the creation of Israel. Emerson has argued in these terms:

> The conception of creating a Jewish national home in Palestine could not possibly be squared with the principle of self-determination, or, for that matter, of democracy, on the basis of any generally accepted criteria. Aside from the fact that many Jews wanted to establish themselves there, the only claim which had any conceivable status was that Palestine had been the ancient Jewish homeland many centuries ago; but to accept the legitimacy of claims to self-determination whose basis is possession broken off two thousand years earlier would be to stir up such a host of conflicting and unrealizable demands as totally to discredit the principle.[21]

It is true that by the normal accepted criteria of self-determination, Zionists could not legitimize their claims to Palestine on the basis of that principle. Even by the canons of nomadic self-determination what was legitimate was at best the right of Jews from different parts of the world to migrate *towards* Palestine – but the creation of a separate Jewish state there had to have another rationale.

Nevertheless, there *was* something rather nomadic about the idea of a 'return' to Palestine after twenty centuries of life in different corners of the earth. The 'nomadic' element would perhaps have been even more pronounced if the state of Israel had been created in *Kenya*, as Joseph Chamberlain had once proposed to the Jews, instead of in Palestine.[22] For a state of Israel in Eastern Africa, consisting of Jews from Eastern and Western Europe, from America, and from Palestine itself, would have introduced an additional dimension to the migratory record of the Jewish people. Yet how consistent such an eventuality would have been with the tribal rights of, say, the Kikuyu is a further factor to be borne in mind in evaluating the ethics of the hypothesis.

Be that as it may, it is with a different kind of nomadic problem that present-day Kenya is involved. Kenya's delegation to the Addis Ababa conference in 1963 described Pan-Somalism as a 'tribalistic doctrine'. Given this conception of the Somalis as a 'tribe', the question was whether self-determination as applied to them would mean transfer of territory or merely transfer of population. The Kenya delegation at Addis Ababa was emphatic about its answer: 'If they do not want to live with us in Kenya, they are perfectly free to leave us and our territory. . . . This is the only way they can legally exercise their right of self-determination.'[23]

In present-day Europe the nearest instance of nomadic self-determination has been in regard to movement of population between the two Germanies. In the Wilsonian sense of the principle, the East Germans were denied self-determination when they were denied the right to vote on the future of East Germany. But in the nomadic sense of self-determination, it was the Berlin Wall rather than merely the denial of free elections which denied the East Germans ultimate determination of their future. By the same token, the Somalis of Kenya would only be completely denied self-determination if Kenya prevented them from moving eastwards into the Somali Republic.

There are, of course, important differences between the issue of East Germany and the issue of the old Northern Frontier District of Kenya. But suffice it to say in this context that when Western observers described the exodus of East Germans westwards as a case of people 'voting with their feet', the observers came near to enunciating the kind of 'self-determination' which operated in Africa before the white man came – and which much later was to be invoked by a Kenya delegation to the Addis Ababa conference as an answer to the Somali problem.

As part of the conclusion of this aspect of the matter, we might re-formulate the principle once again. The old tribal principle of nomadic self-determination seemed to assert a right to decide the fate of the *self* without necessarily deciding the fate of the *area* within which the self had so far found a home. Something approaching such a principle must have been implicit in the tribal migrations which took place in the recent history of different parts of the continent. What the West imported into Africa could not therefore have been this principle. At best it could only have been that which makes this principle so difficult to apply now. If every inch of Africa now 'belongs' to one *State* or another, and territorial frontiers now define units of social organization, the tribal mobility which implied a nomadic principle of self-determination is now hampered by defiantly immobile territorial boundaries. It is the latter phenomenon which bears the label 'imported from the West'.

As for the Wilsonian concept of self-determination, that is even less practical now than it was in pre-colonial tribal days. In the words of the Kenya delegation at Addis Ababa in 1963, 'the principle of self-determination . . . has no relevance where the issue is territorial disintegration.'[24]

This fear of disintegration takes us back to the liberal idiom of English-speaking African nationalism. Since the ethic of self-determination normally connotes, as we have noted, the freedom of *groups*, leaders like Tom Mboya have preferred to emphasize instead the rights of *individuals* regardless of the ethnic group to which they belong. That is why he opposed the idea of regional autonomy as a safeguard of the collective interests of small tribes in Kenya. And that is why he also opposed special safeguards for racial minorities. As he put it once in discussing the latter type of safeguards: 'If there are going to be guarantees, they should not be just for Asians and Europeans, but for all of us as *citizens* of this country.'[25]

In the same speech Mboya referred to the demand for regional autonomy by Kenya's smaller tribes. He condemned it as a demand for 'the fragmentation of Kenya'.

As for Mboya's conception of the African struggle as a whole, he described it elsewhere in the neo-liberal idiom of being 'a struggle . . . based on moral issues and in defence of basic human rights and fundamental freedoms.' He urged Africa to assert even after independence a 'noble emphasis of dedication to freedom for the individual'.[26]

In the colonial struggle the call for individual freedom still made *nationalistic* sense in a situation in which the majority of individuals were *Africans*. And because independence had thus been demanded by appealing to liberal individualism rather than to collective self-determination, there was no inconsistency after independence in denying 'self-determination' to the Somalis and other 'tribal' *groups*. All that the Somalis could demand were their rights as individual citizens of Kenya.

But was there no group identity involved in African nationalism? Some collective identity had in fact to be present if it was to be 'nationalism' at all. As we have argued already the group identity at the beginning of African nationalism was the identity of *blackness* racially. This brings us to the only sense of 'self-determination' that has been present in African nationalism all along – a kind of implied *pigmentational* self-determination. The principle in this case asserted a right which did look at first glance like a Wilsonian sense of self-determination. Nkrumah once framed the case in the following terms: 'The problem of Africa, looked at as a whole, is a wide and diversified one. But its true solution lies in the application of one principle, namely, the right of a people to rule themselves.'[27]

The Jennings' objection raises itself again – What is a people? Nkrumah does not seem interested in a precise definition. For him there is at least one kind of situation where foreign rule is conspicuous – and that is when the rulers are white and the ruled are evidently a different colour. He said in the same speech: 'The idea that when a handful of [white] settlers acquire a living space on our continent the indigenes must lose their right is . . . a serious travesty of justice. . . . I have always emphasized that

Africa is not, and can never be, an extension of Europe. . . .'[28]

It will be seen that *pigmentational self-determination* is not only different from Wilsonian but is almost a rejoinder to Wilson. Stewart C. Easton has pointed out that 'President Wilson's principle of self-determination, though it found answering echoes in European breasts, was not thought of by any European power to be applicable to the peoples of their colonies, who were not fit for self-government – at least not yet.'[29]

Rupert Emerson has gone further and suggested that even Wilson himself did not seem sure whether he wanted the principle of self-determination applied to non-European peoples under colonial rule, in addition to dynastic intra-European empires.[30]

If Woodrow Wilson had believed in *pigmentational* self-determination, his order of priorities would have been reversed. He would have condoned more readily internal European empires while condemning trans-racial European expansionism into Asia and Africa.[31]

But the idea of *some* kind of self-determination assumed importance for Africa not after World War I and Wilson's ambivalent enthusiasm but in the course of World War II and following it. An important contributory factor to the popularity of the principle among African nationalists was the Atlantic Charter which President Franklin Roosevelt and Prime Minister Winston Churchill signed on 14 August 1940. Again the Charter, as a declaration of common Anglo-American principles, did not use the term 'self-determination' as such. But it did say that the United States and the United Kingdom 'respect the right of all peoples to choose the form of government under which they will live; and they wish to see sovereign rights and self-government restored to those who had been forcibly deprived of them.'[32]

This statement was taken by many people in the colonies as a promise of self-government for them too. But in the House of Commons Churchill was soon to disillusion attentive nationalists in Asia and Africa. Churchill said to the Commons:

At the Atlantic meeting we had in mind, primarily, the restoration of the sovereignty, [and] self-government . . . of the States and Nations of Europe now under Nazi yoke . . . so that this is quite a separate problem from the progressive evolution of self-governing institutions in the regions and peoples which owe allegiance to the British Crown.[33]

But Churchill had already exposed himself to demands for an

extension of the principle of self-government to subject peoples elsewhere. The Atlantic Charter stirred the national aspirations of politically conscious West Africans. In April 1943 the West African Students Union in London sent in a demand to the Colonial Office for dominion status. A group of West African editors, with Azikiwe as leader, prepared a memorandum entitled *The Atlantic Charter and British West Africa*, visited Britain, and asked for substantial political reforms. And among the resolutions passed by the Pan-African Congress of Manchester in 1945 was one which demanded that 'the principles of the . . . Atlantic Charter be put into practice at once.'[34]

Yet by limiting the Charter's application to subject peoples in Europe only, Churchill had declared himself to be even less of a believer in *pigmentational self-determination* than Wilson had been. Trans-racial domination was all right to Churchill, given that the ruler was white. It was intra-Caucasian subjugation that his Atlantic Charter protested against.

Nevertheless, the Atlantic Charter, as an affirmation by the two leading Anglo-Saxon powers, remains an important document in the history of nationalism in English-speaking Africa. But, as we shall discuss more fully in a later chapter, a new Charter was born in 1945. It was not long before this new United Nations Charter effectively replaced the Atlantic Charter as the ultimate source of legitimation for anti-colonialism. By 1955 the Bandung Conference was declaring its support specifically for 'the principles of self-determination of peoples and nations as set forth in the United Nations Charter.'[35]

But why have nationalists needed such documents in the formulation of their demands? The main reason why the authority of such Charters was invoked was, of course, in order to lend greater diplomatic weight to the demands of the colonial politicians. And so the names of the Charters themselves, and sometimes some appropriate phrases from the texts, became part of the total linguistic equipment of nationalism. A related question to the one which has just been answered is: 'Why do people make their demands in the particular language in which they do make them?'

A basic reason for the choice of language might simply be that the people know no other. Another reason which the people might have is when the phraseology is old and reassuring. A third reason for preferring a particular idiom is almost the opposite – the idiom is tempting to use because it is new and exciting. This certainly applied to many of the phrases which African nationalists went out of their way to use in their political language – ranging from direct Marxist echoes like 'capitalistic exploitation' to phrases like 'manifest destiny' borrowed from American rhetoric.[36]

But perhaps the most pertinent reason for the choice of a particular way of formulating one's demands is when the formulation is likely either to persuade the addressee into complying with your demands, or to embarrass him if he persists in refusing to comply. Africa's use of the liberal idiom in its nationalism must have been determined by each of these factors at one time or another. And although the specific term 'self-determination' has been used more sparingly than might have been expected, it has at times been used in the specific pigmentational sense of opposition to 'colonialism'.

But what is the nature of this relationship between the idea of self-determination and the concept of colonialism? Both Lord Hailey and Margery Perham have indicated that the term 'colonialism' is, in general, a term of abuse.[37] If they are right, then to use the word 'colonialism' is normally to assert your anti-colonialism. To assert your anti-colonialism is to demand 'self-determination' in at least one sense. The paradoxical conclusion is therefore that the term 'colonialism' *implies* self-determination – that he who uses the former word is often also demanding or applauding the application of the latter principle.

As for the history of the word 'colonialism' it seems to have come rather late into the vocabulary of Afro-Asian nationalism. In her first Reith Lecture, Margery Perham remarked that 'colonialism' was 'a new word, or at least a word that has been used in a new way during the last few years.'[38] Six years before that a Beit Professor of the History of the British Empire at Oxford asserted with greater conviction the newness of the term. Professor Vincent Harlow said: 'It is a word with a short but remarkable history. It does not appear to be more than about three years old: it is not yet in the dictionaries; but it has quickly become a propaganda instrument of great power.'[39]

Harlow himself speculated as to whether the word was 'invented' at the Asian-African Conference at Bandung. In some sense it *ought* perhaps to have been invented at Bandung in any case. This is because colonialism did represent, to use Harlow's words, 'the debasement of the coloured world at the feet of Western Europe.'[40] And Bandung in 1955 represented a moment of solidarity for the coloured world.

Be that as it may, the word 'colonialism' remains a powerful instance of the emergence of a new term to designate an old phenomenon. On the other hand, the post-independence term of *neo*-colonialism is, in a sense, precisely the reverse. It is a case of slightly modifying a relatively old term to designate what might be a new phenomenon in Africa's experience.

Yet why should it be necessary to use an old name for something new? In the relationship between words and abstract ideas, we have already argued that an idea precedes the coining of a single word for it. What we ought now to note is that in the relationship between words and events, or words and concrete phenomena at large, the sequence is less straightforward. There are occasions when a word is coined as a label for a new type of event which has yet to happen – though an event which has, of course, been already thought of or envisaged. However, there are other occasions when political language is left behind political events.

One good, if somewhat digressive, example of the latter eventuality is the case of British constitutional language. In his Inaugural Lecture at Hull in 1962, Professor A. H. Birch argued that the language of British political discourse in the twentieth century had lagged behind changes in the British political system itself. Birch said:

> In the nineteenth century the liberal view of the constitution was in part an idealised picture of existing practice and in part an ideology of reform. As this idealised picture came to be widely accepted so the liberal way of describing the constitution passed into general usage. In this fashion what was once an ideology became a language. In the twentieth century the practice of government does not conform to this picture, but most people continue to discuss politics in liberal terms.[41]

And so a term like 'sovereignty of parliament' continues to be used as if the balance of initiative had not shifted towards the executive. And the principle of 'ministerial responsibility' is invoked with little regard for its practical utility in contemporary British politics. Here then is a case of constitutional language being left behind by other constitutional developments – with significant consequences both for Britain herself and for the history of the central political institutions of former British Africa.

By the same token one of the more pressing *diplomatic* problems of those new African states is that they are landed with a vocabulary of evaluation which developed in the limited political activity of opposition to 'colonialism'. On attainment of independence the new states came to be faced with a wide range of global issues on which they are only just beginning to feel the need for definite opinions of their own. The leaders then have to devise policies, take international stands, and try to influence events. But they have to carry much of this out in an anti-colonialist vocabulary which, in the twilight of imperial rule, often has a ring of sheer obsolescence.

There are occasions when African nationalists are evidently guilty of a misapplication of old evaluative concepts to new situations. But the student of political events must allow for the possibility of a re-interpretation of old concepts to cope with new challenges. A new social conscience in some part of the world might, for example, dictate a re-interpretation of an old idea like 'equality of opportunity'. Or the new conscience might make distinctions between 'negative freedom' and 'positive freedom' in an attempt to give the old word *freedom* a new social dimension. And faced with a new challenge like that of the Common Market, on the one hand, with on the other hand a sentimental British attachment to the old doctrine of the sovereignty of Parliament, advocates of British entry into the European Economic Community could in 1962 set out to re-define the old doctrine of parliamentary sovereignty with the help of phrases like 'expansion of sovereignty' or 'pooling of sovereignties'. All this might be done in order to still one's own doubts, or steal the thunder of one's opponents, or genuinely lend a new depth to an old concept.

But it still remains true that when confronted with a stage crisis which calls for improvisation, the plight of an old artist like Britain who has known a whole range of roles over the years is more fortunate than the predicament of the new star just emerging on the world stage, with a limited equipment of past lines to invoke. In this perhaps lies the case for closer attentiveness to the idiom improvised by the new arrival – just in case there is a level of meaningful subtlety beneath all that exasperating simplicity.

This is why a discussion of 'self-determination' has been important as a prelude to understanding the other principles discussed in the following chapters. In the next chapter we hope to demonstrate that the central concept in African nationalistic thought is not so much self-determination as *self-government*. Given a choice people might, on occasion, as readily 'determine' to be ruled by others as to rule themselves. But when a people do choose to be ruled by a foreigner, they are not in that instance behaving in a *nationalistic* manner. That is why the central concept in African nationalism is not merely a desire for the right to *make* a choice – but is the choice of self-government itself.

Nevertheless, 'self-determination' needed to be given prior analysis in order to indicate the special meanings it had assumed in the context of African nationalistic thought. The implicit notion of pigmentational self-determination is intimately related to the more positive principle of racial sovereignty which the next chapter will examine. Yet the 'sovereignty of the African peoples' as an idea would itself need to be broken down into further theoretical components – including the sheer consciousness of being 'all Africans' and the assertion of some kind of internal continental jurisdiction over African affairs.

The Anglo-Saxon liberal idiom and the English language continue to play a part in African diplomatic discourse. Indeed, to former British Africa the English language is the ultimate medium of participation in international affairs. But although this sharing of the English language imposes a certain similarity of political idiom between Africa and other English-speaking areas, that similarity has got increasingly more deceptive.

What the following chapters seek to accomplish is a theoretical penetration into some of the inner postulates and assumptions of African modes of argument and evaluation as centred on the all-pervasive ethic of self-government.

CHAPTER TWO

ON THE PRINCIPLE OF RACIAL
SOVEREIGNTY

IN THE last chapter we discussed the utilization of the principle of 'self-determination' in the anti-colonial struggle in Africa. We analysed some of the recurrent themes in the language of opposition to imperial rule. This chapter takes the discussion further and links the principle of self-determination to the broader ramifications of *self-government* at large.

Although we are forced at times to talk about 'self-government' as if it was a single principle, we should only do so in the awareness that there are at least five concepts of self-government involved in the politics of anti-colonialism. There is, first, self-government as an absence of colonial rule; secondly, self-government as sovereign independence, with all its ramifications in relations with other countries; thirdly, self-government as internal management of internal affairs, including the maintenance of law and order, a matter which may have serious implications externally; fourthly, self-government in the liberal democratic sense as government supported 'by the will of the nation, substantially declared';[1] and fifthly, self-government as government by rulers manifestly belonging to the same race as the ruled.

In the idiom of nationalism these different concepts of self-government are not always neatly distinguished. Indeed, it has at times taken a Jacques Soustelle to distinguish, for example, between self-government as an absence or termination of colonial rule and self-government as complete sovereign independence. As he himself put it, adroitly addressing an American audience in December 1960 in the course of a television debate with Ghana's Ambassador, Alex Quaison-Sackey:

... there are two ways of giving freedom to the people. The first one is to give them complete independence or a large measure of autonomy, as the United States did with the Philippine Islands and Puerto Rico. The other one is to admit the people of the territory into a nation on a full equality, such as the United States did in the case of Hawaii and Alaska.[2]

By the same token self-government for Algeria did not have to take the form of independence. In fact, to the extent that Algeria had already the status of being 'part' of a free country, France, Soustelle felt that the term 'colony' did not in any case apply to Algeria. He added: 'I think the time is ripe now to go further and to formally admit the Algerian province within the French Republic. That is what we call integration, or "The Hawaiian Way".'[3]

History, as it turned out, was not on the side of Soustelle on the specific issue of the future of Algeria. But for purposes of analysis what concerns us here is the distinction he emphasized. Even if we insisted that the term 'colony' did apply to Algeria at the time that Soustelle was claiming otherwise, it was still theoretically true that Algeria could have ceased to be a colony and still not become a separate independent state.

But even Soustelle was not sufficiently discriminating in his classification of types of self-government. The 'complete independence' of the Philippines and the 'large measure of autonomy' given to Puerto Rico did not amount to one type of self-government but to two distinct ones. The case of Puerto Rico is analogous to that of Southern Rhodesia before the declaration of independence – a 'self-governing colony' at best. This is a third concept of self-government – what we have described above as 'internal management of internal affairs'.

The fourth concept, that of liberal democratic self-government, is at times designated as 'majority rule'. But in fact this designation has led to confusion with that fifth concept of ethnic self-government mentioned above. To put it in another way, two senses of 'majority rule' have tended to be invoked in evaluating African events. One sense of 'majority rule' requires that the rulers should be *popular* and, as far as possible, institutionally answerable to those they rule. This is the usual liberal concept. The other sense of 'majority rule' requires that the rulers should broadly be of the same ethnic or racial stock as those they rule. Both types of rulers were sometimes described as 'representative' – but in the second category the rulers or leaders were 'representative' in the sense of being ethnically 'typical' rather than democratically accountable.

In the history of colonial liberation movements it was more often the ethnic conception of 'majority rule', rather than the orthodox liberal one, which had pride of place in African nationalistic thought. Yet for as long as the nationalist movements had the support of the general populace as a whole, this distinction was merely academic. The nationalist leaders were 'representative' by the canons of both liberalism and ethnic typicality.

Nevertheless, ethnicity as a basis of legitimation in African nationalistic thought cannot be over-emphasized. All the five concepts of self-government converge on it. It is this central point of contact between all the five concepts of self-government that we have called the principle of *racial sovereignty*.

One approach towards unravelling the implications of this concept is to look not so much at what the nationalists themselves say, but at the statements and reactions of others within the same general field of colonial discourse. In November 1960 the United Nations General Assembly was presented with an Afro-Asian resolution calling for a 'speedy' end to colonialism. The resolution included a provision which insisted that 'inadequacy of political, economic and cultural preparedness' should not serve as a pretext for delaying independence. Dismay and scepticism characterized some Western reactions to this resolution. The *New York Times*, for example, was 'dubious' about the provision which rejected the test of readiness for self-government: 'This provision is in obvious conflict with the Charter provisions calling for *prior* development of free institutions in areas where they do not as yet exist. It should be modified to avert new and even more dangerous crises like that in the Congo.'[4]

We might first note that in the paper's reasoning there is a jump from an absence of 'free institutions' to a Congo-type lack of any effective institutions at all. To put it another way, the *New York Times* uses in one sentence a capacity for *democratic* self-government as the criterion of independence; and in the next sentence it switches to the criterion of being able to cope with what are considered to be basic demands of sovereign independence.

There is another thing which emerges from the passage from the *New York Times*. The paper appears here to be putting forward a case for denying independence to those areas where free institutions 'do not as yet exist'. And yet in another editorial only the previous month the same paper found it 'easy to agree . . . that Africa should be developed for the good of its own people and should not be under the control of any outside nation or bloc.'[5]

This is hardly to be interpreted as meaning that the paper would not include Africa, or much of the continent, among areas where 'free institutions' did 'not as yet exist'. Yet if the *New York Times* had found it 'easy to agree' that Africa should not be under the control of an outside power – in spite of lacking free institutions – what had happened to the paper's stand that only those areas with such institutions should have independence?

There was, in effect, neither a retraction nor a contradiction involved in the two stands taken by the paper. Taking the Congo as a case in point, one might say that the reconciliation between the two stands lay in the fact that the first stand ('No independence without free institutions') applied to that territory up to 29 June 1960 and no further. The second stand (that the Congo 'should not be under the control of any outside nation') assumed validity from 30 June 1960 when the independent Republic of the Congo was inaugurated.

What emerges from all this reinforces John Plamenatz's deceptively simple observation: 'There are many countries independent which are not free, and no one would suggest that they ought to be deprived of their independence in order to be made capable of freedom.'[6]

But the Congo itself was not so much a country which needed to be made, in Plamenatz's phrase, 'capable of freedom', as a country which needed to be made capable of authority. But to the extent that freedom in this instance needed some authority, and that where there were no effective institutions at all, there could not be meaningful 'free institutions', the Congo might serve as an extreme case of incapacity for freedom. Nevertheless, people who might have protested against independence for the Congo before it was granted, on grounds of such incapacity, have been known to object to a withdrawal of that independence after it was granted. A representative of no less a colonial power than France – herself a firm if inconsistent believer for so long in the dictum that independence outside Europe and North America was for those who were capable of it – could virtually embrace the view that, capable or not, the Congo after 30 June 1960 was to keep her independence. Answering the accusation of the representative of the Soviet Union in the United Nations that the Western powers wished to infringe the independence of the young Congolese state, Armand Berand of France argued that it was the kind of United Nations' interference demanded by the Soviet Union at the time which would amount to 'attacking the independence of that state'. The Frenchman went on to assert: 'My delegation and my Government would in no circumstances whatsoever be able to follow him along that course of action.'[7]

One question which arises is: Why not? From the point of view of the moral legitimacy of one people governing another who were 'not ready to govern themselves', why should withholding independence have been different from withdrawing it? The 'incapacity' for freedom or self-government was presumably still there – the only difference in the case of the Congo was that such 'incapacity' had, by 1960, ceased to be a hypothetical and convenient presumption by the ruling Belgian administration and had become a demonstrated actuality for all to observe. This should have reinforced rather than invalidated the moral case for getting the Congo to be governed by others once again. Why then had it not?

Plamenatz sees the distinction in terms of its being 'one thing to intervene in other people's domestic affairs, and quite another to wash your hands of them when you have long been responsible for running their affairs.'[8] One presumption behind Plamenatz's distinction seems to be that colonial rule did not constitute 'intervening in other people's domestic affairs'. But since he himself could hardly deny that by ruling the Congolese the Belgians were ruling a people other than themselves, why was Belgian rule not intervention in 'other' people's domestic affairs?[9]

This is where the idea of formal *sovereignty* as understood in Western diplomatic experience comes into play. A Plamenatz who sees a distinction between 'the domestic affairs' of the Congolese after independence and their affairs before they attained that status might indeed have sympathized with the United Nations' insistence in September 1960 that Belgian troops should leave the Congo. A Westerner might even have agreed that those Belgian troops in September 1960 were now 'troops of aggression'[10] – though the same Westerner could have regarded the presence of such troops in the Congo before the end of June in that same year as being perfectly legitimate.

Such an ambivalence in a Westerner is not difficult to understand considering the extent to which attitudes are conditioned by accepted phraseology. If the Congo before the end of June 1960 was a Belgian 'colony' then, by definition, 'sovereignty' over it resided in Belgium – and the term 'Belgian troops of aggression' could therefore hardly apply while the Congo still 'belonged' to Belgium. The African nationalists themselves have been, to some extent, restricted within the same conceptual prison walls of international discourse. They have, however, been trying to break out of them in relation to the position of colonialism in international law.

But what are the conceptual prison walls of the language of 'aggression' and 'sovereignty'? A step towards an answer can be taken by defining 'aggression' in the classical Western sense as 'attempted diminution by force of a territory's sovereignty'. The diminution can be territorial – annexing part of the country itself – or it can be in terms of trying to reduce the internal power and jurisdiction of the country's government. In the classical Western sense the word 'attempted' in the definition is crucial. When the diminution of sovereignty has actually been accomplished, and recognized by others as so accomplished, the phase of 'aggression' has passed. In other words, aggression in this Western sense ceases to be aggression when it is totally successful and recognized as such. This is particularly so if the aggression has taken the form of territorial annexation, for success in this is tangible and easier to establish as a fact. If, then, sovereignty is definable to the Westerner as 'power and jurisdiction over a given area and answerability for that area to other nations under international law' aggression as an attempt to encroach on that power ceases when there is no more power to encroach upon. The phase of aggression is passed when sovereignty, as that power, changes hands.

It is these underlying implications of 'aggression' in the classical Western sense that constitute the prison walls of the language of international discourse. And the dilemma of the anti-colonialist is particularly marked among the so-called 'moderates' of Afro-Asian nationalism. In the heat of that first controversy over the legitimate government of the Congo in 1960, President Habib

Bourguiba of Tunisia, for example, implied a distinction between the legitimate exercise of sovereignty from the point of view of the country's own constitution before some trouble arises and legitimacy from the point of view of external relations. 'Does anyone in Egypt, Iraq, Pakistan, Nepal or South America ask whether the local government is constitutional or not?' And the moral Bourguiba drew was that 'in international relations today the Government that can maintain order and properly conduct the affairs of the state is considered to be the legitimate one.'[11]

This is the criterion of *de facto* control. But it has considerable complications for the anti-colonialist. Is it really enough to render it legitimate that a Government be in effective control? Where then rested Bourguiba's own challenge – little more than a page later – of French control over Algeria at that time and Portuguese control over Angola and Mozambique?

It can, of course, be retorted that in both stands Bourguiba showed consistency in his distrust of mere constitutional texts. Just as he found that Lumumba fell short of being the head of a 'legitimate' government merely because a constitution said so,[12] Algeria, Angola and Mozambique fell short of being integral parts of their respective metropole for the same reason:

Portugal . . . still denies that Angola and Mozambique are colonies because the text of the Portuguese law decided that they were an integral part of the national territory. A similar text decided the annexation of Algeria to French territory as from 1834. . . . The myth of integration does not guarantee the Algerians equality of rights with the French, but renders impossible all attempts at dissociating the two countries.[13]

There can be no doubt that Bourguiba is being just as sceptical here of mere constitutionality as he was in evaluating Lumumba's claims. And yet his concession that a constitutional 'myth' made it 'impossible' at that time to 'dissociate' Algeria from France surely amounted to an admission that, myth or not, the French were in relatively effective control of Algeria. At least their control was more effective than that of Ferhat Abbas' Provisional Government at the time in exile in Tunisia. What then made the latter, in Bourguiba's eyes, more 'legitimate' than the former?

To dismiss French control of Algeria at the time as colonial rule would not solve this problem – for it would still be pertinent to ask what rendered illegitimate an effective government set up in the territory by a colonial power.

One way of answering the question would be to insist that the criterion of *de facto* control applied to countries which were already sovereign. But if France was sovereign and was willing to extend that sovereignty to include Algerians, Soustelle might well have asked what rendered this less legitimate than French sovereignty over, say, Corsica? What rendered French rule over Tunisia itself illegitimate for as long as it was effective?

The dilemma, in fact, arises from an easy transition from the notion of sovereignty to the notion of legitimacy. Ironically enough, the transition starts from the premise that it is wrong or illegitimate for one nation to encroach on the sovereignty of another. Nation A then 'usurps' the sovereignty of Nation B. When the usurpation is complete and effective control established and recognized it becomes wrong or illegitimate for Nation C to encroach on the sovereignty of Nation A over B. In other words, it became wrong for India to usurp the sovereignty of Portugal over Goa. From the notion of the illegitimacy of usurping someone else's sovereignty it is an easy transition to the notion of the legitimacy of that sovereignty itself.

In the case of the colonization of Africa the position was complicated by the fact that if Nation A was European and Nation B was African, Nation A barely recognized Nation B as a 'nation' at all – and the idea of encroaching on the sovereignty of another 'nation' seemed therefore somewhat inapplicable to the situation. This is so ingrained in the minds of some Africans themselves that the Lukiiko of Buganda found it relevant to base their right to independence as late as 1960 partly on the argument that, in a recognizably Western sense, 'Buganda was a real sovereign state before and at the time the British bestowed their protection.'[14]

This whole line of thought also has its roots in the assumptions of traditional international law. One important characteristic of international law as it now stands is that it is a law which was born in Europe and was originally intended to govern inter-European relations. Today that law remains essentially Western in its conception of the world and in the rules of behaviour which it lays down. Yet some of the challenges which have been advanced by nationalists in Asia and Africa have been challenges directed at the West – and questioning some of the old assumptions about the boundaries of legitimacy in relations between groups.

One point at issue concerns the unit of humanity whose behaviour is to be controlled by international law. Is international law to concern itself only with relations between *states*? Or should it also permit into relevance relations between races, tribes, or other units of human identity? Traditional international law as it evolved in Europe came to concern itself only with relations between one state and another – not between one state and a clan or tribe. And so Britain could be expected to follow scrupulously the Law of Nations in her relations with France, but not in her relations with, say, a tribe in New Guinea. It made sense to ask Britain to respect the sovereignty of a fellow 'state' or 'nation' but it did not make sense to ask her not to violate 'the sovereignty of a tribe'.

But what was a 'state'? In the final analysis it came to mean the type of internal social and political organization which Europeans could recognize as similar to theirs. That was why *civilization* came to be a criterion for determining which countries had rights under international law. In other words, the Law of Nations came to mean in effect 'the Law of Civilized Nations'. Even that prophet of Western liberalism himself, John Stuart Mill, could argue in the following vein:

To characterize any conduct towards a barbarous people as a violation of the law of nations only shows that he who speaks has never considered the matter. . . . Barbarians have no rights as a *nation*, except a right to such treatment as may, at the earliest possible period, fit them for becoming one.[15]

Twenty-five years after Mill published these words the Berlin Conference of 1885 was held – to ratify the partition of Africa. These were the days when – as Frederick Starr once contended – 'the practical man, the businessman, the man of affairs, the philanthropist, the missionary', all agreed that 'civilized folk have a perfect right to interfere with any native tribe too weak to resist their encroachment'.[16]

The climate of opinion in this matter was not, however, without its paradoxical overtones. On the one hand, a people's right to independence (in, say, Africa) rested, if Starr is correct, on their not being 'too weak to resist encroachment'. On the other hand, it was also possible to hear that right based on their not being 'too strong' – at least, not strong enough to encroach on neighbouring tribes and be a rival to the Europeans' own scramble for the continent. This would seem to have been the line which Sir Harry Johnston, for example, took when, at about the turn of the century, he argued that

> Abyssinia ... for many reasons connected with its history, its religion, and its sturdy assertion of independence, deserves more than any other state of Africa to preserve her independence, provided she will abstain from offence and recognize her true geographical limits.[17]

Actually, the criterion of 'sturdy assertion of independence' would seem to echo Starr's postulate that the natives should not be 'too weak', while the closing criterion in Johnston's statement invokes the condition that the natives should not imagine themselves too strong – at least, not in their territorial ambitions.

But it is the increasing consciousness of what Johnston calls 'true geographical limits' for a people, with its connotations of defined *state* frontiers, which is crucial in any attempt to determine the kind of associations evoked by the concept of 'sovereignty' in the European mind. At any rate, it is safe to say that any arguments *against* colonial annexation in areas like Africa were seldom couched in legalistic terms of 'encroaching on the sovereignty of an independent tribe'.

However, since tribes in Africa varied in degree of comparability with European political units and systems, a qualification must be made. The Rhodesian historian of the twenties, H. Marshall Hole, argued that

> ... if ... it is admitted that it is in itself a good thing, or a necessary thing, that native territories should pass under the control of a civilizing Power, there are only three ways in which this can be accomplished – occupation by force ... gradual penetration ... and occupation with the consent of the native tribes or their rulers. ...[18]

Which method was used depended, in part, upon how recognizable a tribe was as something approaching the European concept of a 'state'. Gradual penetration tended to work with the looser, weaker tribes. The device of concluding 'treaties', either with or without some violent show of strength following resistance, was what was invoked with tribes sufficiently developed to have a 'seat of sovereignty' recognizable to the European. Resemblance to what was European was the scale of respect for sovereignty. The British arriving in Buganda, for example, 'saw in the institutions of the Buganda Kingdom familiar instruments

of government. This led to collaboration with the Baganda. . . .
The Baganda became a most favoured nation.'[19]

Respect for Buganda's 'sovereignty' was not, of course, of the
degree that could save Buganda from annexation. The explorer
H. M. Stanley was impressed by Buganda and considered its king
'a prince well worthy of the most sympathies that Europe can
give him'. But the three thousand soldiers of Mutesa impressed
him only because they were 'nearly' civilized and the law and
order of Buganda 'astonished' him only because it was of the
standard of 'semi-civilized countries'.[20] Of course, respect for
sovereignty was far from absolute in Europe itself. But the point
here was that such respect was extended to Africans only in
proportion to how nearly European in their political organization
they were. Hence the ease with which Johnston singled out
Abyssinia from the African map and found it most deserving of
independence. Hence, indeed, the fact that as late as 1958
M. Pierre Wigny, at one time Belgium's Minister of Colonies,
could proceed to legitimize the original colonization of the Congo
by the Belgians in terms like these: 'When the Belgians came to
Africa the natives had to be taught everything. . . . They had no
idea what a nation was, or a state, or even a slightly developed
political organization.'[21]

It just so happened that M. Wigny overlooked what has been
described as 'the only remarkable nation-state known to have
existed in that part of the world'[22] – the kingdom of the Bakongo –
though at the time of the actual arrival of the Belgians this
kingdom was well past its prime. This, however, does not affect
the argument to any great degree. Even if the kingdom of the
Bakongo was not overlooked, even if it was flourishing at the time
of the arrival of the Belgians, even if it was not 'remarkable' by
being the only one, Stanley's epithet 'semi-civilized' as applied to
the Baganda would have applied to the Bakongo. And European
scruples about annexation – weak as they were in Europe itself –
would have been weaker still in the case of the Bakongo tribe.

And so the European delegates at the Berlin Conference of
1885 were not unduly impressed by arguments which invested
some kind of sovereignty in native rulers. It was, in fact, the
United States' Plenipotentiary at the conference who came
nearest to putting forward a doctrine of tribal sovereignty.
According to this American, 'modern International Law follows

closely a line which leads to the recognition of the rights of native tribes to dispose freely of themselves and of their hereditary territory.'[23]

Yet even this sovereignty which the American invested in the African was a sovereignty of self-alienation. It was giving the African the right to surrender his rights to someone else. This is the sort of reasoning which led to the myth of negotiation between a colonial power and those African chiefs who were on the verge of being dispossessed. As we have noted, solemn treaties were sometimes drawn up between, say, Queen Victoria and tribal potentates – and the doctrine of 'colonialism by consent' was born.

The whole idea of a people's 'consent' was, of course, a powerful political norm in Western tradition. But in the case of the colonies the Western colonial powers qualified the norm with an implied capacity for *rational* consent. In other words, behind the treaties entered into with native rulers was a persistent conviction that a people should be ruled only with their consent provided they were rational enough or civilized enough to be entrusted with the option of *not* consenting. If self-government is then viewed as government by consent, the right to it was for those who were capable of a rational exercise of it.

Thus, many of the arguments in support of colonial rule tended to take it for granted that all one had to do to 'prove' that colonial rule was justified was to 'prove' that the territory was incapable of governing itself in this or in some other sense. What was often overlooked was that there was a logical jump from the premise that such a territory could not govern itself to the conclusion that it had 'therefore' to be governed by others.

Later on African nationalism came to question this jump. As Lord Milverton is reported to have once put it, '. . . when we talk of the premature grant of self-government the adjective presupposes a point of view which is not admitted by Africans.'[24] But in the eyes of the colonial administrator the adjective remained a fundamental guide to action – a principle of what to avoid in the years ahead.

For Lugard the doctrine of the consent of colonized peoples took a somewhat different form. For him a colonial power retained sovereignty over her colonies once the people had alienated it to her – but that colonial power could not *transfer* that sovereignty to another power without the consent of the people in the colony. He felt that such a transfer 'without the willing consent of the people concerned' would be a breach of the principle of trusteeship in dependencies and would be inconsistent with the national honour of the imperial country. Lugard quoted Sir William Beveridge's remark that 'the principle that millions of human beings should not be transferred without regard to their wishes or their interests is worth a war'. Lugard shared the view that an 'arbitrary surrender' of British sovereignty over a colony would be

tantamount to dealing with the people for whose welfare we are responsible as though they were slaves or chattels, and mere possessions which could be transferred at will, regardless of the fact that the inhabitants of the Crown Colonies are British subjects.[25]

But for Lugard, sovereignty over the colonies resided, in the ultimate analysis, in Britain herself and not in the native rulers or inhabitants of those colonies. 'Undisputed sovereignty was one of Lugard's principles', his biographer, Margery Perham, has stressed.[26]

What Afro-Asian nationalists have now come to challenge are two of the basic assumptions which we have attributed to Lugard and to the general logic of Western reasoning on colonization. That the sovereignty which needs to be respected under international law is the sovereignty of Western-type states is one of the assumptions now being questioned. The other is the old Western presumption that aggression was no longer aggression if it was completely successful.

For many nationalists in Africa and Asia the right to sovereignty was not merely for nation-states recognizable as such in a Western sense but for 'peoples' recognizable as such in a racial sense, particularly where differences of colour were manifest. It might well have been primarily in this latter sense that the Ghanaian National Assembly understood President Tito of Yugoslavia when he told the Assembly in 1961 that the success of anti-colonialist movements had established that international relations could not be 'consolidated without the recognition of the genuine and full equality of all *peoples*'.[27] And the equality included, above all, the right to sovereignty.

It is from this fundamental consideration that there emerges not so much national sovereignty as *racial* sovereignty in terms at least of the colour of the skin. It was on the basis of such sovereignty that Nkrumah could say: 'I am most happy about India's annexation of Goa, which I consider long overdue.'[28] It must have been on similar assumptions of the inherent sovereignty of each race that many other leaders in Asia and Africa supported Nehru's action on Goa.

Less obvious as an emerging concept of nationalists in their international outlook is that this racial sovereignty is considered to be more than just a 'moral' basis for opposition to the old Portuguese sovereignty over Goa. It was increasingly advanced as a 'legal' basis for such opposition.

On the moral side, this amounted to a divorce between the notion of 'legitimacy' and the notion of 'sovereignty'. The divorce was not entirely a new idea. When on 17 October 1899 the American Anti-Imperialist League protested that a 'self-govern-ing state cannot accept sovereignty over an unwilling people',[29] it was implying that American sovereignty over the Filipinos would be 'illegitimate sovereignty' without suggesting that this was a contradiction in terms. The criterion advanced here for legitimate sovereignty was the willingness of the territory concerned – the aforesaid criterion of consent.

On the quasi-legal side of the argument the American League, even at that early stage more than half a century ago, 'insisted' that 'subjugation of any people is "criminal aggression". . . .' But their Policy Statement aptly put the words 'criminal aggression' in quotation marks, for both the word 'criminal' and the word 'aggression' are, except figuratively, legal terms. And the League virtually conceded that international law was perhaps on the side of the 'aggressors'. At any rate it conceded under protest that there was 'a doctrine of international law which permits the subjugation of the weak by the strong'[30]– at least if the weak were non-Westerners.

It is this old doctrine which has been 'under fire' from Afro-Asian nationalists in our own day. The challenge, in effect, extends the notion of 'illegitimate sovereignty' to a paradoxical notion of 'illegal sovereignty'. Given this, the logical door was open for Krishna Menon to describe colonialism as 'permanent aggression'. Menon started invoking this concept of 'permanent aggression' to reporters even before he arrived at the United

Nations to defend India's annexation of Goa. W.E.Abraham, the Ghanaian former Fellow of All Souls, lent philosophical backing to Menon's approach by reaffirming that 'colonialism is aggression'.[31]

Early in the same year of 1962 the twenty-one-member committee, which the General Assembly established in 1957 to advise it as to when to reconsider the question of defining aggression, had held further meetings. The Liberian delegate, Nathaniel Eastman, stressed that twenty-two new states – most of which were African – had joined the Organization since the committee's previous session in 1959 and that they needed time to submit their views. For the same reason Ghana supported a motion for adjournment for a few more years. Jan Polderman of the Netherlands captured the mood of the new states when he said that what was needed was a definition of aggression which would serve the interests of the small countries, particularly those which had recently attained independence. But he, like the delegates from Ghana and Liberia, did not think the circumstances were any more propitious for such a definition than they had been in 1959.[32] It seemed clear that the new states were not as yet ready to embody their fears about colonialism in a specific legal formula.

Yet, following India's annexation of Goa, the idea that colonialism was 'permanent aggression' was already becoming part of Afro-Asian argumentation. When the General Assembly finally gets round to a formal discussion of a comprehensive definition of 'aggression', it seems almost certain that Portuguese pretensions to Angola and Mozambique would, as had Portuguese rule over Goa be cited as one type of 'aggressive' presence. Given this postulate it was meaningless for the British Foreign Secretary in 1962 to complain that the United Nations was excessively preoccupied with colonial problems. Lord Home – as he then was – would not have complained if the United Nations were preoccupied with problems of 'aggression'. The jump which he had to take to catch up with Afro-Asian nationalistic thinking was to see problems of colonialism as, in effect, problems of aggression. The reasoning involved was that if it was illegal to usurp the sovereignty of a people of different colour, it could not be illegal to attempt the restoration of that sovereignty. If, in other words, Portuguese possession of Goa was 'aggression', it could not have been aggression to put an end to it. On the contrary, to put right what was illegal was not only legal itself – it was worthy of the aims of the United Nations.

What the notion of 'permanent aggression' amounts to today is a rejection of the old Western notion that aggression was no longer aggression when it was completely successful. According to this older notion, once Goa became a colony of Portugal, Portuguese aggression (if there ever was any) ended by definition – for one cannot commit aggression against a non-sovereign country. Thus India's invasion of Goa came to be deemed to be 'aggression' not against Goa but against Portugal, just as the landing of Indonesian paratroops in West New Guinea, say, in June 1962, came to be taken as 'aggression' against the Netherlands rather than against West New Guinea.

When to this is added the sister-notion that a state cannot commit aggression against its own sovereignty, Portugal's occupation of Goa or Dutch occupation of West New Guinea was legally safe to the Westerner as soon as it appeared 'permanent'. And because of this the very idea of 'permanent aggression' verged on being a contradiction in terms. It is precisely this reasoning then that the new members of the international scene now reject, for since effective colonial control amounts to a permanent violation of racial sovereignty it must remain permanently an 'aggression'.

This is not to say that they do not concede what may be termed 'colonial sovereignty'. It is surely on the basis of such a sovereignty that many of the new states would insist on making Britain answerable for Rhodesia as a British colonial responsibility. And it was on the basis of the same sovereignty (reinforced by specific United Nations Trusteeship obligations) that many insisted on the withdrawal of Belgian troops from Rwanda and Burundi as speedily as possible *after* their independence – the presence of the troops after 1 July 1962, pending evacuation, being urged to be 'without prejudice to the sovereign rights of Rwanda and Burundi'.[33] Such concessions to 'colonial sovereignty' are considered temporary concessions, and as such, not inconsistent with the fundamental stand that colonial sovereignty is in violation of racial sovereignty and ought to be speedily terminated.

This brings about a fundamental change in the criterion referred to by Plamenatz that 'a country is capable of self-government when it can produce native rulers strong enough and responsible enough to respect international law.'[34] The challenge to this again takes the form either of rejecting it as a criterion for fitness for self-government or of denying that it can form the basis of deciding which countries may legitimately be ruled by others.

But here a further subdivision takes place, for the point at issue can become not only what constitutes 'capacity for self-government' but also what constitutes 'respect for international law'. In his work on *International Law in an Expanded World*[35] Professor B.V.A. Röling divides the history of international law into the period of 'Christian nations' (1648–1856), the period of 'civilized nations' (1856–1945) and the period of 'peace-loving nations' (from 1945 onwards). He goes on to criticize the inadequacy of international law in the present time mainly on the grounds that it is a system of law of Christian European origin and its concepts do not necessarily commend themselves to the emerging Asian and African countries.

If, then, colonialism was all right according to international law in the phase of 'Christian nations', if it was even more widely extended with the blessing of international law in the period of 'civilized nations', it had become, in the words of Nkrumah, 'a horrifying anachronism' in this latest phase.[36] And if the United Nations itself is for 'peace-loving nations', it was open to Nkrumah to view possession of colonies as 'now quite incompatible with membership of the United Nations'.[37]

If, then, to be able to govern yourself is to be 'responsible enough to respect international law' the colonizer is as 'incapable' as her colony. And to the argument that the former is objectively at least '*strong* enough to respect international law', the answer would surely be that the graver is the offence of not respecting it. In other words, to take over a territory because it is incapable of respecting international law is to be guilty of an even greater disrespect for that law.

What has happened then to the nationalist's stand (in regard to, say, India's annexation of Goa) that it cannot be illegal to put right what is illegal? How can it be disrespectful to international law to ensure that international law is respected? What, for instance, was legally wrong with Anthony Eden trying to get Nasser to respect international treaties over the Suez Canal? What could be wrong with recolonizing the Congo, as Roy

Welensky once suggested, if the Congolese Government was incapable of protecting foreign nationals within its territory?

The nationalist's stand would presumably be based on the premise that what is illegal can never be 'put right' by a more serious illegality. Certainly in regard to the Congo, forceful intervention by other powers was to be deemed by Ghanaian standards as 'amounting to aggression'.[38] And since the worst kind of intervention was intervention by the wrong race, the worst kind of aggression was aggression against racial sovereignty. As Nkrumah said to Tshombe in a letter dated 12 August 1960: '. . . you have assembled in your support the foremost advocates of imperialism and colonialism in Africa and the most determined opponents of African freedom. How can you, as an African do this?'[39] How, in other words, could any African be an accessory to the violation of the racial sovereignty of an African country? It was not only 'contrary to nature': it was unwise. It compromised the race as a whole and militated against the emergence of the sovereign African – the one who consents to obviously *African* rule and to nothing short of that. And yet Tshombe's own financial intervention in Northern Rhodesian elections in 1962 on the side of Nkumbula aroused relatively little hostility – primarily because it was *intra*-African. What all this means is that while in Europe 'aggression' was, for historical reasons, most easily recognizable if it was committed by one European country against another, in Africa 'aggression' has yet to become clearly recognizable if it is committed by one African country against another. That is why government charges of 'treason' in Nigeria in 1962 sounded somewhat hollow when levelled against Nigerians who might have intrigued on behalf of Ghana. In other words, against the background of the notion of racial sovereignty, the idea of 'treason' as between Ghana and Nigeria had yet to command immediate comprehension.

Nonetheless, it should not be inferred that the principle of racial sovereignty is intended to *replace* that of state sovereignty. Like the Monroe Doctrine, the principle of racial sovereignty merely introduces an additional dimension to the doctrine of non-intervention. To take a non-African example, Saudi and Egyptian 'intervention' in the Yemen was thus a 'domestic' affair of the Arabs according to racial sovereignty, but an *external* violation of the rights of the Yemenis according to state sovereignty. A new level of externality would have been introduced by any *non-Arab* intervention.

By the same token, any Ugandan 'interference' in Congolese affairs in 1964–5 was interstate interference, but American and Belgian 'interference' in the Congo was both interstate and interracial.

In conclusion, let us clarify further the relationship between this principle of racial sovereignty and the five concepts of self-government with which we opened the chapter. To the extent that colonial rule in Africa's experience has denoted the rule of one race over another, colonialism is, as we have noted, a violation of racial sovereignty. But what if Algeria's colonial status had been ended not by independence but by honest democratic integration with metropolitan France? Perhaps with more feeling than logic Nkrumah for one could not conceive of such a merger between different peoples. We shall discuss this point more fully subsequently, but for the moment suffice it to quote Nkrumah's emphatic if confused assertion that 'Algeria is African and will always remain so, in the same manner that France is French'.[40]

As for self-government in the sense of internal management of internal affairs, the most important instance of violation of racial sovereignty at such a level was the case of Rhodesia. As Joshua Nkomo, Rhodesia's leading African nationalist, put it in 1961:

> You might have been led to believe that Southern Rhodesia is a self-governing country. . . . The name Southern Rhodesia embraces 3,000,000 Africans, 250,000 white settlers and 20,000 Asiatics and coloureds. Of these groups only the 250,000 white settlers have been and are still monopolising ALL functions of government to the total exclusion of the African. Therefore Southern Rhodesia is NOT self-governing but the settlers in the country are self-governing.[41]

In claiming that the African's 'exclusion' was 'total', Nkomo might have been overstating his case. But the essential point was that there was a minority of white settlers having ultimate control over Africans many times their number. Rhodesia was therefore a self-governing colony which involved a violation of racial sovereignty.

Nkomo's article from which the above passage is drawn was entitled 'One Man One Vote – The Only Solution in Southern Rhodesia'. And the passage in question cites population figures in order to assert that in Southern Rhodesia there was no 'majority rule'. Here then we touch self-government in that liberal sense of majority rule. Yet Nkomo discusses the issue not in terms of how many people voted for the government in Rhodesia at the last election but in terms of how many Africans there were in the country in comparison with white settlers. What was at issue here then was not merely whether the Rhodesian government was 'representative' in the liberal sense of institutional accountability but also whether it was 'representative' in the sense of ethnic typicality. Again the principle of racial sovereignty was at stake.

But before the coming of the white man had sovereignty in Southern Rhodesia resided in the people or in the native rulers? As we have indicated, there were occasions in the history of colonization when tribal chiefs were made parties to formal treaties of annexation or 'protection'. In a limited sense such treaties did imply a recognition of chiefly authority. The white minority government in Rhodesia was later to revert to this recognition as a way of demonstrating African consent to white leadership. In 1964 Ian Smith displayed that he had the backing of African chiefs even if he should decide on a unilateral declaration of independence. The suggestion here was that the African people were indeed being governed with their consent since they were governed with the consent of their chiefs. The question of violating the 'sovereignty' of the African people 'did not, therefore, arise'. As the Pastoral Instruction of the Catholic Bishops of Rhodesia once put it:

That methodical action of an organised people towards another whose development is evidently insufficient, or similar action upon a vacant territory – that work which we call 'colonisation', is not of its very nature an evil thing . . . provided that in all circumstances *the right of sovereignty of the indigenous rulers* and the property rights of their people are respected.[42]

But by continuing to attribute ultimate authority to native rulers, both Ian Smith and the Catholic Church were talking in an idiom which antedated the emergence of African political consciousness in the modern sense. Smith carried this obsolescence into the speech which accompanied his unilateral declaration of independence on 11 November 1965. He asserted that his declaration did not mark a diminution in the 'opportunities' which Africans had in Rhodesia to 'advance and prosper'.

Far from this being the case, it is our intention, in consultation with the chiefs, to bring them into the Government and Administration as the acknowledged leaders of the African people on a basis acceptable to them.[43]

His whole conception of controlled African participation in government was in defiance of the new political norms in Africa. Among the most pervasive of those norms was the principle of racial sovereignty. Unproclaimed, it was nevertheless implicit in much of African nationalistic behaviour. It coloured African conceptions of self-government in all its varied forms.

The anomaly of a white-controlled Rhodesia was just one more obstacle that the principle of racial sovereignty had to overcome before attaining paramountcy in the continent as a whole.

CHAPTER THREE

ON THE CONCEPT OF 'WE ARE ALL AFRICANS'[1]

IN MARCH 1957 Ghana achieved uniqueness by being the first nonwhite and non-Arab country in Africa to emerge from colonial rule. In May 1963 Nkrumah achieved uniqueness at Addis Ababa by being the boldest and most radical Pan-Africanist in his proposals. As a believer in a speedy formation of a continental union Nkrumah was virtually isolated at the conference which created the Organization of African Unity. We shall discuss more fully in a later chapter the place of Ghana in the development of African political thought. What concerns us in this chapter is the general ideological background to this dual uniqueness of Ghana – the first in freedom and the first in Pan-African daring. Our area of concentration in this chapter will be the meeting point between the quest for freedom and the feeling of continentalism. What factors in Africa's historical experience could conceivably give meaning to an assertion like that of Nkrumah that 'Ghana's freedom would be meaningless if it was not linked with the total liberation of the entire continent of Africa'?[2] In strict terms, our concern here is neither with Ghana's freedom as such, nor with the liberation of the African continent. It is with the alleged *link* between the two.

We shall, therefore, first grapple with the problem of defining what is 'an African'. Implicit in this is the issue of defining 'Africa' itself. The argument will take us to the notion of an indivisible African freedom as implied by the above quotation from Nkrumah. We shall then try to discern the ultimate values of African nationalism as a continental phenomenon.

Bernard Lewis once grappled with the question 'What is a Turk?' and finally put forward, virtually as part of the *definition*, the 'sentiment of Turkish identity' – simply thinking of oneself as a Turk.[3] Now the course of world history is being much affected by people who on occasion speak of themselves collectively as 'Africans'. How important to the definition of an African in politics is the quality of thinking of oneself as an African?

In many respects, Melville Herskovits maintained, Africa is a geographical fiction. 'It is thought of as a separate entity and regarded as a unit to the degree that the map is invested with an authority imposed on it by the map makers.'[4] The argument here is presumably that climatically the range in Africa is from arid deserts to tropical forests; ethnically, from the Khoisan to the Semites; linguistically from Amharic to Kidigo. What have all these in common apart from the tyranny of the map maker?

One possible answer is that they have a negative common element: they are alike one to another to the extent that they are collectively different from anything in the outside world. It is perhaps this question-begging assumption which makes Nkrumah insist that 'Africa is not, and can never be an extension of Europe.'[5] That argument was used against the notion that Algeria was part of France, and it continues to be used against Portuguese 'integration' of Angola and Mozambique. In a televised New York debate with Jacques Soustelle when the future of 'French' Algeria was still in question, Ghana's Ambassador Alex Quaison-Sackey employed the argument not merely as a variant formulation of the thesis that 'Algeria had to be independent of France' but as a piece of evidence in support of that thesis.[6]

Did Quaison-Sackey and his President mean that no nation could – on account of some logical difficulty – overflow across continental boundaries? Was it to be inferred that since, say, the United Arab Republic was at the time an instance of 'Africa' (represented by Egypt) overflowing into 'Asiatic' Syria, Nkrumah's argument was an implicit prediction of the break-up of that union? And what of Bernard Lewis' Turkey – was it Asia overflowing into Europe or Europe spilling over into the Orient?

It seems more likely that Nkrumah's use of 'can never' (in his 'Africa . . . can never be an extension of Europe') is not one of incapacity, but of moral rejection. Europe 'can never' *legitimately* extend into Africa, however practical the extension might be empirically.

And yet the element of strict incapacity is not entirely absent from the Ghanaians' exposition of the thesis. It continued to be presented almost like a logical impossibility – the reasoning being something to the effect that if Algeria was part of Africa, and Africa was a separate continent from Europe, then Algeria could not be part of a part of Europe at the same time. The argument sounded persuasive, and continues to sound persuasive in regard to Portugal's 'projections' into Africa. But, by itself as an *argument*, it sounds persuasive only if one accepts what Herskovits describes as 'the preconceptions that arise from according continental designations a degree of reality they do not possess.'[7]

Herskovits himself referred to the description of Africa by the Geographer Royal of France in 1656 as a 'peninsula so large that it comprises a third part, and this the most southerly, of our continent.'[8] And a case can certainly be made for the thesis that North Africa was in a sense an extension of Southern Europe for a long time – and if the connection with Europe was to an extent broken with the advent of Islam, it was only to turn North Africa into a western extension of the Arabian peninsula and the Fertile Crescent rather than a northern continuation of the area south of the Sahara.

And yet Nkrumah insists that not even 'an accident of history' can 'ever succeed in turning an inch of African soil into an extension of any other continent.' To him it was self-evident – and 'colonialism and imperialism cannot change this basic geographical fact.'[9]

The reasoning implicit in this assertion seems to accord greater importance to 'geographical facts' than to 'accidents of history'. Yet the choice of terms could surely be interchanged. To the Frenchman who opposed Nkrumah's thesis, the argument could just as well have been framed in the reverse semantic order that no accident of *geography* could change the basic historical fact that Algeria had had a longer connection with Europe than with, say, the Congo or Tanganyika. Geographical facts are as much 'accidents' as historical accidents are 'facts'. In the politics of Africanism, which aspects are really important?

The very term 'Africanism' seems to imply that geography matters more, since 'Africa' is a geographic designation. Nkrumah's stand can therefore be taken as further evidence for Max Beloff's argument in another context that 'it is easier to understand the contiguities of geography than the continuities of history.'[10]

And yet in regard to Africa, the argument cannot rest there. History can be apprehended and felt without being 'understood'. Indeed, what makes geography important in politics is very often the history behind it. The whole span of historical development may not be relevant. The effect of a period of history is not always to be measured by the number of years it covers. Africa is certainly one instance where a few decades of history led to greater changes than the several centuries that preceded them. One of the changes that these decades have brought about is perhaps a new consciousness of 'geographical contiguities' and a new response to them. And so, while acknowledging wide differences in culture, language and ideas between various parts of Africa, Nkrumah could still insist that 'the essential fact remains that we are all Africans, and have a common interest in the independence of Africa.'[11] That they are 'all Africans' may be no more than a recognition of a geographical fact: that they have 'a common interest in the independence of Africa' is a 'continuity' of history.

But is there an implied 'therefore' between the two parts of Nkrumah's statement? At first glance it may seem plausible to suppose that if there is some kind of causal relationship between being Africans and being interested in African independence, the latter must follow from the former. This is true, but only partly. The other side of the argument is, paradoxically, that they are 'all Africans' because of the common interest in independence; that until a craving for independence was born they were not 'Africans' but Ibo, Kikuyu, Balunda, Egyptian, Somali and Zulu. In other words, if Nkrumah's 'We are all Africans' is an assertion of a self-conscious collectivity, then the collectivity is as much an effect as a cause of the self-consciousness.

Taking the argument a stage further, the craving for independence presupposes, of course, an absence of independence,[12] i.e., in this instance, the advent of the colonization of Africa. Are we then to conclude that it was colonization which made it possible for Nkrumah to say 'We are all Africans'? And if so, what has happened to Nkrumah's repeated argument that the process of colonization had included 'the policy of divide and rule'?

The two arguments are not impossible to reconcile. Certainly Julius Nyerere seemed to subscribe to both. In his furious letter to *The Times* (London) just before he resigned as Prime Minister in 1962, he accused the paper's news-reportage of trying to drive a wedge between 'the Government and the people of Tanganyika on the one hand and the people of Kenya on the other.' And, like a true nationalist, he wanted to 'state quite categorically that the time for the policy of divide and rule has passed.'[13] Yet Nyerere had been known to argue in a way which suggested that if the imperialists divided (as a policy) in order to rule, they also united (in effect) by the very act of ruling. At a symposium at Wellesley College almost two years earlier Nyerere had emphasized that 'the sentiment of Africa', the sense of fellowship between Africans, was 'something which came from outside'. He said: 'One need not go into the history of colonization of Africa, but that colonization had one significant result. A sentiment was created on the African continent – a sentiment of oneness.'[14]

Carried to its logical conclusion this says that it took colonialism to inform Africans that they were Africans. I do not mean this merely in the sense that in colonial schools young Bakongo, Taita and Ewe suddenly learned that the rest of the world had a collective name for the inhabitants of the landmass of which their area formed a part – though this was certainly one medium by which Africans were informed by colonialism that they were Africans. A more important medium was the reaction against colonialism leading, as it did, to a new awareness of the 'geographical contiguities' mentioned above, and the new responses that this called out. The result was felt even by the Arab North – so that a new type of Egyptian told his countrymen:

... we cannot, in any way, stand aside, even if we wish to, from the sanguinary and dreadful struggle now raging in the heart of the continent between five million whites and two hundred million Africans. We cannot do so for one principal and clear reason: we ourselves are in Africa.[15]

Perhaps for the first time in that country's history a ruler of Egypt was taking a stand to awaken his countrymen to an implication of the 'geographical fact' that they too were 'in Africa'. Almost as emphatically as his Ghanaian counterpart the Egyptian President was to commit himself to the policy of 'We are all Africans'.

But is the Egyptian an African in the same sense that Nkrumah is one? The answer must be a qualified 'No.' To the extent that they are both within a continent that underwent some form of colonial rule in recent history, and to the extent that this gives them a certain sense of fellow feeling, the Egyptian and Nkrumah are both 'Africans'. But while the Egyptian is an African only in the sense that Nehru was an Asian, Nkrumah is an African in a more significant meaning. To put it in another way, Egypt as a national entity is old; Ghana is new. Nasser is therefore an Egyptian in a deeper sense historically than Nkrumah is a Ghanaian, but he is an African in a shallower sense emotionally than Nkrumah is an African. The continental feeling built up by colonialism was more emphatic in Africa south of the Sahara than it ever was either north of the Sahara or in Asia. The particularly marked artificiality of the sub-Saharan 'nations', even when compared with those in Asia or North Africa, is certainly an important part of the explanation. The question then arises, from what is this importance derived?

One approach to the answer is to examine the individual side-effects of this sub-Saharan artificiality. Among these were the collective labels that the colonial powers had to give to the multiplicity of tribes within each territory. The British administrator in India, for example, did not have to call Indians 'Asians'. When he did not call them Hindus or Muslims, Gujerati or Punjabi, he lumped them together as 'Indians'. Such sentiment of oneness as this created was therefore limited to the Indian sub-continent instead of encompassing the entire Asian continent.[16] There was, to be sure, a degree of fellow feeling with other Asians. But this led to very little talk in Asia about a 'United States of Asia', realistic or not. Nor was there the same degree of conviction behind any inchoate sense of belonging to the 'same' race on a continental scale. As Lord Hailey observed, the spirit of Asianism had not 'involved the emergence of a concept of pan-Asianism in the East.'[17]

In sub-Saharan Africa, however, there was often no territorially exclusive term to designate the indigenous inhabitants in a given territory – at least, not when these were being distinguished from the immigrant races. In India an exclusive club could have a sign 'No Indians admitted'. In Tanganyika or Kenya it would not have been racially specific to say 'No Tanganyikans' or 'No Kenyans' since these terms had little natural ethnic content.[18] The term 'African' seems to have gained currency in some

instances as a euphemism for the term 'native'. When the Legislative Council came into the multi-racial territories of East Africa,
the seats for the races were allocated in continentalistic terms –
'African' seats, 'European' seats and, after the Indian partition,
'Asian' seats.

Thus, to use Nyerere's rhetoric, 'Africans, all over the continent, without a word being spoken either from one individual
to another or from one African country to another, looked at the
European, looked at one another, and knew that in relation to the
European they were one.'[19] In relation to another continent, this
continent was one: this was the logic of the situation.

Nevertheless, he was putting it too strongly when he talked to
Africans 'all over the continent'. For where the 'nations' were not
entirely artificial it was possible for the colonial powers to think of
and describe the natives as 'Somalis' and 'Sudanese' without
resorting to the all-encompassing 'Africans'. And to the extent
that the narrower terms did not emphasize affinity with the rest
of the continent, the 'spirit of Africanism' of the Somalis or the
Sudanese is not of the same depth as that of the 'Tanganyikans'.
Indeed, this applies even to those natural nations within artificial
ones, like the Baganda of Uganda. The point to remember is that
where colonial boundaries approximate very closely to ethnic
ones, and where there is a degree of homogeneity within the
boundaries to give the concept of 'nation' some substance over
and above the mere existence of legal boundaries on the map,
there is less of a pull toward identity with what Nyerere calls
'Africans all over the continent'. As Lord Hailey put it in connection with some such homogeneous, if especially small, territories,
'Africanism is seen there mainly in terms of the maintenance of
the national identity of the indigenous community concerned'.[20]

It nonetheless holds that if, as Herskovits claimed, Africa was
'a geographical fiction', Tanganyika and Ghana were greater
fictions. As an English settler in Africa wrote:

> The administration of some of these artificial divisions have made a
> practice of trying to foster a synthetic patriotism towards 'Tanganyika'
> or the 'Gold Coast'. . . . These loyalties to a wholly artificial and un-
> realistic administrative boundary . . . tend to obscure and undermine the
> underlying sense of oneness across the continent which I have heard
> expressed in the constantly reiterated phrase 'We Africans'.[21]

But if the feeling of 'We Tanganyikans' or, more recently, 'We

Tanzanians' is beginning to undermine the feeling of 'We Africans', for how long can we continue to think of the latter as less 'synthetic' than the former? If Nigerians are developing a greater loyalty to 'Nigeria' than to 'Africa', for how long can it be maintained that they are less Nigerians than they are Africans? It is all very well, one might argue, for the sympathizers of African unity to lament that

... the youthful generations of Africans ... have seen in school coloured maps of Africa . . . all the forty divisions clearly demarcated by thick black lines; and it is hard for them to remember that such concepts as 'Nigeria' or 'Tanganyika' are of very recent origin and are wholly artificial.[22]

But if a 'youthful generation' finds it hard to remember that a fiction is a fiction, for how long can it remain so?

Here we come to the different levels of what has come to be known as 'African nationalism'. In 1944 a British Colonial Office Advisory Committee on Education in the Colonies drew attention to the finding that travel and contact with other nationalities had given rise among Africans to a 'dawning realization of themselves as Africans, even as "nationals" of a territory like Northern Rhodesia, playing a part in world affairs.'[23] It was, in other words, a consciousness not only of being 'Africans' but also of being Africans from a particular territory. This distinction in levels the term 'African nationalism' very often fails to make. It is used to denote any form of nationalism *in* Africa and involving *Africans* – the nationalism that looks inward territorially, like that of Nigerians after independence; the nationalism that looks inward tribally, like that of the Kikuyu in the 1940's and 1950's; and the nationalism that looks outward continentally or regionally and envisions the submergence of the colonial units into a larger creation.

When, however, a distinction *is* made between these different meanings, the tendency is to think of the narrower territorial or tribal nationalisms as being in some sense 'less nationalistic' than the wider continentalistic brand. The Nigerian who is for exclusively Nigerian interests thus becomes less of a 'real Nationalist' than a Nkrumah or a Touré who seems prepared to sell his country's sovereignty for a vision of continental unity.[24]

Perhaps here the contrast with Europe is particularly striking. The rebellion against dynastic empires in Europe was, in a sense, a rebellion against large, multi-ethnic or multi-lingual states – a rebellion which could not easily be reconciled with pan-Europeanism. And even today that Englishman is nationalistic who is opposed to giving up the sovereignty of England for the sake of a united Europe. Why then is the particularist Nigerian less of a nationalist than the pan-African Nkrumah?

Both in Africa in its recent history and in Europe in the wake of 'self-determination' after World War I, nationalism had denoted a commitment to what Nkrumah has described as 'the application of . . . the right of a people to rule themselves.'[25] This is just another way of expressing opposition to foreign rule in moral terms – and in an idiom that African nationalism inherited from European nationalisms. Where Africa parts company with Europe is on the crucial issue of what is a 'foreigner'.[26] In Europe the 'foreign' ruler was generally himself a European. To have rebelled against him and then subscribed to the idea of 'uniting' with him in a pan-European spirit was politically illogical.

In the case of the continental brand of African nationalism this difficulty does not arise since the 'foreign' ruler is a ruler from outside the continent altogether. It is therefore quite consistently 'nationalistic' to win independence for Ghana, set out to build it as a nation, create a sense of patriotism toward it, and at the same time declare an intention to submerge its 'national' identity within a giant state on a continental or sub-continental scale. But even if this is conceded to be consistently nationalistic, what could make it a more justifiable definition of 'the real nationalist' than the particularism of the Nigerian who refuses to give up his Nigerian 'identity'?

One answer might be that the Nigerian is resigning himself to the arbitrary frontiers imposed by colonialism and therefore deserves to be regarded as less of a nationalist. This line of reasoning sometimes goes to the extent of implying that the creation of a 'United States of Africa' would not be something entirely new but rather in effect a return to things as they were before the advent of divisive colonialism. The same Nyerere who said at Wellesley College that colonization gave birth to African fellowship told the Royal Commonwealth Society that it was *pre*-colonial African history which demanded that 'African unity must have priority over all other associations'[27] as if the colonial period had interrupted a fellowship that went far back before it.

The argument here had virtually become 'We were all Africans until colonialism split us into Ugandans, Kenyans and Nigerians'. It is certainly true that they could not have been Nigerians and Ugandans before the advent of colonialism, since colonialism created Nigeria and Uganda. The logical jump is in the assertion that they must 'therefore' have previously been just 'Africans'. Nor is it a simple case of the very word 'African' being itself *non*-African in his inception, however true that may be. Rather, it is a case of the inhabitants of the continent having known other, often *narrower* group classifications than the 'Ugandans' and 'Nigerians' of post-colonial days.

And yet there is a persistent reluctance in the continentalistic type of African nationalism to acquiesce in the map drawn up at Berlin in 1884–5.[28] Indeed, the Berlin Conference which partitioned Africa served as the inspiration of the first All-Africa people's conference held in Accra in December 1958. One observer maintained at the time that the connection between the two conferences occurred to the Chairman of the Accra Conference, Mr Tom Mboya.[29] Mboya's slogan 'Europeans, scram out of Africa' was meant not only to echo the phrase 'European scramble for Africa' but also to amount to a demand that Europeans should pull out now, so that Africans could set about putting Africa 'back together again'.

Anyone, then, who did not subscribe to this vision of putting Africa back together again was something short of a true African nationalist. There might be differences of opinion over how far into the future this aim was to be pushed, and over the form and pattern in which Africa was to be put together. But a considerable consensus had developed at least on the point that African unity was possible only when the European ruler has 'scrammed out' of the continent as a whole. In the words of Sekou Touré, 'the liberty of Africa is indivisible.'[30]

This doctrine of indivisibility is persistent in the language of nationalism in Africa. In part it arises out of the same factors which led the colonial powers to apply the broad term 'African' to indigenous inhabitants of different parts of the continent. In one sense the African nationalist has to think of Africa as 'indivisible' because the rest of the world tends to think of it as such. At least outside Africanists' circles, it is frequent enough to hear an atrocity in the Congo being stretched in significance and deemed a reflection not merely on Congolese but also on African capacity for, say, self-discipline. In the face of such generalizations, actual or anticipated, a nationalist from Ghana may decide that if he cannot defend himself by pointing out that he is not Congolese, he might as well defend himself by defending the Congolese – by discovering exclusively 'external' causes for the troubles of that country.

At this level, then, the African image of their own indivisibility is a reflection of the image of Africa that the outside world has tended to hold – going back to the days when Africans were classified together as 'all backward' or 'all primitive' with little regard for the enormous variations of social and political development in different parts of the continent. It is significant that the reflection has become more real than the original before the mirror of time – and empty European generalizations like 'They are all Africans' are becoming less empty as the Africans themselves, in fellowship, affirm that so they are indeed.

But the doctrine of African indivisibility has intellectual as well as psychological roots; and the New World has certainly played a part in this. It was, for example, from Abraham Lincoln, as well as from John Stuart Mill, that Julius Nyerere says he learned of Western notions of institutionalized democracy.[31] And yet Nyerere himself was not educated in America. Clearer traces of American influence are to be discerned in those African nationalists who did spend formative years in the United States – the most famous of these being Azikiwe of Nigeria, Nkrumah of Ghana and Banda of Malawi. Pan-Africanism has then a root in the New World not only because Afro-Americans like DuBois and Garvey launched it on to a world stage but also because many even of the African fathers of Pan-Africanism were themselves exposed to elements in American political thought.

It is, of course, dangerous to single out specific ideas in African thought and trace them to the New World. But one can at least hazard an estimate and even point to certain American thinkers who were especially influential. American writers today sometimes give the impression of putting Thomas Jefferson first as a persistent intellectual force in the world.[32] In doing so they are in danger of projecting their own estimate of important American thinkers on to the rest of the world. Actually, for every African who has heard of Thomas Jefferson, probably several knew of Abraham Lincoln – even if only as the liberator of Negro slaves in his country. Some may well have acquainted themselves with the kind of arguments Lincoln used in support of that liberation – especially, that the Union could not 'permanently endure half slave and half free'. This was, in fact, a classic formulation of the doctrine of the indivisibility of freedom; and it has been echoed down the generations since. In 1899 the American Anti-Imperialist League was already extending Lincoln's ideas to colonialism at large and asking America not to betray Lincoln by persisting in colonizing the Philippines.[33] By 1947 an African leader, Nnamdi Azikiwe, was arguing in West Virginia that 'one half of the world cannot be democratic and the other half undemocratic'[34]– and the conclusion to be drawn was that the colonies must be liberated.

By 1962 America, which had dramatized that argument nationally by a Civil War a century ago was being asked by an old defender of white settlers in Africa, Mrs Elspeth Huxley, to make it clear to the now independent African governments that their countries could not 'any more than others, contract out of the rule that freedom is indivisible.'[35] In regard to the position of the white settlers – of whose rights she had long been champion in opposition both to Margery Perham[36] and to African aspirations – the colonial wheel had come just about full circle.

But if the Africans were now betraying the ideal of an indivisible freedom, what had their struggle been all about?

The question can best be answered by first examining what any nationalism is all about. Frederick Hertz once defined national consciousness as 'the combined striving for unity, liberty, individuality and prestige.'[37] Need these four aspirations be of equal weight? Must liberty, for example, be as important as, say, prestige to any people with a national consciousness? Can the precise combination of the different elements vary in importance not only within the 'consciousness' of a single nationalist but also between one nationalist and another?

This opens up the relevance of the particular circumstances which give rise to national consciousness. If there have been occasions of what John Stuart Mill might describe as 'collective humiliation',[38] it would make a difference what form the humiliation took. Did it just deal a blow to a people's 'prestige'– as by, say, beating them in a space race to the moon? Did it go further and actually deprive them of their 'liberty'? Did it 'divide' them in order to do so? On the answers to such questions would rest the aspirations of such a people within their national consciousness, and indeed their very aptitude for realizing them.

For example, one of the major differences between English-speaking and French-speaking Africans is as we have noted that the latter have been the more culturally creative of the two. It has been pointed out often enough that Léopold Senghor of Senegal was a poet, Keita Fodéba of Guinea a producer of ballets, Bernard Dadié of the Ivory Coast a novelist and Cofi Gadeau a playwright, before they held office in their respective states. One reason advanced to explain this is that the Africans who were ruled by France were more exposed than their British counter-parts to 'collective humiliation' in the cultural field. Their creativeness was thus a response to the assimilationist assumption that African culture was inferior to that of France.[39]

And yet, curiously enough, far less talk of 'our British heritage' is heard among English-speaking Africans than of 'our French cultural background' among at least the Brazzaville group of former French subjects. The latter's rebellion against French cultural arrogance has not really taken the form of a determined attempt to tear away from the French influence – in spite of Senghor's homage to *Negritude*. Theirs, in fact, is less a rebellion than the paradox of rebellious emulation. While Nkrumah and Nyerere would at least like to believe that such a thing as 'African Socialism' is fundamentally indigenous, Senghor prefers to talk in the more rational but less nationalist terms of a 'socialism based on the seminal cultural values of both Africa and Europe.'[40] This approach, even if more persuasive, surely constitutes a lesser degree of insistence on the distinctiveness of an African personality. Sekou Touré is in many ways unrepresentative of the French-speakers – and it was perhaps because of his stronger Africanism that at his meeting with Senghor in 1962 on the question of settling African differences he was informed once again of Senghor's belief that Africa should be 'open to all the pollen of the earth and to all the fertilizing contributions of the various civilizations and continents'.[41] The reason for Senghor's insistence is that to him the concept of 'We are all Africans' is, if equated with what he calls 'continentalism', a form of autarchy

– and 'like all autarchies it denies the interdependence of peoples. . . .'[42]

On such occasions Senghor comes dangerously near to joining those 'cosmopolitans' whom Rousseau once accused of trying to 'justify their love of their country by their love of the human race and make a boast of loving all the world in order to enjoy the privilege of loving no one.'[43] Presumably it would then be the English-speaking Nkrumah with whom the nationalistic Rousseau would be in sympathy. In Rousseau's terms Nkrumah at least justified his love for Ghana by his love of the African rather than the human race. And even when he made a boast of loving all the world, it was but to love a continent. 'We are all Africans – and the rest of the world is not', was the essence of his outlook.

Yet it is possible to exaggerate the difference between these two African views. No one acquainted with the varied sides of Senghor's philosophy can doubt that he, too, has a deep emotional attachment to his own race. To say that he and Nkrumah differed only as to the means for achieving a common end would be not only platitudinous but also somewhat inaccurate unless that end is given a broad name like 'Africa's assertion of herself'. The two African outlooks would still differ in their interpretations of what would constitute such an assertion.

Nevertheless, agreement even on broad objectives must be deemed significant for the future course of African history. It remains now to examine the impulse behind those objectives and the nature of the quest. What is the central aspiration in the national consciousness of the emerging African?

The language of African nationalism in recent times has tended to suggest that the central aspiration was liberty, indivisible or not. Single word slogans like *Uhuru*, *Kwacha* and 'Free-Dom' have emphasized this. So has the understandable conceptual framework which makes 'anti-colonialism' a demand primarily for 'liberation' – and proceeds from there to the precarious conclusion that the basic motivation behind African nationalism is a desire for 'freedom'. That African freedom is immensely important to the African nationalists is, if course, beyond doubt. But it is not to be hastily assumed that the average African really shares Lord Acton's conception of liberty, not as a means to a higher political end but as itself the highest political end. The average African does not rate liberty even in the sense of 'independence' so high. Instead, there are higher political ends that such liberty is, as a means or prerequisite, needed for.

One alternative end which might suggest itself is equality. And it is certainly an end now obscured in all the chanting of 'independence' in the remaining colonies and 'freedom from neo-colonialism' in the countries already sovereign. Even in Kenya, which emerged late from being a 'White Man's Country', the cry for political equality has all but disappeared from the vocabulary of the African nationalist. The days when *Pan-Africa* could carry an article by a Kenya nationalist under the heading of 'Kenya Today: Equality is Our Slogan'[44] seem to have really receded into history.

All the same it must be emphasized that nationalism in Africa is still more egalitarian than libertarian in its ultimate aspirations. This is not to underestimate the logical complications in any attempt to disentangle the concepts of equality and of liberty – complications that may be suggested by recalling that the first Declaration of Independence from British colonial rule opened with the premise that 'all men are created equal'. And yet disentangling the two concepts can surely be carried at least to the extent of suggesting that whereas the Americans proclaimed 'equality' in pursuit of independence, the African nationalists have now sought independence in pursuit of equality. Indeed, the development of African nationalism is a progressive metamorphosis of what would be acceptable as an adequate expression of racial equality.

In that development can be traced a transition from the notion that 'freedom is indivisible' to the notion that 'equality is indivisible' – that until all Africans are regarded as the equals of Europeans, no African can be sure that he is accepted as an equal. To substitute Tom Mboya's phraseology, 'as long as any part of Africa remains under European rule, we do not feel that Africans will be regarded in the right way.'[45] What this means is that 'the manumission of mother Africa from the foreign yoke'[46] is essential not only for its own sake, but also for elevating the African in the eyes of the world – and in African eyes too. The underlying logic of this belief is that the slave needs his freedom to be the equal of free men, as well as to exercise it.

On closer analysis, however, the African quest combines the aspiration of equality with those two other nationalistic aspirations which Hertz described as 'individuality and prestige'. The obvious designation for the combination is 'dignity' – a word even more imprecise than 'equality'. Perhaps it is useful to coin a term like 'dignitarianism' for such a movement, and then give it some precision by definition. It can, for example, be defined to *exclude* the nationalism that takes its minimal or strictly 'human' dignity for granted and only seeks to reunite, say, Germans with fellow-Germans across an artificial border. African examples of such unification-minded nationalisms include the Bakongo, confident of themselves in relation to their neighbours, but seeking to unite with fellow-Bakongo. Then there are the Ewe, still restive at division. In their cases 'dignity' has been a vague incidental to the central aspiration of reunification – no matter how often it was used as a rallying slogan.

Sub-classifications are possible within the dignitarian forms of nationalism. There is the nationalism that seeks to protect its 'dignity' from some impending danger, real or imaginary. Examples are the nationalism of the Afrikaners of South Africa and, in a different context, that of the immigrant elite in Liberia and of the Amharic aristocracy in Ethiopia. These peoples have had no doubt about their own 'dignity' as they have seen it. Their recent preoccupation, in varying degrees of intensity, has been with how to ensure its continuation. This then is protective dignitarianism.

The nationalism of re-unification like that of the Arabs, or even of the Bakongo, can be dignitarian if unity is envisaged as a means of *recovering* some lost dignity in a glorious past. Here again it is a question of degree of emphasis rather than of the complete absence of this or that aspiration. As Thomas Hodgkin put it, 'since Byron reminded the Greeks of Sappho and Marathon every nationalist myth has included this element of past greatness.'[47] But Hodgkin goes on to note that although 'no Western European seriously questioned the fact that there had been periods in the past when Arab and Indian civilizations, owing little to European stimulus, flowered . . . the case of the peoples of Africa is different.'[48] For them it is not a simple case of recovering a dignity which everyone concedes they once had. It may indeed be an attempt to recover their own respect for themselves, but it is also an endeavour to win for the first time the respect of others. Self-respect and respect by others, difficult to separate as they usually are, are in the Africans' case even more so. Theirs then is an assertive rather than strictly 'restorative' dignitarianism – the kind that impelled Jomo Kenyatta early in 1962 to advise the Europeans of Kenya to learn for the first time to address the African as *Bwana*.

And when, out of similar convictions, Milton Obote on the achievement of Uganda's independence refused to extend his country's recognition either to South Africa or, in spite of the Commonwealth link, to the Federation of Rhodesia and Nyasaland, that old Lincolnian notion of an indivisible freedom had found its ultimate maturity in the concept that the dignity of man was indivisible.[49] On such a level, the African nationalist of whatever shade of Africanism, becomes Rousseau's 'cosmopolitan' – rising from the emotion of 'We are all Africans' to the aspiration of 'We are all men.'

The emotion is likely to persist for as long as the aspiration is no more than an aspiration. Nationalism feeds on ambition, and ambition feeds on 'conflict' or competition with others. The ambition is the creation of a respected image of *Bwana Mwafrika*,[50] and the conflict is with the forces in the way. Nkrumah's proposals for a speedy formation of a continental union were unique among heads of states only in being the most ambitious manifestation of the assertion of 'We are all Africans.' There remains an area of life within which Africans of different shades of commitment continue to feel that they are, in Lumumba's phrase, 'brothers in race, brothers in conflict.'[51] That is what the Organization of African Unity is all about.

To the question whether they are brothers because of 'race' or because of the 'conflict', it can only be said that the two merge together and become virtually indistinguishable.

CHAPTER FOUR

GHANA AND AFRICAN DIPLOMATIC THOUGHT

KWAME NKRUMAH has fallen from power. Yet on many of the themes of African thought that we hope to discuss his views will continue to have some bearing. No contemporary figure has had a greater ideological impact on sub-Saharan Africa than Nkrumah has had. It does not necessarily followed that there are more people in Africa who would agree with Nkrumah than would agree with some other leader. But it does mean that Nkrumah, even out of power, continues to be the kind of person with whom many would at least be *conscious* of being in disagreement. If he is not a leader of African opinion, he has been a great initiator of African debates. He has often articulated the kind of ideological hypotheses which the rest of Africa has then proceeded to debate.

Part of the explanation of Nkrumah's impact lies, of course, in the man himself and in his flair for controversy. But at least as important has been the fact that he led the Gold Coast to the distinction of being the first black colony to attain independence. His triumph was a historic precedent in the fortunes of African nationalism.

Although nationalism in the Gold Coast was born as a reaction to what was happening *within* the country, it later came to seek ultimate fulfilment *without*. But here again Nkrumah's country was only the first of many. Among the distinctive aspects of sovereign statehood is simply the conduct of authoritative diplomatic activity. And so the self-centred principle of 'self-determination' matured into a cult of participation in international affairs for many a new state.

But the nature of African nationalism had been such that on attainment of sovereign status African countries started devising a two-tier structure of diplomatic activity. One tier concerned

relations between African countries themselves; the other concerned relations with the outside world. Yet in effect these two
levels had lines of inter-connection between them, and the nature
of inter-African relations could not always be distinguished from
the nature of international relations at large.

Nevertheless, the distinction between these two levels of
African diplomacy should not be overlooked, for, as we hope to
demonstrate in later chapters, it does sometimes have practical
consequences in situations like that of the Congo.

In this chapter we are limiting ourselves to the impact of
Nkrumah's Ghana on these two levels of African diplomatic
thought. Some of the themes which emerge will be taken up
again later for more comprehensive analysis.

In our discussion of the theme of intra-African diplomacy we
shall include the lingering allegiance which Nkrumah has paid to
the Pan-Negro origins of contemporary Pan-African thought. We
shall then assess Ghana's role in those themes of unity which have
often characterized African politics since Ghana's own independence. As we move out into that second *extra*-continental level of
African diplomatic activity, we shall first assess Ghana's contribution to the general ideology of African international relations. The
chapter will conclude with an evaluation of Ghana's general
record in public diplomacy at large.

As regards the lingering attachment to Pan-Negroism – it was
perhaps fitting that the first black African country to be liberated
from colonial rule should have been led by someone with such
close connections with Negroes in the United States as Nkrumah
had. As we know, Nkrumah was himself educated in the United
States. And his activities among American Negroes had ranged
from dating Negro girls to preaching in Negro churches. The
book that had the biggest impact on him in his formative years
was, he tells us, a testament of Marcus Garvey.[1]

At a state dinner to mark Ghana's independence many years
later, Nkrumah had occasion once again to recall Garvey. But
just before he mentioned Garvey's name to illustrate a point, he
invoked the dramatic device of asking the band to play Ghana's
new national anthem. Then he made his point, saying:

Here I wish I could quote Marcus Garvey. Once upon a time, he said,
he looked through the whole world to see if he could find a government
of a black people. He looked around, he did not find one, and he said

60

he was going to create one. Marcus Garvey did not succeed. But here today the work of Rousseau, the work of Marcus Garvey, the work of Aggrey, the work of Caseley Hayford, the work of these illustrious men who have gone before us, has come to reality at this present moment.[2]

Earlier in the speech Nkrumah had reaffirmed Pan-Negroism in the following terms:

There exists a firm bond of sympathy between us and the Negro peoples of the Americas. The ancestors of so many of them come from this country. Even today in the West Indies, it is possible to hear words and phrases which come from various languages of the Gold Coast.[3]

In the history of Pan-Africanism the most important Negroes of the Americas remained George Padmore from the West Indies and W.E.B.DuBois from the United States. To these historic figures Ghana opened her doors on attainment of independence. They died citizens of Ghana. The whole phenomenon was a 'Back to Africa' event of unique symbolism.

A year after Ghana's independence Nkrumah visited the United States at the invitation of President Eisenhower. Being his first visit there as Prime Minister of the newly independent Ghana, Nkrumah looked upon the occasion as, in a sense, 'the fulfilment of the hopes and dreams of my student days at Lincoln University.'[4] Among the places he visited during his stay in the United States was Harlem in New York. Nkrumah has recorded that 'the spectacular and spontaneous welcome given to me by the people of Harlem remains one of the happiest memories of the whole tour.'[5]

In the spring of 1961 it was as President of the Republic of Ghana that Nkrumah once again visited Harlem. He addressed a Negro rally there. He reminded his audience that Harlem had once been a home for him. As visiting Head of State, Nkrumah was careful about what he said on civil rights in his host country. In fact, he hardly mentioned the specific Negro problem of the United States. To some extent his audience was disappointed. Yet his very presence in Harlem as President of an African country was a moment of excitement to the audience and perhaps to Nkrumah.[6]

Yet back in Africa Nkrumah's consciousness of being black has been allowed to be operative only in specific areas of policy. In a speech in April 1960 Nkrumah asserted:

When I speak of Africa for Africans, this should be interpreted in the light of my emphatic declaration, that I do not believe in racialism and colonialism. The concept of 'Africa for the Africans' does not mean that other races are excluded from it. It only means that Africans, who naturally are in the majority in Africa, shall and must govern themselves in their own countries.[7]

Putting 'racialism and colonialism' together in this way signifies, in the case of Nkrumah, a deeply established association of ideas in his mind. As has emerged in previous chapters, Nkrumah has subscribed to what we have called pigmentational self-determination. He is often conscious of being a black man when he is attacking 'colonialism'. But while the consciousness of being black can powerfully sustain opposition to European rule, that same consciousness could endanger the kind of continental solidarity advocated by Nkrumah. Perhaps more than any other black African leader Nkrumah has strongly been a *continentalist* – a believer in the unity of *both* sides of the Sahara. Within months of Ghana's attainment of independence, Accra was getting ready for the first conference of independent African states. Explaining the significance of the conference to his countrymen Nkrumah said in a national broadcast:

For the first time, I think, in the history of this great continent, leaders of all *the purely African* states which can play an independent role in international affairs will meet to discuss the problems of our countries. . . . [8]

It was significant that the countries which Nkrumah was recognizing as 'purely African' were in fact Tunisia, Morocco, Egypt, Sudan, Libya, Ethiopia and Liberia. These were the countries whose representatives he welcomed on 15 April 1958. He affirmed to them a slogan which he at least often tried to live up to: 'If in the past the Sahara divided us, now it unites us. And an injury to one is an injury to all of us.'[9]

In practice it was into three major categories that Africa could be divided. The categories were Arab Africa, English-speaking Negro Africa and French-speaking Negro Africa. Nkrumah began by trying to establish closer ties with each. Within twelve months of each other he contracted two symbolic marriages. One was his own personal marriage to an Egyptian girl – a quiet trans-Saharan marriage of Pan-African significance. The other was the token territorial union between Ghana and Guinea on 23 November 1958 – a loudly proclaimed marriage between the first black colony to achieve independence from Britain and the first to get it from France.

But in the years which followed Nkrumah's role in bringing together the different segments of Africa varied according to segment. In relations between Arab Africa and Negro Africa Nkrumah was, on the whole, a unifying factor. But in relations between English-speaking Negro Africa and French-speaking Negro Africa Nkrumah was, on balance, a divisive factor.

To some extent the two effects that Nkrumah had were, at least in the earlier days, causally related. The causal relationship was at one time connected with the issue of Algeria's independence. Nkrumah was unequivocal in his support for the FLN in their fight against France. At a meeting with the Press when he visited the United States soon after Ghana's independence Nkrumah said he supported the Algerians in their struggle for freedom 'because Algeria is on the African continent'.[10] Two years later, when Ghana was celebrating her attainment of Republic status, Nkrumah paid tribute to 'the gallant men and women who had laid down their lives for the liberation of Algeria.'[11] In the same year Nkrumah repeatedly condemned France for an additional act of defiance – for having 'arrogantly exploded this nuclear device on our soil'.[12] The soil in question was, of course, Algeria. By the time that Nkrumah addressed that historic United Nations General Assembly in the autumn of 1960 when many delegations were led by Heads of Government, Nkrumah was more convinced than ever that France could not win a military victory in Algeria. He said:

Indeed, any person who thinks that France can win a military victory in Algeria, lives in a world of utter illusion, and time will prove me to be right. . . . This utter waste of the flower of youth of France and Algeria as a result of a senseless war must now stop.[13]

Nkrumah went on to call upon the United Nations to take on the 'responsibility' for stopping the war and getting the parties to negotiate. By thus seeking some kind of United Nations' role in the Algerian problem, Nkrumah was lending support to the wishes of the FLN itself, which was at the time lobbying at the world body.

It is precisely this kind of open support for the FLN which, on the one hand, brought Nkrumah closer to the Arabs and, on the other, helped to widen the difference between him and French-speaking Africa at large. Later in that same year the Ivory Coast, Senegal, Congo (Brazzaville), Upper Volta, Niger, Dahomey, Chad, Gabon, the Central African Republic, Cameroun, Mauritania and Madagascar, all met at Brazzaville to explore areas of possible joint action by them. On the issue of Algeria the Brazzaville Group, while applauding General de Gaulle's own acceptance of the possibility of self-determination in Algeria, fell short of recognizing the FLN. As for the possibility of the kind of United Nations' role which Nkrumah and others had envisaged, the group asserted that:

They do not want to associate themselves with the hardly practicable and negative solution, consisting in an illusory resort to UNO, for the organisation and control of a referendum in a country which does not come under the guardianship of UNO.

Anxious lest their motives be misunderstood, the group went on to say that

Although not belonging to the Community, they have not hidden their friendship for France. But it is not this friendship which dictates their behaviour today.[14]

They were fearful of the consequences of prolonging the war in Algeria and wanted it ended in 1961 'it being understood that political guarantees would be granted reciprocally to both sides.'[15]

In some ways the Brazzaville Group was indeed 'realistic' in their conception of how the Algerian conflict might be ended. But what they gained in realism they lost in nationalistic solidarity with the Algerians. A certain anti-Arab tendency has sometimes been discernible among French-speaking African leaders – perhaps in part inherited from France and her own anti-Egyptian 'tradition'.[16] In any case the Brazzaville group took a strong stand against inviting the Algerian rebel leader to the summit conference of African states in Lagos in January 1962. They made this stand clear to their prospective Nigerian hosts well in advance. On January 21 a meeting in Ghana took a counter stand to that. The foreign ministers of the Casablanca group of African states issued a statement from Accra saying that they could not attend the conference in Lagos because the Algerian Provisional Government had not been invited. When the organizers of the

Lagos summit conference would still not invite the Algerians to it, Tunisia, Libya and the Sudan joined those who boycotted the conference. When the depleted conference assembled on January 25, feelings were reportedly high. On the 26th the Heads of Governments confirmed their foreign ministers' reiterated refusal to invite the Algerian Provisional Government. And speeches against the 'white Africans' of the North were reported from Lagos.[17]

It will be seen that the division between African countries was not neatly between French-speakers and English-speakers. What was 'neat' was that not a single Arab country found it possible to attend the Lagos conference. On that occasion the continent could easily have divided itself into Arab Africa as against Negro Africa. What spared the continent such a division was the fact that Ghana, Guinea and Mali were on the same side as the Arabs. Racially, Guinea and Mali had almost as little in common with the Arabs as Ghana had. But religiously they had more, since Guinea and Mali were Muslim countries. Ghana was therefore the only black African country which sided with the Arabs for reasons which could not be attributed to religious solidarity.[18]

Almost exactly a year earlier Nkrumah became the only non-Muslim African leader publicly to join in a condemnation of Israel. Nkrumah was a signatory to the African Charter of Casablanca of January 1961. The Charter's resolution on Palestine noted that

Israel has always taken the side of the imperialists each time an important position had to be taken concerning vital problems about Africa, notably Algeria, the Congo and the nuclear tests in Africa, and the Conference, therefore, denounces Israel as an instrument in the service of imperialism and neo-colonialism not only in the Middle East but also in Africa and Asia.[19]

There was so much surprise about Nkrumah being a party to such a condemnation that Ghana's President had to reiterate the position. In fact, there was little conviction behind Ghana's denunciation of Israel on that occasion. She maintained technical co-operation with Israel. What the whole episode illustrated was how far Nkrumah was prepared to go to maintain a trans-Saharan image of solidarity.

In some ways this Arab-Ghanaian accord was surprising – particularly since Nkrumah and Nasser were sometimes regarded as rivals for leadership in Africa. This, at any rate, was the assessment of the *West African Pilot* of Nigeria in one of its attacks against Nkrumah. On the question of leadership in Africa, the newspaper taunted Nkrumah in the following terms:

Until recently it was a tournament between Nasser and Nkrumah but Africa today contains many stars and meteorites, all of them seeking positions of eminence.[20]

But given these strong feelings against Nkrumah which Nigerians have sometimes expressed, does it still remain true that Nkrumah's political impact on the continent resulted in dividing the French-speakers from the English-speakers? Is it not just as arguable that nothing could have brought the English-speaking Nigerians closer to Francophone Africa than a shared hostility towards Ghana under Nkrumah?

This is a pertinent objection to raise against our original hypothesis. We might remind ourselves that the hypothesis was to the effect that, on balance, Nkrumah had been a unifying factor as between Arab and Negro Africa and a divisive factor as between English-speakers and French-speakers within Negro Africa itself. If we examined the feelings which were expressed at the time of both the Monrovia conference in May 1961 and the Lagos conference in January 1962, it might appear that Nkrumah was, in a twisted paradoxical sense, a unifying factor all round. By maintaining links with Arab Africa he had helped to avert a division of the continent into Arab and Negro blocs. And by antagonizing Nigeria, he had helped to forge a bond of shared hostility to Ghana at least as between the largest English-speaking country and the Brazzaville group.

Yet this bond of a shared antagonism towards Nkrumah disguised a more fundamental divide as between the two linguistic blocs of Negro Africa. In March 1964 French-speaking African states dissolved their Afro-Malagasy Union (the UAM) on the ground that its existence as a sectional organization militated against the spirit of broader political accord which the Organization of African Unity stood for. By February 1965 the Francophone states were seriously considering the UAM's revival. Nkrumah's policies were an important contributory factor to this reappraisal. Nkrumah had helped to force the old Brazzaville group back to their former self-conscious exclusiveness.[21]

In part, the root of the trouble went back to Nkrumah's increasing conviction in the course of 1960 that many of the newly independent Francophone African states were, in effect, 'client states, independent in name'.[22] Their lukewarm attitude towards the FLN was only one manifestation of their continued dependence on France. This view of France's relations with her former colonies influenced Nkrumah's judgment on the issue of African association with the European Economic Community. He even viewed the Treaty of Berlin of 1885 as a kind of precursor of the Treaty of Rome of 1957 which set up the EEC. Nkrumah said:

The former treaty established the undisputed sway of colonialism in Africa; the latter marks the advent of neo-colonialism in Africa . . . [and] bears unquestionably the marks of French neo-colonialism.[23]

Nkrumah's attitude to the European Economic Community affected the attitudes of the other English-speaking African countries. On this issue, more perhaps than on any other single issue, Nkrumah set the pace for the policies of other English-speaking African countries. After the Commonwealth Prime Ministers' conference of 1962 there was general speculation in Britain as to why the Nigerian Government, noted for its cool-headed pragmatism, should have rejected out of hand the idea of being associated with the European Economic Community. A persuasive suggestion was the one which was made by, among others, Walter Schwarz in an analysis on the European Service of the BBC. Schwarz argued that

Nigeria's Government, always open to attack from its own youth for being too lukewarm about its nationalism, simply finds it politically impossible to lag behind Ghana on this issue.[24]

Since then there have been some changes both in the European Economic Community's methods of dealing with Commonwealth Africa and in the attitude of Nigeria and the East African countries towards the possibility of some kind of arrangement with the European Community. This point will be taken up again later when we discuss more fully the concept of 'neo-colonialism' and the relationship between Pan-Africanism and Non-alignment. But for the moment suffice it to note Nkrumah's leadership in a policy which had the effect of emphasizing the difference between Francophone and English-speaking Africa.

A further factor which alienated Francophone Africa from Ghana was the hospitality which Ghana continued to extend to political rebels from her French-speaking neighbours. In part this also arose out of Nkrumah's conviction that most of his neighbours were in any case under 'puppet regimes'. It was therefore proper for Ghana to harbour and even sympathize with the native opponents of those regimes. This factor, perhaps more than any other, was what aroused the anger of the French-speaking African states at their meeting in Nouakchott in February 1965. And it was this factor which made them threaten to boycott the meeting of the Organization of African Unity which was scheduled to take place in Accra later in 1965. The price which they momentarily extracted for their attendance in Accra was a new 'Good Neighbour' policy to be followed by Ghana, especially in regard to the rebels from French-speaking Africa. Ghana could still give political asylum, but she was no longer to afford the rebels a public platform for their grievances or a training ground for their resistance.[25]

However, all indications were that Ghana would find it hard to maintain the kind of 'good neighbourliness' demanded by her neighbours. On the contrary, the general evidence would suggest that Ghana was prepared to alienate herself from most of the present regimes of Francophone Africa in the hope of a more militant Pan-African partnership in the future. Nkrumah seemed to be of the opinion that time was on the side of the more radical French-speaking Africans in opposition to the present regimes.[26]

But what kind of regimes would meet Nkrumah's criteria of ideological acceptability? This is what brings us to the more specific concepts which Nkrumah has contributed to African diplomatic thought.

Nkrumah valued distinctiveness in African diplomatic behaviour. Out of this attitude emerged Nkrumah's concept of 'the African personality' – perhaps his most famous single contribution to African ideology. Robert W. July has suggested that the idea is no older than Ghana's independence – 'President Nkrumah's concept of the African personality appears to have been first enunciated no earlier than 1957 or 1958.'[27] On the eve of the first conference of independent African States in Accra early in 1958 Nkrumah certainly used the concept in terms of newness. He said in a broadcast to the nations

For too long in our history, Africa has spoken through the voices of others. Now, what I have called an African Personality in international affairs will have a chance of making its proper impact and will let the world know it through the voices of Africa's own sons.[28]

However, the concept's first implementation was perhaps the very decision to change the name of the Gold Coast. The idea of 'personality' in this context implies the idea of *identity* – and a country's name is an important aspect of its total identity. According to Nkrumah, the main objection to the name 'the Gold Coast' was that it had a translatable meaning. Any name which was translatable militated against distinctiveness and was therefore a dilution of identity. In a speech to the Ghana National Assembly on 12 November 1956 Nkrumah argued in the following terms:

The name Gold Coast . . . is internationally regarded not as a name but as a description. It has therefore been the habit of each European country to give to the Gold Coast in its own language not the English title of 'Gold Coast', but a name which in the language of that European country means 'gold coast'. The Government consider it very undesirable that the Gold Coast should begin its independent international life with as many names as there are languages represented in the United Nations.[29]

But why was the name *Ghana* chosen to replace that of the Gold Coast? Here too questions of identity and personality were involved. David E. Apter has pointed out that new nations often revel in the vision of 'rebirth' and the innocence of youth.[30] But even more important for a sense of national identity is a myth of being old and wrinkled as a nation. As Northern Rhodesia later came to do, the Gold Coast could have *contrived* a new name for itself. But the Gold Coast selected instead an identity with a wealth of history behind it. Though a new state it preferred the grey-haired dignity of an ancient name. As Nkrumah romantically put it in the course of the independence celebrations:

It is our earnest hope that the Ghana which is now being reborn will be, like the Ghana of old, a centre to which all the peoples of Africa may come and where all the cultures of Africa may meet.[31]

In the very name he adopted for the new member of the international community, Nkrumah sought to lend a historical dimension to the impact of his 'African personality'.

As for the conference of independent African states which was convened soon after, nationalists in other parts of the continent came to view it as marking 'the birth of the African personality' in the *diplomatic* field. And hopes of a 'united will of all Africans' at the United Nations began to be expressed.[32]

Both from Nkrumah's romantic conception of Ghana as 'a centre to which all the peoples of Africa may come' and from the general optimistic assessment of the significance of the first conference of African states, it will be seen that the idea of an African personality was linked from the start with the myths of Pan-Africanism. These myths are in turn another area of African thought influenced by Nkrumah's general views. We have already noted the effects of his policies on alignments as between Francophone Africa, English-speaking Africa, and the Arab part of the continent. What we might glance at now is his theory about a continental union.

The union between Ghana and Guinea mentioned earlier did not assume much vigour. But at least it was evidence enough of Nkrumah's readiness to approach the issue of African unity on a piecemeal basis.[33] But by the time that he and other heads of African states assembled at Addis Ababa for the conference which gave birth to the Organization of African Unity, Nkrumah was no longer a believer in a step-by-step approach to unity. His book *Africa Must Unite* was released in time for the conference, and in it he made a vigorous plea for immediate continental union. He was isolated at the conference – but he gave nationalists everywhere a major hypothesis to argue about.

What was the essence of that hypothesis? Voltaire had once asserted that 'the best is the enemy of the good'. In his theory of African unification, Nkrumah reversed the order and seemed to be arguing that the good was the enemy of the best.[34] He was saying that while modest functional co-operation might be good in itself, it would reduce the impetus for a more ambitious degree of integration. By the same token, movements for regional unification like the one which aspired to an East African federation would militate against the cause of a broader continental union. As Nkrumah himself put it:

The idea of regional federations in Africa is fraught with many dangers. There is the danger of the development of regional loyalties, fighting against each other. In effect, regional federations are a form of balkanization on a grand scale.[35]

Ugandans came to use this as a rationale for their own growing opposition to the federal aim in East Africa. But Julius Nyerere was emphatic in his dismissal of Nkrumah's thesis. On 9 December 1963, Nyerere said:

> We must reject some of the pretensions that have been made from outside East Africa. We have already heard the curious argument that the continued 'balkanisation' of East Africa will somehow help African unity. . . . These are attempts to rationalize absurdity.[36]

In this context of an East African federation in relation to the prospects of a continental government, Nyerere was probably right and Nkrumah wrong. 'We believe that the East African Federation can be a practical step towards the goal of Pan-African Unity', Nyerere and his East African comrades asserted in their declaration to form such a federation in June 1963. And plausibility was on their side.[37]

And yet Nkrumah's argument that narrower forms of union harm the cause of broader unions is not always implausible. Nyerere and his Government described Tanganyika's union with Zanzibar as a step towards the goal of an East African federation. In this latter case Nyerere was wrong. The narrower unification of Tanganyika and Zanzibar has harmed the ambition of a broader unification of East Africa as a whole. Nothing could have dramatized more effectively the problems which would attend a prospective East African federation than the problems already met in relations between Zanzibar and Tanganyika. Even in external affairs it has not always been certain that the central government in Dar-es-Salaam could speak for the union as a whole. The prolonged argument as to which of the two Germanies was to have an Embassy in Tanzania was one case in point.

The moral of this whole experience is that there are occasions when a *blind* plunge into union is what is needed to make the union take place at all. The union of Tanganyika and Zanzibar did itself constitute such a sudden plunge. But once that took place, East Africa as a whole could no longer federate *blindly* – for the smaller union had opened the eyes of the region as a whole to the difficulties involved in such a venture. Nkrumah's hypothesis has therefore found some kind of evidence in East Africa's experience after all.[38]

As for Nkrumah's philosophy in regard to international affairs at large, he seems to have put considerable emphasis on broad participation. For him it would not do to limit the African personality to those affairs which are of direct relevance to Africa. The African presence in world politics should be felt beyond the issues of immediate concern to the African continent. The result of this reasoning is that Ghana has gone further than any other single African country to get herself involved in broad international issues.

In a sense, it began with Nkrumah's decision to remain within the Commonwealth. Given that Ghana was the first black African colony to attain independence, the future of the Commonwealth in Africa depended a good deal on what kind of precedent Nkrumah set. The Sudan before him had declined membership of the Commonwealth. Would Negro Africa now accede to it? Ghana set the precedent of African accession. There was surprise in some quarters, but Nkrumah clearly believed in the grouping. As he himself observed during that visit to America which followed independence:

> Some Americans have expressed surprise that Ghana, after emerging from colonial status, should choose of its own free will to remain within the Commonwealth. . . . But we believe that the evolving form of the Commonwealth is an institution which can work profoundly for peace and international co-operation. . . . No policies are imposed on it from above. It does not even seek unity of policy. But it provides a unique forum in which men of different culture and different approach can sit down together and see what can be done to lessen tensions and to increase the economic and social well-being of themselves and their neighbours.[39]

There have been occasions since then when Nkrumah has felt that lessening world tensions at large was more important than Commonwealth goodwill. One such occasion was when he reprimanded Prime Minister Macmillan for giving India military aid when India was attacked by Communist China. Nkrumah was afraid that aid to one side in the Sino-Indian dispute might all too easily result in aid being given to the other side by someone else – with all the risks of escalation.[40]

In nuclear politics, too, Ghana has sought to be a participant. In June 1962 Accra was host to a 'World without the Bomb' conference attended by almost all organizations in the world which were opposed to the threat of nuclear warfare.[41]

But perhaps to be a participant in the science of the atomic age postulated not merely an opposition to nuclear warfare, but some kind of involvement in nuclear science itself. Or so Nkrumah implied when he said in December 1964 that in this 'age of atomic revolution' neither Ghana nor Africa could afford to lag behind other nations. He declared:

We must ourselves take part in the pursuit of scientific and techno-logical research as a means of providing the basis of our socialist society. Socialism without science is void.... We have therefore been compelled to enter the field of atomic energy because this already promises to yield the greatest economic source of power since the beginning of man.

Nkrumah was speaking at a ceremony at which he laid the foundation stone of Ghana's Atomic Reactor Centre at Kwabenya near Accra.[42]

In the summer of 1965 it was in a different kind of international participation that Ghana was involved. Ghana's High Commissioner in the United Kingdom became Ghana's special envoy to Hanoi in a bid to break the South Vietnam impasse. The mission was not successful, partly because the United States rejected Ghana's suggestion to stop the bombing of North Vietnam. But the fact that Ghana attempted at all was one more illustration of Nkrumah's assertion of an African presence in world affairs. One of the tragedies of his career is that he fell from power when he was on one of these missions in Peking in February 1966. His diplomatic participation abroad made it easier for his opponents to force him out of office.

Perhaps it was also fitting that the first African to be elected President of the United Nations General Assembly fourteen months before the Ghana *coup*, should have been Nkrumah's Ambassador, Alex Quaison-Sackey. And just as fitting was Sackey's own description of the election as a fulfilment at last of 'the African personality' in the world organization.[43]

In the chapters which follow we shall continue to draw, as we have already drawn in previous chapters, from Nkrumah's utter-ances and declarations of policy on different aspects of inter-African politics and international affairs. Behind the utterances remain Nkrumah's unique place in the development of African diplomacy, ranging from his role in Arab-Negro relations to his active intrusion into the highest levels of international politics.

CHAPTER FIVE

NEO-DEPENDENCY AND AFRICA'S FRAGMENTATION

WE POINTED out in the second chapter that an end of colonial rule is not synonymous with independence. In this chapter we propose to look at one implication of this statement. We might start from the truistic premise that there are degrees of independence. What we should go on to ask is whether there are gradations of colonial status as well. Is the condition of being a 'dependency' relative? Is there such a thing as a state of neo-dependency – a status below the level of meaningful sovereign initiative but disguised as something higher?

One affirmative answer came from the All-African People's Conference held in Cairo towards the end of March 1961. The conference gave collective recognition to a relatively new concept in African nationalistic thought. The name given to this idea was 'neo-colonialism'. As for the phenomenon which the term designated, it was viewed by the conference as indirect political and economic manipulation, designed to perpetuate external control in Africa in more subtle ways.[1] Neo-colonialism is then the actual *activity* of manipulation which an external power might carry out or attempt to carry out. But we might use 'neo-dependency' to describe the *status* of an African country which was being so manipulated.

Perhaps no term in African nationalistic vocabulary has had a harder time establishing its respectability among Western audiences than has the term 'neo-colonialism'. There are reasons for this linguistic handicap. Perhaps before we analyse the term itself we should evaluate its 'social standing' as a concept of diplomatic discourse.

One handicap which the term has suffered from is precisely its etymological nearness to the word 'colonialism'. This has tended

74

to give the term 'neo-colonialism' a ring of obsolescence. The British, for example, are reconciled to the end of colonialism. They therefore cannot see how the mere prefix of 'neo-' can save African protests from being a simple case of flogging a dead imperial horse. Moreover, these particular Anglo-Saxons are in any case instinctively prejudiced against new English words which are not English-born.

Across the English Channel, however, the reaction against the term 'neo-colonialism' might arise out of a simple continental attachment to 'precise' definitions. 'What does it mean?' a continental European might ask – convinced *a priori* that it could not mean anything. M. Spaak was unhappy once about the lack of a precise definition of 'neo-colonialism'.[2]

Yet we need to remember that what is vague is not necessarily meaningless. In trying to determine how meaningful 'neo-colonialism' might be, we propose in this chapter to test the term against a specific type of relationship which some nationalists have described as 'neo-colonial'. The relationship in question is African association with the European Economic Community. At the time that Britain was applying for membership of the Community, most of Commonwealth Africa declared its opposition to being institutionally associated with the European Community. And the opposition was, in part, based on the assumption that African associates of the EEC were in effect neo-dependencies. How meaningful was that assumption? And how was it related to the weakness which seemed implicit in the fragmentation of the African continent into small states?

Yet before the term 'neo-colonialism' can be tested against this particular issue of African association with the EEC a minimal definition is called for. And one definition we might usefully examine lies in Nkrumah's description of neo-colonialism as 'a logical development of the discredited theory of indirect rule.'[3]

In a sense this does indeed shift the problem of definition on to the concept of 'indirect rule'. But some idea of Lugard's policy preferences is perhaps all we would need for our purposes. In regard to Northern Nigeria Lugard felt that it was 'desirable to retain the native authority and work through and by the native emirs.'[4] In regard to the internal control of Uganda Lugard asserted that 'the object to be aimed at in the administration in this country is rule through its own executive government.'[5]

It was presumably on such evidence, on paper and in practice, that Nkrumah worked out his own definition of indirect rule – in his own words, 'to let the African Chief appear nominally in control while actually he was manipulated from behind the scenes by the colonial power'.[6] Neo-colonialism is, then, a more refined form of this process. The African 'Chief' is now granted a flag, a national anthem and a seat in the United Nations – but essentially he is still being manipulated behind the scenes either by the former master or by a new one. The nature of the strings of manipulation has changed from 'the rights of conquest' to 'the rights of he who pays the piper'. In both instances it is a case of appearing to grant formal autonomy, and even proclaiming to the world that the Africans were free, whereas in practice Africa's rulers remained Europe's subjects.

Curiously enough there were times when Lugard himself, perhaps only as an answer to world criticism of British annexations, talked as if indirect rule as practised in the colonies amounted to giving back the country to its own people, as independence is supposed to amount to today. In 1938, for example, Lugard was addressing a Conference in Oxford in these terms:

> When lately Britain protested against Italy's attack upon Abyssinia, it was argued that during this era of acquisition she had done the same thing herself . . . [as in the case of] the conquest of Ashanti, the protectorate over Uganda, and the overthrow of Fulani Rule in Northern Nigeria. Putting aside the fact that the action was in each case practically forced upon us, we may remind our critics that in every instance without exception the country was restored to its previous rulers.

This, of course, fell short of what today would be called even formal independence – the native rulers were reinstated with powers only restricted in the interests of justice and good government.[7]

Within his ideological responses in turn, what Nkrumah feared a generation later was a policy of having African rulers reinstated by formal independence – 'with powers only restricted in the interests of "justice" and good business.'

But if neo-colonialism is something new, and is to be distinguished from old colonialism by its *indirectness* what was 'direct' about the colonialism of old – if it worked though 'a system of indirect rule'? Can the ideological analyst penetrate into the comparative logic of the two concepts?

When colonialism in the old days used Chiefs it was, as Lugard has told us, primarily for *internal* rule. What was to be direct and absolutely certain was the issue of 'sovereignty' residing in Britain. 'Undisputed sovereignty was one of Lugard's principles', his biographer has, as we have noted, emphasized.[8] And in its international sense, particularly in the case of the self-governing colonies like Southern Rhodesia at the present day, the residual core of sovereignty which still remains with Britain is the right to conduct the international affairs of the territory, and to speak for it to the world at large.

Neo-colonialism, however, is a reshuffling of roles between the new 'Client Chief' of an African country and the big power behind him. Sovereignty in its international sense is, in fact, passed on to the Chief – and more often than not the big power under neo-colonialism sets about manipulating the Chief not so much in the Chief's relations with his own people as in his relations, in the Cold War context, with other states. As of old the big power is still the power behind the Chief's stool, but as of now the power is more interested in the directives the Chief gives to his Foreign rather than to his Home Secretary – except in so far as domestic policies have vital foreign implications.

For this control of foreign policy the neo-colonial power may indeed pay. In fact, the whole concept of neo-colonialism leaves the United States just as vulnerable to African attacks as the ex-colonial powers themselves. The suspicion is that the big powers are trying to buy allies in the cold war – and to such bids Nyerere, for one, has retorted that although Africans desired to be friendly to every country, 'we have no desire to have a friendly country choosing our enemies for us.'[9]

The one major issue on which the client Chief's domestic policy may get mixed up with the foreign policy he is intended to pursue is the whole question of what system of government to adopt. Of course, underlying Lugard's whole idea of 'Indirect Rule' is that people should be ruled through institutions they can understand. And yet when, on attainment of formal independence, Africans proceeded to discard the imported models of government and start experimenting with new ones, the Westerner all too often concluded that this was the thin end of the wedge that would not only destroy democracy but introduce communism into the African country. Certainly the Americans have not always distinguished between Eastern-oriented foreign policies and new systems of government within the newly independent states. And, in the words of Chester Bowles,

When we relate all our [American] actions to the presence or absence of a Communist threat in any nation, we tend to turn communism into a natural resource like uranium or petroleum which may be exchanged for dollars at the United States treasury.[10]

If neo-colonialism in this sense means pouring money into a poor country in order to control it politically, it presents another significant contrast to colonialism of old. Today it is not very often that one hears the argument of 'exploitation for European interests' used by *defenders* of colonialism. In the new climate of opinion, that seems more like something a prudent imperialist might cover up with other arguments – such exploitation having now become more a weapon of attack against colonialism than a shield in its defence.

And yet at the turn of the century Sir Harry Johnston, for example, could – without a trace of cynicism – put forward as a sound British policy that a territory like India was to be ruled in such a way that

The European may come in small numbers with his capital, his energy and his knowledge to develop a most lucrative commerce and obtain products necessary to the use of his advanced civilization.[11]

On Africa Sir Harry put forward this exploitation argument in defence of colonization in even clearer terms. He said:

Since we have begun to control the political affairs of parts of West Africa and the Niger Basin our trade with these countries, rendered secure, has risen from a few hundred pounds to about six million pounds. This is sufficient justification for our continued government of those regions and their occasional cost to us in men and money.[12]

The point to remember is that Sir Harry was not being defiantly honest and blunt. His line of defence was not unrepresentative of his time. How representative he was can be further illustrated by a reference to what an opponent of colonization across the Atlantic was saying some years later. Frederick Starr, in the first of that series of articles on the Congo in the *Chicago Tribune* of half a century ago, maintained that he did not approve of 'the exploitation of native population by outsiders for their own benefit.'

'Nor do I feel', he said, 'that even the development of British trade warrants interference with native life, customs, laws and lands.' If the 'even' in the sentence – used, as it was, without any undue cynicism – is not sufficiently revealing Starr makes matters plainer by adding: 'I know, however, that these views are unpopular and heretical.'[13]

Starr's stand on exploitation is not 'heretical' by today's standards. And this change even by itself is a measure of the difference between old colonialism and at least one form of contemporary neo-colonialism. When Sir Harry Johnston argued that six million pounds a year for British enterprise justified 'our continued government' of West Africa, he was in effect saying that it was worth establishing political control in order to get money *out* of a country. When John Foster Dulles argued to the United States Senate that it was 'enlightened [American] self-interest' to give aid – with political strings attached – he was, in fact, saying that it was worth putting money *into* a country in order to establish political control. Not all conditional aid is necessarily 'neo-colonial' but Dulles did tend to think of aid as a manipulative device. Here then was a reversal of means and ends between classical colonialism and at least one form of contemporary neo-colonialism. And if Persia's Dr Amini, when resigning as Premier in July 1962, could demand as of right more American money for Persia because of Persia's position in the cold war, then here also was, in a sense, a reversal of roles between exploiter and exploited.

But the position is made more complicated by Dr Amini's claim that the neutrals got more money than a committed country like Persia.[14] If freedom from old colonialism then meant, in part, freedom from exploitation by the big powers, freedom from neo-colonialism now could have the more positive quality of being freedom to exploit the big powers – to sell a recurrent danger of communism to Western countries and a tantalizing hope *for* communism to Eastern. And if 'enterprise' in competition with, or at the expense of other lands is to be praised by the norms of Sir Harry Johnston, to be 'noncommitted' in foreign policy is not entirely unenterprising. As Nkrumah put it, it was 'nonalignment in action' to accept eighteen million pounds from the United States and Britain for the Volta River Project while negotiating with Russia for a project to develop power from the Bui. It had become possible for a small country, if uncommitted, 'to enter into financial and commercial relations of such magnitude with foreign powers without in the least affecting its independence.'[15]

The qualification that must now be put forward is that this reversal of roles between exploiter and exploited is best exemplified only in those former colonial territories that have turned out to have little else to auction but their foreign policies. In those countries which still have resources which Western countries need or want, the old idea of legitimizing Western control in terms of Western *economic* interests has yet to disappear. Sometimes such arguments are even addressed to Africans themselves, and sometimes by people whose sincerity and lack of material interest in the resources are not in question. Where a case can be made that the exact location of the resources was not inhabited, the case for colonial exploitation is easier still. Even bishops, addressing their multiracial flock in a place like Rhodesia, have been known to argue that colonization is, or could be, 'everything that is praiseworthy' if it involves 'the appraisal and harnessing and making available to the rest of the world the untapped natural resources of an unoccupied territory.'[16]

Of course, the bluntness of Sir Harry Johnston is much rarer now than it was in his time, if for nothing else than the fact that colonization now, unlike in his time, has to be defended against more critics than those of the metropolitan countries themselves. And even these latter are more numerous now than they were in Sir Harry's day.

Nevertheless, in business circles, for example, it has perhaps continued to make sense to justify Western control in terms of productivity, security, prices – 'Supervised child care at Bakwanga diamond mine is one way of raising Bantu health and productivity levels', the argument would go; but more important for productivity was the denial of political rights. After all, when in 1952 the Bantu of Kenya were already enjoying some political rights, atrocities ensued – and atrocities are regrettable because 'the economy is affected, the Bantu's stake is reduced, the British stake unimpressive, and the free world, which needs strategic materials, is poorly served.'[17]

It is such business circles which in 1962 rallied to a Katanga lobby in the United Kingdom, Belgium and the United States. And it is perhaps their vested interests that would seek to ensure that, in Nkrumah's words, 'the new Balkan States of Africa will not have the independence to shake off the economic colonial shackles. . . .'[18]

It is up to the Africans themselves to seek ways of loosening these shackles. Nkrumah himself has tended to argue not so much to the effect that economic co-operation between Africans must look forward to political integration but almost to the effect that there cannot be meaningful economic co-operation between Africans unless there is political integration. The reasoning involved is that short of a political union there would remain, among other things, fratricidal competition between Africans themselves – and within the language of an 'indivisible' Africa fratricide is little short of suicide.

Given, however, that Nkrumah is almost the only African leader who would argue that African unity must *begin* with political integration, Ghana under him had to settle for other forms of a 'beginning'. In 1962 she looked upon the easing of customs 'barriers' between herself and the Upper Volta, and the declaration of Tema as a free port for all African states, as among 'practical steps towards the creation of an African Customs union.'[19] With this Nigeria's Nnamdi Azikiwe agreed.

'Another economic factor which can bring political unity nearer is the establishment of a common market', the Nigerian went on to add.[20] And in April 1962, Ghana, for one, was already committing herself to plans for the formation – at least with the other Casablanca Charter States – of an African Payments Union, a Permanent Council for African Economic Union and Economic and Technical Co-operation.

Yet while Nkrumah was giving support to the idea of an African Common Market, he was at the same time voicing objections to the European common market. It is with the arguments which surrounded the latter issue that we should now concern ourselves. For our purposes the period which best illustrated the neo-colonial fears of Commonwealth Africa was the period between Britain's submission of her application for EEC membership in 1961 to President de Gaulle's veto against British entry in January 1963. Three attitudes were discernible among those Africans who were critical of the idea of African association with the European Economic Community. One attitude was hostile to the very notion of a united Europe – the hostility arising in part out of a suspicion of the Community's motives. Another attitude was to the effect that Europe could do what it wanted but Africa should be no part of it. The third and more realistic attitude was the hope that Africa should benefit by the increased wealth of a united Europe – but not on the formal standard terms and institutional ties implicit in associate membership as then defined for Africa. These three stands were not necessarily taken by different people but were sometimes discerned in the arguments put forward by the same leaders.[21]

It is not the purpose of this chapter to disentangle those attitudes. What we need to note is that in each attitude there did recur the fear that Africa might remain economically backward – and therefore subject to manipulation by those on whom the viability of her economy depended. The fear that Europe's union might retard Africa's economic development rested on the estimated impact that Europe's union might have, firstly, on closer integration between African countries, and secondly, on the *type* of economy which would characterize the African continent.

On the issue of Europe's impact on prospects for unity in Africa, a study made in 1961 put forward the suggestion that 'there is a much greater hope of unity in Africa if the ex-French and ex-British territories are all on a par in their relationship with Europe.'[22] But French-speaking Africa was already enjoying associate membership with the European Common Market, while English-speaking Africa could only do that if Britain decided to join the European Six and if the Six decided to give Britain's former colonies the same terms as the former French and Belgian colonies. If African unity then depended on African countries being 'on a par in their relationship with Europe', and if the parity of relationship open was associate membership of the EEC, then African unity was becoming dependent on decisions which were to be made in Brussels, London and some other *European* capitals. Of course, all would be well from this point of view if all the African countries decided to devise a parity of relationship with Europe that entailed *renunciation* of associate membership by those who already had it. But the temptation to remain associate members was already too great for those who were already in the club.

Indeed, in 1962 the French-speaking areas were so jealous of their status that they rigorously opposed allowing Commonwealth countries to benefit from preferences and aid provided under the Rome Treaty unless, in the words of an Ivory Coast diplomat, 'they become members of the club'.[23] As often as not they were less generous than that. A review of events pointed out that on the question of giving similar associate status to Commonwealth African countries 'France and the existing AOT object, as preference loses its value when it is more widely extended.'[24] This made it difficult for African states to achieve parity of relationship with Europe even if those who opposed the European Common Market swallowed their pride and applied for association.

Then there were some of the legal implications of the Rome Treaty itself vis-à-vis any changes of political boundaries in Africa. In 1961 Tom Soper drew attention to the fact that only that part of Somalia which was once Italian could legally participate in the benefits of the Treaty of Rome; and if any grants under the special development fund were made, they were legally to be spent only on the ex-Italian part of the now single Republic of Somalia. There was then the proposed union of the former French and former British Cameroons pending. 'It is not at all easy to see how all this would be sorted out with the proposed union . . . or with any possible wider associations among ex-British and ex-French territories', Soper commented.[25] But if it was not sorted out in advance, it could be seen as a possible obstacle to such 'wider associations'.

Soper himself argued that because the Rome Treaty required associate members to extend the most favoured nation treatment to each other, it, in effect, required of them to 'create the basis of a Common Market among themselves in Africa'. Considering this, Soper maintained that the Rome Treaty 'provided a positive incentive for closer union among African countries'.

But, like the Aga Khan at a Commonwealth Day reception in Cambridge, Soper made a lot of the argument that 'economically . . . Europe and Africa have become naturally complementary' – and went on to point out that trade between African countries was negligible and likely to remain so for many years partly because 'their products are similar'.[26]

What value was there in the Rome Treaty's 'incentive' to get the Africans to form a basis of a Common Market of their own? If such a basis was important when the Rome Treaty helped to create it, it was surely important if the Africans were to create it on their own initiative. Nor was it self-evident that if countries produced 'similar products' then there is little value in having a common market. After all, the whole idea of that Principle in the Rome Treaty which stood for 'the establishment of a system ensuring that competition in the Common Market is not distorted'[27] was based on a recognition of the obvious fact that the economies of European countries were substantially *competitive*. That was the whole point of bringing down tariff barriers which were intended to protect the domestic industries of each member, and was the whole point of the affirmation of the principle of 'fair competition' as recognized by the Declaration of the Heads of the States forming the European Economic Community. Indeed, many of the European countries were competitive both in their industrial and in their agricultural produce. And a convincing case had yet to be made that while it benefitted them to have a Common Market in spite of producing similar products, it would harm Africans to have a Common Market because they were producing similar products. The range of potential specialization in agricultural produce was indeed narrower than the range in industrial, but given an open market specialization was possible at least on a region-to-region basis in Africa. Certainly a convincing case had yet to be made for the proposition that while Europe would benefit by having a common policy as a basis for selling their cars to outsiders, West African countries would suffer by having a common policy for selling their cocoa to outsiders.

For the more purely psychological reasons for an African's objection to the European Common Market, one must examine some of the presuppositions of African nationalism itself. Nationalism derives sustenance either in opposition to or competitively with other nations. As we have seen, nationalism in Africa sprang out of a philosophy of what Nkrumah simply called 'the right of a people to rule themselves'.[28] It would be a mistake to suppose that such a philosophy must necessarily form a part of every instance of nationalism. The philosophy of the right to self-rule may be a negligible factor in a nation to whom such a right is not at issue. German nationalism, for example, may well have derived sustenance at one time not so much out of a philosophy that the Germans had a right to govern themselves as out of a conviction that they had a right to govern others – though the latter, no doubt, presupposed the former. French nationalism in the colonial wars of Indo-China and Algeria was also rooted not in a belief in some universal right to self-rule but in a conviction of a French right to rule others. In the words of Premier Mamadou Dia of Senegal, Europe was the 'mother of nationalism and . . . by a strange destiny, mother of colonialism'.[29] The scramble for Africa more than half a century ago was thus a clash between a number of European nationalisms quarrelling between themselves in pursuit of the colonies. Out of these European nationalisms of ruling others, then, empires were built. And now out of the African nationalism of self-rule empires have disintegrated. What has been crucial in the two types has been the impetus of opposition to, or rivalry with, other nations.

African nationalism started with the element of opposition rather than rivalry as its sustenance. With the attainment of at least formal independence by most of Africa, African nationalism has needed in part a change of diet. To change the metaphor, the theme of opposition has been slowly retreating to give way to a growing impetus of rivalry. To the extent that there is now a Nigerian nationalism and a Ghanaian nationalism, the rivalry may be strictly inter-African – motivated by what the nationalists themselves would condemn as the aforesaid fratricidal and suicidal instincts. To the extent that there is an *African* nationalism, however, the rivalry is primarily with the Western Europe which had once ruled Africa – not so much a rivalry to maintain equality but a rivalry to achieve equality with Europe.

And yet, thanks to the emergence of the temptation to be *associated* with Europe economically, the furthest in Pan-African sentiment that a hundred parliamentarians from French-speaking Africa could go at a conference with the EEC European Parliament in June 1961 was that the new association envisaged for 1962 should be open to all African states 'on condition that none of them should belong to another economic group whose objectives were incompatible with those of the association itself.'[30] This might have been implicit in the logic of economic competition. But it made it difficult to construct an African unity which was designed to build up Africa to a level of competitive economic equality with Western Europe.

Another factor involved was that although the Pan-Africanists originally viewed unity as a means for achieving equality with Europe, it was originally a case of creating a united Africa to be the equal of a divided Europe. That this would have fallen short of a conclusive assertion of racial equality in, say, technological aptitude was not fully apprehended. What was inspiring was the relative immediacy of the prospect in the eyes of the Pan-Africanists. But by 1961 the idea of a European Common Market, with a partially accepted aspiration to create a fuller European Community later, was more clearly seen to militate against the aspiration of trying to achieve an African equality with the old divided Europe.

Moreover, there had been, in the language of African unification, the implied assumption that even if a united Africa, materially on a par with a divided Europe, did not establish African equality in technological achievement, it would have established African *superiority* in moral terms. The (Nigerian) Action Group Policy Paper on a West African Union issued in 1960 could thus view the creation of such a Union as a means by which Africans were to have proved to the world that 'Negro States, though the last to come, are the first to use their brains for the conquest of the forces that have kept men apart.'[31] Such Negro States would have been almost the first multilingual sovereign states formally to renounce their sovereignty for the unity of at least one group of peoples. And to that extent they would have established a superiority over a Europe which in recent times had had two enormously costly 'civil' wars, more literally fratricidal as well as suicidal – a Europe which still remained in acute competition with itself both internally and in the advantages that each segment of Europe sought from the outside world.

The European Economic Community now would still leave Europe competitive internally, but by gradually achieving a harmonization of European interests externally, it showed signs of outpacing the Africans to the distinction of being the first in this kind of achievement. The moral superiority that the African had hoped to accomplish by the mere act of uniting – regardless of what the unity itself could in turn accomplish materially – was being neutralized as a motivating aspiration of African nationalism.

In those African countries with white settlers articulate enough to ridicule African hopes for unity, the frustration felt by the Pan-African nationalist could be particularly keen. The *Sunday*

Post of Nairobi, Kenya, is not the only organ of settler opinion that has taunted Africans with remarks like:

If Europe, which has been a continental entity for well over a thousand years, heir to the even older civilizations of Greece and Rome, and unified by the Christian faith is, even now, only groping towards unity, it is absurd to suppose that primitive Africa can do better.[32]

Such racial taunts were, of course, older than the European Economic Community. With some African nationalists it even became a matter of racial vindication to achieve unity before 'civilized' Europe achieved it – and thus establish that Africa had a greater capacity for transcending 'primitive tribalism' than the Europe that had taunted and laughed at Africa for that very tribalism for so long.

And should that African nationalist belong to a country like Kenya where even territorial unity was yet to be achieved, his sense of wounded frustration could be greater. To him, as to Tom Mboya, it was now 'ridiculous and hypocritical' to talk about the fragmentation of Kenya when 'even in Europe the trend today is for a people to work together in unity'.[33] Unity had become the twin paramount African political value to Freedom in the wake of decolonization. Tanganyika had the two values together – *Uhuru na Umoja*, Freedom and Unity – for its national motto. The Ghana-Guinea Union declared its motto as 'Independence and Unity'. And the Charter of Casablanca pledged its signatories 'to promote the triumph of liberty all over Africa and to achieve unity'.

About a year before the Casablanca Conference the Action Group of Nigeria was in its turn arguing that their own sovereignty was not to be an end in itself but a means towards ends which included winning respect for people of African descent 'by the creation of a Negro world'.[34] Part of the reasoning involved was that, given that civilization was the sum total of a people's development, and the real importance of a people in the world was to be judged by their contribution to the sum total of human achievement, the Action Group concluded that 'we must ensure that we make a distinct and worthwhile contribution to the civilization of the world'.[35] For Nigerians to make that contribution, Nigerians had to unite. But in itself Nigerian unity, as just another nation-state, could not be distinctive. For Africans to make contribution Africans had to unite – and even by itself that was to be a distinct contribution since it was then expected to be virtually unprecedented, at least as a conquest of multi-tribalism and multi-lingualism.

This is the frustrating significance which came to be implicit in the European Community in relation to what would have been the *intrinsic* value of African unity as a moral achievement. But what of the significance of the emergence of a united Europe in relation to the *instrumental* value of African unity?

This side of the question has already been touched upon but it needs elaboration. It needs, first of all, to be stressed that the Action Group was not unrepresentative of African nationalistic thinking in viewing the first end of African sovereignty as being to bridge in the shortest possible time the technological gulf between Africa and the more developed world.[36] If a United Europe would make the gulf between Africa and the richer nations even greater, that fact alone could be enough to make it psychologically difficult for a proud African to welcome with enthusiasm the prospect of a united Europe. Even as matters now stand the gap between the rich nations that are already in economic orbit and the poor ones that have yet to take off is growing wider rather than narrower – and without a united Europe it is already true that this gap is one of the dominant issues that are bedevilling international politics, and may continue to do so as the century wears on. If the development of the Western world has sparked off what Adlai Stevenson called 'a revolution of rising expectations'[37] the more developed the Western world becomes, the higher will rise the expectations of the poor countries – and the greater will be the gulf in those countries, firstly, between the aspirations they have and the actualities they face, and, secondly, between themselves and the richer nations abroad.

When Commonwealth Africa was discussing the implications of the EEC at the time Britain applied for membership, it did indeed seem unfair to expect Europe to remain technologically static just in order to enable the poorer parts of the world to catch up with it. And yet there did remain in the logic of European unity the aforesaid opposition to, or rivalry with, non-Europeans. In part, this was rivalry with other primarily white countries like the North American ones or the Soviet Union. Indeed, these white rivals are *the* short-term rivals. But other future rivals were under review. Writing for the *New York Times* in December 1961

James Reston claimed that Britain believed in a continuing dialogue with the Russians for considerations of future protection against the pressure of races far more numerous than the white races. Looking at the same long-range future, a French official, talking to Reston, forecast that 'the great conflict at the end of the century will not be ideological, but racial.'[38]

Reston himself conceded that all this might be wrong but, in his own words, 'it is being said, not by broom philosophers, but by some of the most influential officials in the Western world.' And the late Hugh Gaitskell, also addressing Americans in 1962 in reference to underdeveloped countries, expressed the fear lest the European Common Market should develop into something 'inspired by its own form of nationalism behind a high tariff wall.'[39]

But even if Reston was merely theorizing, Gaitskell unduly fearful, and the issue of race undiscussed in the councils of Europe, that issue was still, in the estimation of many Africans, implicit in the logic of European plans. Inevitably Europeans had both a geographical and a racial identity. In relation to Americans, Europeans might be little more than inhabitants of another continent – cousins, perhaps, across the Atlantic. In relation to Africans or Asians, however, Europeans were both inhabitants of another continent and members of another race or group of races. European competition with Africans, actual or presumptive, could not therefore free itself from a racial tinge, and the racial element could gather momentum as the competition becomes less presumptive and more actual. Europe could for the present show a generous inclination to admit African countries to associate membership of the Common Market. But the United Nations Commission for Africa expressed a widespread fear when it said:

If the associated countries were to try to diversify their economies, by increasing the protection of their local industry against the competition of the EEC countries, it is doubtful if the EEC countries would continue to offer the same advantages to the export of primary products by the associated countries.

In other words, associate membership presupposes, in effect, that African countries shall be primary producers. And the Commission goes on to note that there is a danger that the associated African countries might prefer the short-run advantages of tariff concession from the EEC to the long-term advantages of industrial expansion.[40]

If this were to happen, nationalists in Africa may well view associate membership of the European Common Market as just a glorified, twentieth-century version of a role that was assigned to Africans way back from the slave days. 'Hewers of wood' Africans could remain indefinitely if producers of raw materials they remained perpetually – such at least was the reasoning of Ghana's High Commissioner to the United Kingdom when he addressed fellow Africans in London in the spring of 1962.[41]

A Western critic like Tom Soper might, however, retort: 'If wood is wanted and people are prepared to pay for it, I fail to see what is lost by being a hewer of it.'[42] Producing raw materials was itself a scheme of development – or could be. The Western capital that, in the nineteenth century, went seeking raw materials in the colonies was an instrument for development in those colonies themselves, and there developed what has been called an 'interdependence' between a metropolitan centre of industry and a colonial periphery of producers of raw materials.

There have, however, been significant changes since then that have not always been properly understood in this connection. An article on EEC associate membership in 1961 drew attention to the fact that while prices of manufactured goods had been moving slowly upwards for a decade or more, the trend of primary products over the same period has too often been downwards. And yet the same article found it possible to argue that it was not European groupings which threatened the African economies as this instability of commodity prices.[43] If a European grouping could be instrumental in at least delaying the emergence of African manufactured goods and prolonging African dependence on unstable commodities, it was difficult to avoid viewing the European grouping as a threat to Africa's ultimate economic interests.[44] There was at least a measure of plausibility in the observation of the United Nations Economic Commission for Africa that unless certain precautions were taken 'association with EEC can easily tend to perpetuate economic dependency and thus turn out to be a long-term disadvantage to the country concerned.'[45]

All this relates to the significant shift which had taken place in the old 'interdependence' between a Europe in the grip of an industrial revolution on the one hand, and its sources of raw materials in the colonies on the other. In the initial stages of that 'interdependence' Europe needed her colonies more than the colonies consciously needed Europe. But from about the 1930's Europe's internal production had grown more rapidly than its need for imports, and some of the previously imported raw materials could by 1960 be produced within the West's own frontiers. Barbara Ward who has studied the economics of under-development in relation to the richer countries, draws attention in 1962 to the emergence of such items as artificial rubber, new fabrics for textiles, petro chemicals and 'conceivably even ersatz chocolate'. She noted that the Western world's 'pull of develop-ment' on the outside world had declined in magnitude since the early days of the West's economic expansion. 'We have been filling the gap with extraordinary economic assistance,' she says. 'But we do not look on this "job" as a settled commitment. It is still a precarious expedient; and in any case it is too small.'[46]

If Western aid was a precarious expedient and arises sub-stantially out of a conceivably transient ideological division within the white world itself, the African in 1962 had no way of knowing for certain how much longer that aid would be forth-coming. If Western technology had already produced a number of substitutes for raw materials, the African had no way of telling how many other Afro-Asian primary products would become dispensable in the wake of a stronger Europe. There was, of course, the need for food in Europe. But the Economic Com-munity's plans to increase 'the individual earnings of persons engaged in agriculture' were already being interpreted as a sign of the quest for a more self-sufficient Europe even in terms of agricultural products. This is not to mention President Kennedy's vision of an Atlantic Community which could add the food surpluses of North America to the self-sufficiency of an integrated white world. Given all this, Africa as a whole might learn too late that she could not, in Nkrumah's words, improve even her standard of living by remaining an agricultural continent in-definitely or 'improve the skill and ingenuity of her peoples by keeping them solely as workers in rural areas'.[47]

Within the context of this reasoning, the European Common Market was a new emphasis that 'class' or national-income divisions on the global scale partly coincided with race divisions as between white and coloured peoples. And to the extent that the European Common Market had already tempted the bulk of the French-speaking African countries with the carrot of associate membership, and might tempt others, that Market could be taken as one of those devices which Sekou Touré had already condemned as calculated 'to make of all Africa the continent of the proletarian peoples'.[48]

Proletarianism on this inter-continental scale differed from its position in inter-class struggles within national boundaries or within the industrialized region of the world by itself. Unlike the Marxist proletarian, the African had more to sell than his labour. He might have the mines of Katanga or of what was then Northern Rhodesia. He might have the agricultural products of Ghana, Nigeria and the French-speaking areas. He might be concluding his own commercial and industrial agreements – and might even appear to be the very image of a Marxist bourgeois. The point at issue was not whether he had nothing more to sell than his labour, but what price was paid for that labour for what it helped to produce. Nor was this a simple case of the labour theory of value, for what African labour produced in Africa was primarily African not only because African labour produced it, but also, perhaps more important, because the African continent was where the resources were located.

Should the Western community become self-sufficient even in the primary products that African labour produced, or should it devise substitutes for them, that Western Community would ultimately buy African only if that was cheaper than the alternative. And the African might well have to sell at that price. To look at the problem from another angle, if Africa itself was far from self-sufficient in industrial products, if it failed to industrialize by succumbing to the belt of associate membership of the European Community, then the continent as a whole would remain no more than a cheap African market for that European Common Market. There would indeed be an exchange of products. The African may retain that appearance of a bourgeois doing business with another bourgeois. But the basis of that exchange would be a new form of exploitation. It would, if you will, be the neo-exploitation of post-colonial days.

Marx predicted that the poor in the Western world would get poorer, that the rich richer. This did not convincingly come about – and Lenin produced imperialism as the means by which the Western workers were saved from the abject poverty that was predicted for them. Now the Western empires were disintegrating. What could save the Western worker from the long-expected impoverishment under capitalism was allegedly this neo-exploitation of the underdeveloped world that was emerging after 1960. Most African leaders are socialists of one shade or another, though it is not certain how many of even the Marxists among them view this new phenomenon as an extension of Lenin's theory of imperialism. What is certain is that there are some even today who would agree with Nkrumah that

The Treaty of Rome . . . can be compared to the treaty that emanated from Berlin in the nineteenth century. The former treaty established the undisputed sway of colonialism in Africa; the latter marks the advent of *neo-colonialism* in Africa . . . [and] bears unquestionably the marks of French *neo*-colonialism.[49]

What the Africans therefore needed was a central authority of their own to co-ordinate their economic and political defence against this threat.

An interesting point that emerged in all the discussion surrounding the EEC is that Nkrumah's line of reasoning was not far removed from the sort of reasoning involved in the plans of the Europeans themselves – to *defend* Europe against something approaching neo-colonialism. That is to say, that whether certain Europeans admit or not, or want to do anything about it or not, or even consciously realize it or not, Europe was beginning to feel the need for the kind of centralized authority that Nkrumah envisaged for Africa. And Europe felt that need partly because it found itself already with a centralized authority – only this authority was from outside Europe. This was certainly a line that a European federalist might frankly take in the face of the situation that confronted Europe following World War II. Altiero Spinelli, for example, pointed out in 1962 how economic reconstruction after World War II required a central authority for Europe which would distribute aid in a way which would promote a balanced recovery of the various countries; how the political reconstruction of Germany had to take place in such a way as not to generate mistrust and disagreement between victors and vanquished; and how military defence and related foreign policies had to be harmonized. But, argued, Spinelli:

Europe, founded on the principle of national sovereignties, was organically incapable of undertaking such tasks alone. The American hegemony, willingly accepted by the European states in the dramatic period after the war, supplied the supranational power which Western Europe needed but did not possess.[50]

What this meant was that the Europeans were having to give up a little of their old sovereignty – but to someone outside Europe. Certainly in the area of foreign and military policy, each European government was having to exercise its responsibilities substantially through the Atlantic Alliance – an alliance which Spinelli described as 'not a classical alliance but rather a true military confederation'.[51]

Of course, the United States, too, had commitments to this alliance. But, unlike its European allies, America had such a dominant place within the alliance that it was able to preserve a 'substantial measure of its sovereignty'.[52] If the original American colonies then united in order to preserve their collective sovereignty as against Europe, they had more than just succeeded. The supranational authority they had created for themselves had finally gone towards making their collective self a supranational power on the world scene. Created as a defence against Europe, that collective self was now a defence *for* Europe. And it was on Europe that the agony of choosing had now fallen: the choice 'between two forms of supranational power – one constituted by American hegemony, the other by an over-all European government'.[53]

This choice that Spinelli saw as facing Europe continues to bear a resemblance to the choice which Nkrumah saw as facing Africa – if for the notion of an American hegemony in Europe is substituted the notion of a European or white hegemony in Africa. There is the further difference that whereas Europe's dependence on America is, at its most obvious, dictated by military considerations, Africa's dependence on Europe is more in the field of economic needs. But the essential resemblance in choices is still there – such that a De Gaulle can at one and the same time look forward to the expendability of the American presence in Europe and work to make indispensable a European presence in Black Africa.

It is such comparability in situations which might now make it possible to *translate* the term 'neo-colonialism' and make it more meaningful to Western ears. To General de Gaulle an African nationalist might say that what he meant by decrying 'neo-colonialism' was that he was as keen to eliminate or mitigate the European hegemony in Africa as the General himself was keen to eliminate or mitigate the American hegemony in Europe.[54]

To Britain the African might similarly have to invoke an ideological translation which could command comprehension in the context of Britain's own historical experience. The African might make the observation that since Britain ceased to be a full 'giant' herself internationally, she has sought to be part of another 'giant' – first by a 'special relationship' with America, then by seeking membership of the European Community, and back to the Anglo-American special relationship again and now perhaps slowly back to Europe. Because Britain is indeed both 'European' and 'Anglo-Saxon', the belief of being part of either or both 'giants' should be relatively easy to cultivate. But being tied to a 'giant' with which one cannot convincingly identify oneself is what can so easily become a status of neo-dependency.

As for getting himself understood by Walter Hallstein, President of the EEC Commission, an African nationalist might simply say that he shared the view which the Professor expressed to Americans when he visited them in April 1962. On Europe's relationship with America, Hallstein had argued that a 'partnership cannot be founded on disproportionate economic ability and resources'.[55] The African, too, feared a so-called partnership so founded.

But perhaps the easiest translation of 'neo-colonialism' which an African could make is if he was trying to communicate his sensitivities to a Latin American. Given the probable ideological responses of a Latin American in the context of his own historical experience, all that the African nationalist would need to say to define 'neo-colonialism' is to explain that he did not want to see Africa play a Latin America to Europe's United States. 'I have forebodings about Europe becoming the Colossus of *our* North', a Nkrumah might assert.

Translated in these terms perhaps even M. Spaak might be less exasperated about the absence of a clear-cut definition of 'neo-colonialism'.

Africa's jargon is indeed different from De Gaulle's, from Hallstein's, from the idiom of Britain under Macmillan, and from the language of Latin American nationalists. But perhaps there is a level of experience on which their instincts become substantially similar. The impulse to escape from a state of neo-dependency, or to resent such a state while it lasts, is perhaps one such level of comparable experience. And one possible form of escape continues to be the conquest of fragmentation within one's own region of the world.

Yet even unity would not be enough. It would still be pertinent to ask this question: How can Africa overcome her economic weakness without first going through the stage of economic dependence on others? This is the dilemma which will confront nationalists for a generation to come. A military regime in Ghana might restore cordiality with the West. A dynamic political regime in Tanzania might explore new relationships with the East. Nigeria might associate herself with the European Economic Community while Zambia contemplated withdrawing from the Commonwealth. A profound ambivalence will persist for years to come in Africa's relations with those who are more powerful than she is. Perhaps there is something to be said for this ambivalence. To be in need of help and afraid of help might well be the essence of dignified indigence.

CHAPTER SIX

THE PAN-AFRICAN IMPLICATIONS OF SOCIALISM AND THE ONE-PARTY STATE

A FORMER Labour Party Colonial Secretary, Arthur Creech Jones, once remarked that he did not consider it the duty of that office to impose socialism on the colonies.[1] In the case of Africa it has now turned out that such an imposition was not necessary. No ideology commands respect so widely in Africa as the ideology of 'socialism' – though, as in Europe, it is socialism of different shades. In Guinea and Mali a Marxist framework of reasoning is evident. In Ghana Leninism was wedded to notions of traditional collectivism. In Tanzania the concept of *Ujamaa*, derived from the sense of community of tribal life, is being radicalized into an assertion of modern socialism. In Kenya there is a dilemma between establishing socialism and Africanizing the capitalism which already exists. In Nigeria, Senegal and Uganda some kind of allegiance is being paid to the ideal of social justice in situations with a multi-party background. There are places, of course, where no school of socialism is propagated at all. But outside the Ivory Coast there is little defiant rejection of the idea of 'socialism' in former colonial Africa.[2]

Yet the kind of socialism which Arthur Creech Jones would have propagated was a socialism operating in the context of a multi-party system of politics. What is more common in Africa, however, is a socialism wedded to a one-party structure of government.

The preoccupation of this chapter will be with the Pan-African implications of both socialism and the ethic of one-party states. It will examine the extent to which these two aspects of African thought help or retard the ambition of broader integration in Africa.

Let us take socialism first. And in this regard a distinction

97

needs to be noted between socialism as an *ethic of distribution* and socialism as an *ideology of development*. At a broad level of generality it can be argued that the birth of socialism in Europe was inspired by a quest for *distributive* justice. In the wake of a *laissez-faire* industrial revolution in England, socialism was not primarily associated with ways of development. Such ways did indeed feature in socialistic thought but the basic ideal of socialism was what later came to be called 'social justice'. And social justice was conceived in terms of greater equity in the distribution of the wealth of the community.[3]

In Africa, on the other hand, socialism after independence has drawn its greatest appeal from its image of efficiency in development. An ethic of distribution is all right where there is already enough wealth to be distributed. But in communities of limited wealth and 'rising expectations', an ideology of development is often more to the point. And 'socialism' is invoked as a comprehensive term for five-year plans, governmental control of the economy, attempts to 'mobilize the masses', and a general assertion of 'rationality' in dealing with the problems of the country.[4]

Yet this distinction between the ethic of distribution and the ideology of development should not be pushed too far. Both elements are present in African socialistic thought. All that needs to be noted is that *after* independence the quest for an ideology of development has gained a slight ascendancy over the distributive aspect of socialism in individual countries. The qualifications which need to be made will emerge in the course of the discussion.

From the point of view of Pan-Africanism, we hope to demonstrate that socialism as an ethic of distribution has been of service to the cause of Pan-Africanism. We then hope to go on to show, however, that socialism as an ideology of development has started to militate against that same cause.

Historically, the distributive aspect of African socialistic thought is older than the developmental one. It might therefore be useful to examine the older aspect first.

The idea of distributive justice has implied or involved three related concepts. These are, first, opposition to 'exploitation'; secondly, egalitarianism; and thirdly, a general sense of social fellowship. We should take each in turn in the context of African thought.

One factor which made 'socialism' attractive to African

nationalists before independence was not something in socialism itself, but something attributed to *capitalism*. Hobson's and Lenin's thesis on the nature of imperialism might have over-simplified the phenomenon.[5] All the same, historically, the growth of capitalism did have some connection with imperial expansion. Out of this link between capitalism and imperialism emerged the links between European socialists and Afro-Asian nationalists. And this in turn later led, in some cases, to a marriage between nationalism and socialism as ideologies in the new states. The reasoning of the transition from stage to stage was perhaps of the following order:

> Socialism is against the capitalist;
> Nationalism is against the imperialist;
> But the capitalist and the imperialist are either the same man or two men in alliance;
>   Therefore
> Nationalism and socialism in Africa can be either the same ideology or two ideologies in alliance.

Not every African nationalist followed Nkrumah in embracing the Leninist thesis on imperialism.[6] But almost all nationalists shared the view that Africa was being 'exploited' for the primary benefit of the metropolitan powers. The *distributive* principle of imperial exploitation was among the major targets of nationalistic attacks. This common conception of the economic fate of Africa was itself a point of solidarity in Pan-African terms – as well as being a basis for sympathetic dialogue between African nationalists and socialists in the metropolitan countries.[7]

The second point we derived from the ethic of distribution was egalitarianism. As we have already argued in a previous chapter, African nationalism itself is a movement whose main inspiration has been, in the ultimate analysis, a desire for equality rather than for freedom. But the equality which had inspired European nationalism had been equally between *classes*.[8] The equality which has inspired African nationalism is equality between *races* primarily. Nevertheless, the mere presence of an emphatic egalitarian element in socialism – however different in ultimate orientation – was enough to inject a socialistic dose into African nationalism. Here again then socialism served that aspect of Pan-Africanism which rebelled against the racial arrogance of European imperial rule.

This brings us to the third related concept we derived from the ethic of distribution – the concept of a general sense of fellowship. In African socialistic thought, the fellowship is sometimes seen in two related perspectives. One perspective links modern socialism in Africa to the fellowship of tribal life. It often goes on to assert that traditional life in Africa was classless. The other perspective, instead of stressing an old classless Africa, goes out to emphasize that contemporary Africa as a whole is one class within a global class-system – and it is a poor class.

Sometimes the sense of solidarity derived from the latter perspective is not simply Pan-African but 'Pan-poverty'. Mamadou Dia, the former Prime Minister of Senegal, called the first section of his book 'The Revolt of the Proletarian Nations'. He pointed out that Africa and Asia were among the poorest of the peoples of the world, and quoted Gabriel Ardant's powerful line that, 'the geography of hunger is also the geography of death'.[9] Sékou Touré has seen the international system more specifically in terms of class struggle. He has passionately asserted:

The analogy between the proletarian class of the modern world and of proletarian peoples is not fortuitous; it is in the ineluctable consequence of the plundering . . . that the colonial powers practised illegitimately by various means wherever they could implement themselves and rule.[10]

In English-speaking Africa Julius Nyerere, as we will note again later, put it in the following terms:

Karl Marx felt that there was an inevitable clash between the rich of one society and the poor of that society. In that, I believe, Karl Marx was right. But today it is the international scene which is going to have a greater impact on the lives of individuals. . . . And when you look at the international scene, you must admit that the world is divided into the 'Haves' and the 'Have-nots'. . . . And don't forget the rich countries of the world today may be found on both sides of the division between 'Capitalist' and 'Socialist' countries.[11]

This then is the image that African socialists sometimes have of their continent as a 'proletarian continent'. Socialism might therefore be deemed to have created a bond of romanticized poverty between them – and has therefore contributed to Pan-African sentiments at large.

Another romantic image that socialism had fostered occurs in

African conceptions of traditional tribal life. Tom Mboya has put it in the following vein:

In Africa the belief that 'we are all sons and daughters of the soil' has always exercised tremendous influence on our social, economic and political relationships. From this belief springs the logic and the practice of equality, and the acceptance of communal ownership of the vital means of life – the land.[12]

Mboya goes on to assert that the acquisitive instinct, 'which is largely responsible for the vicious excesses and exploitation of the capitalist system', was tempered in African traditional life by a sense of togetherness. 'There was loyalty to the society, and the society gave its members much in return: a sense of security and universal hospitality.'[13]

Given this 'data' Nyerere could in turn proceed to conclude:

We, in Africa, have no more need of being 'converted' to socialism than we have of being 'taught' democracy. Both are rooted in our past – in the traditional life which produced us.[14]

On the issue of classes themselves, Nyerere uses linguistic evidence. He is doubtful whether the word 'class' exists at all in any indigenous language. He regards this linguistic evidence as important – 'for language describes the ideas of those who speak it, and the idea of "class" or "caste" was non-existent in African society.'[15]

But there was no real equivalent of the word 'socialism' in indigenous African languages either. Yet African leaders like Tom Mboya have insisted that 'socialism' existed in traditional Africa in spite of a lack of name for it. Answering a critic's letter in an East African journal, Mboya accused his critic of 'confusing the word socialism with its reality, its practice'. Mboya asserted:

I have not suggested that we have to go delving into the past seeking socialism. It is a continuing tradition among our people. Does the writer of the letter think that socialism had to be given a name before it became a reality? It is an attitude towards people practised in our societies and did not need to be codified into a scientific theory in order to find existence.[16]

In assessing the validity of linguistic evidence on its own Mboya is more plausible than Nyerere. The absence of a name for a phenomenon does not, as we indicated, necessarily prove an absence of the phenomenon itself. Africa might have had 'classes' even if no African language had a name for them. Nevertheless, the myth of a classless traditional life is another aspect of the ethic of fellowship in contemporary Africa. It therefore constitutes yet another area of mutual reinforcement between Pan-Africanism and the distributive branch in socialism.

But what of the development aspect of socialism? David E. Apter, in discussing the role of ideologies in new states, has described nationalism as an ideology of 'parochial solidarity' and socialism as 'more universalistic' in its tendency.[17] To a certain extent Apter missed the point about the relationship between these two ideologies in the African context. The remarkable thing about them in Africa is that, on balance, it is developmental socialism which is parochial from country to country and African nationalism which has been 'universalistic' in its outlook. It is indeed true that African nationalists themselves see 'socialism' as a kind of ideological link with the outside world. Even those who have sought to ethnicize 'socialism' in Africa by attributing it to the cultural genius of the African race have been reluctant to break the cord of universality. As Tom Mboya put it after asserting the tribal origins of African socialism:

It might be argued from what I have just said that African socialism stands in a class by itself. This is not true. The basic tenets of socialism are universal and we are either socialists by these basic principles or not at all.[18]

But the most which can be claimed for socialism in Africa is that it has sometimes helped to reinforce the sense of fellowship already created by *nationalism* as an anti-colonial movement. Mboya, for one, sees African socialism as an added dimension of solidarity to Pan-African nationalism. In his own words:

You all know that Pan-Africanism is a movement based on our common experience under the yoke of colonialism and is fostered by our sense of common destiny and the presence of traditional brotherhood. I strongly believe that in the field of economic relations we can similarly be guided by the traditional presence of socialist ideas and attitudes in the African mental make-up.[19]

But even as an aid to Pan-Africanism, it is the distributive aspect of socialist fellowship which can have such an effect. The developmental aspect has not in practice been unifying. Even if one thinks of development in terms of closer economic integration between African countries, it is to Pan-African *nationalism* that one needs to appeal. It is perhaps not without significance that the headquarters of African unity, Addis Ababa, is the least 'socialistic' of African capitals.

But what would make developmental socialism in Africa 'parochial'? A major reason is that the socialism of planning and economic priorities postulates some control of economic factors. And this control in turn postulates frontiers of jurisdiction. No African government has jurisdiction beyond the immediate territorial boundaries of its country. Planning and governmental control of the economy heighten a consciousness of these boundaries as the limits of jurisdiction. The economy of the country is not, of course, self-sufficient and consideration needs to be given to the impact of the outside world on the home economy. But adaptability to this impact does itself require not only suitable arrangements with external countries in trade and economic co-operation, but also a command of the internal aspects of the economy for purposes of adjustment.

The disintegrative function of socialism in Africa is best exemplified in East Africa. East Africa attained independence as an economic community. The region had a common market and a common services organization. The common market consisted in a flow of goods between the territories which was almost completely free. The common services included a common currency. Both these factors became a hindrance to Tanzania as she developed a planned economy within her own borders. At a 'secret' conference on the co-ordination of economic planning in East Africa held in Entebbe on 17 March 1964, Tanzania's ministerial delegate Nsilo Nswai announced that Tanganyika was considering leaving the common market and setting up a separate currency. This helped to precipitate a crisis which culminated in the Kampala Agreement. The Agreement allowed for quota restrictions on imports from each other, as well as allocated specialized industries to each partner.[20] The common market principle in East Africa was thus seriously diluted.

Yet even this was not enough for the kind of planning that Tanzania now wanted to embark upon. On 10 June 1965 it was revealed from Nairobi that Tanzania was to withdraw from the East African Currency Board and introduce her own monetary system. And control of imports from Kenya soon became more stringent.[21] The situation continued to substantiate the assertion once made by Haas and Schmitter that East Africa's long period of economic association is no guarantee of its own continuation. To use their own words:

Kenya, Uganda and Tanganyika have been united in a common market for thirty-seven years and have maintained a common services organization for a number of costly and important administrative functions for almost as long; yet there is evidence of political disintegration in their relations since they achieved independence.[22]

A major reason for the disintegration is the developmental socialism which had made Tanzania increasingly impatient of economic factors over which she had inadequate jurisdiction. And so this was a case of socialism militating against Pan-Africanism at the level of economic union in East Africa.

And now we must turn to the implications of the party structure in this regard. Nyerere links African socialism to the ethic of the one-party state. He does this by first asserting a connection between the multi-party system and the class structures of the Western societies within which it operates. He has argued:

The European and American parties came into being as the result of the existing social and economic divisions – the second party being formed to challenge the monopoly of political power by some aristocratic or capitalist group.[23]

The assertion here is that Conservatives and Labour, Republicans and Democrats, and the multiplicity of political factions in France are all a reflection of class antagonisms in the West.

But just as multi-party liberalism emerged out of class distinctions, so did European socialism itself. Nyerere refers to Europe's experience of an agrarian and an industrial revolution. He then goes on to assert:

The former [revolution] created the 'landed' and the 'landless' classes in society; the latter produced the modern capitalist and the industrial proletariat. These two revolutions planted the seeds of conflict within society, and not only was European socialism born out of that conflict, but its apostles sanctified conflict itself into a philosophy.[24]

But the socialism of Africa was, Nyerere claimed, an ideology born of a pre-existent classlessness. And because of the need for a continuing absence of class conflict in contemporary Africa, the one-party system was the best answer.

One Pan-African implication of this line of reasoning lies in the appeal once again to the traditional ways of Africa. Nyerere opens his discussion of democracy and the party system with a quotation from Guy Clutton-Brock: 'The Elders sit under the big tree, and talk until they agree. . . .'[25]

The claim here is that this was the essence of traditional African democracy. In effect, there are two doctrines being asserted in this account. One is the doctrine of government by discussion ('they talk . . .'). The other is a doctrine of decision by unanimity ('they talk till they *agree*'). It is this latter doctrine of 'decision by unanimity' which is sometimes regarded as the ancient tribal genesis of the modern African one-party state. And the appeal to traditional norms converts the ethic of one-partyism into a Pan-African slogan of a shared political culture.[26]

Another point of contact between Pan-Africanism and the one-party ethic hinges on the notion of 'unity'. The reasoning which is sometimes put forward is something to the following effect:

If Africans in one country like Uganda cannot unite into a single political party, how can Africans in the whole continent ever unite to form any meaningful organization?[27]

Nkrumah has sometimes argued that the appearance of unity in those countries which were already independent was a strategic necessity for those countries which were still struggling against colonial rule. Talking about the old internal wrangles with the Opposition in Ghana, Nkrumah has argued that

The impact of this internal division on the movements for liberation in the rest of Africa could be . . . unfortunate. It was likely to cause despondency in their ranks and friction between us and their leaders, who might have no means of recognizing the falsity of opposition attacks upon us. The colonial powers would also not be unmindful of these happenings and possibly use them as a pretext for delaying their departure from . . . colonial territories by citing the magnified political 'battle' in Ghana as a frightening example of premature independence.[28]

But what about the impact of one-party systems on prospects for African unity *after* independence? This is where the one-party system might militate against Pan-Africanism as a quest for full political integration. Here again the best concrete example for study is the East African situation. If we assume that federal hopes might conceivably be revived, the situation is that

discussion ('they talk . . .'). The other is a doctrine of decision by
Tanganyika is a one-party state *de jure*, while Uganda and Kenya
have fluid party systems with no laws against the existence of
opposition parties. What are the implications of this for federal
prospects in East Africa?

In his classic work on the nature of federalism, K. C. Wheare
argues that 'of all the factors which produce the desire for union,
the one which at the same time produces best capacity for union
is similarity of social, and particularly political institutions.'[29] If
that is the case, then the mere fact of having Tanganyika as a
one-party state *de jure*, while Kenya and Uganda have fluid
party systems, introduces a diversity in the East African situation which would make federation difficult. The new federal
party that Nyerere might form could compete for seats in the
regional assemblies of Kenya and Uganda, but the *de jure*
one-party structure in Nyerere's own country would forbid
Kenyatta and Obote from competing in a similar way in Tanganyika elections.

It is, of course, possible to have a standard formula to the effect
that only Kenyans or Ugandans would be allowed to compete for
regional elections in Kenya or Uganda respectively on formation
of federation. This would keep Nyerere's competitive spirit out
of these two countries as effectively as he would keep Obote and
Kenyatta out by his legalized one-party structure. But such an
arrangement would constitute a serious loosening of federal
links between the three countries.[30] Another possible solution,
theoretically, is a merger of the Uganda People's Congress, the
Tanganyika African National Union, and the Kenya African
National Union into a new Pan-East-African party. But the three
parties are at present organized in such fundamentally different
ways that it is not clear how they can, in fact, be merged. Obote,
for example, would have serious difficulties with the local units
of his party if he ever tried to reorganize them in the direction of
greater similarity with TANU. In any case, can a federation be
under a one-party system without becoming a unitary state? This
is a question which has been repeatedly asked of 'federalism' in
the Soviet Union. And few students of federalism outside the
Communist world have recognized the Soviet structure as really
federal. The risk in East Africa is that any attempt to create a
single party to rule East Africa as a whole could all too easily

develop into an attempt to impose a unitary system on the area. And the suspicion which unitarism would arouse might jeopardize the chances of even the more moderate and looser integration of genuine federalism.

But if each of the East African countries developed a one-party system, would this not provide precisely the similarity of political institutions which would help the cause of federalism? The answer here must be 'No'. There are indeed institutions whose relevance for federalism is limited to whether they are shared by each of the constituent parts. To take a rough example, it might not matter for federal stability whether each constituent unit chooses its federal representatives by direct elections or by indirect provided the same system applies in each unit. But the relevance of the one-party system for federalism is less simple than that. You cannot in this case say: 'It is immaterial whether the units are one-party systems or multi-party systems provided they are all the same.' The very fact that the units are all 'similarly' one-party can still be an anti-federal factor. One-party constituent units would give you a loose confederation. A one-party system at the federal level would be an adventure in unitarism which, in the East African situation, could be highly unstable. In either case one-partyism emerges as inherently anti-federal.

But here there is one qualification which ought to be made. K. C. Wheare has, in his study of federalism, distinguished between factors which produce a desire for union and factors which produce a capacity for union. He assumes that similarity of political institutions produces both. So far what we have attempted to indicate is that similarity of one-party institutions is *not* conducive to capacity for operating federal institutions. But is that similarity conducive to some initial resolution to form a union in the first place?

This is certainly arguable. There can be no doubt that a decision to federate with another country is one of the most serious decisions a sovereign state can take. If there is more than one party in a country, and the ruling party wants to federate with another country, the opposition party could play on local micro-nationalism and arouse hostility towards the governing party for proposing 'a loss of the country's identity'. It can therefore be argued that Obote has had to be much more circumspect and cautious about the issue of East African Federation than either Nyerere or Kenyatta. At least until the middle of 1964 Obote had to be careful lest the opposition parties in Uganda succeed in arousing enough local Uganda loyalties to pose a serious challenge to Obote's more pan-African inclinations.

If this reasoning is sound, then the emergence of one-party systems in all three mainland countries is a factor which should facilitate the task of *deciding* to federate. But once the decision has been taken, those very one-party structures would, as already argued, militate against the successful operation and *maintenance* of federal institutions.

This then is the complex web of inter-relationships between the ambition of broader integration in Africa on the one hand and the implications of internal territorial structure on the other. In English-speaking Africa Pan-Africanism is older than either socialistic affirmations or the ethic of the one-party state. The question which now arises is whether Pan-Africanism will *survive* the consequences of these new aspects of African thought.

TOWARDS A PRINCIPLE OF CONTINENTAL JURISDICTION

WE HAVE discussed the risk of neo-dependency and the assertion of that 'African unity' as a safeguard against that risk. We have also analysed the concept of 'We are all Africans' and examined Nkrumah's attempts to make the word 'African' comprehensive enough to include both Arabs and Negro Africans. Yet we have also suggested that leaders of thought like Nkrumah take for granted such underlying assumptions as racial sovereignty and pigmentational self-determination. What we need to ask more specifically now is how these assumptions are reconciled with the multi-pigmentational membership of the Organization of African Unity. By what criteria of race or colour can Arab intervention in, say, the Congo in 1961 and 1964 have failed to be a violation of racial sovereignty or pigmentational self-determination?

In this chapter we shall first analyse this issue of the African-ness of the Arabs. We shall then examine the emergence of continental consciousness and the evolution of a theory of continental jurisdiction. Points of comparison and contrast between such a theory and the Monroe Doctrine will form part of the method of analysis.

In our examination of Ghana's impact on African diplomatic thought we suggested that anti-Arab feeling has sometimes been most keenly articulated in the attitudes of Francophone Negro Africans. Yet perhaps few African leaders have been as open and frank in their discussion of the issue than Awolowo used to be. In his autobiography Awolowo argued in the following terms:

It is true that, physically and geographically, Egypt is in Africa. But apart from the fact that her entire political heart is in the Arab world, she has never regarded herself as having any social and cultural affinity with the black races of Africa.[1]

Yet Awolowo was unaware of the great paradox about Egypt's position in Africa. Egypt is at once the least 'African' of the Arab states and the most '*Pan-African*'. It is the least African because it has been more deeply involved in Arab politics outside Africa than any other country in Africa. This is both a symptom and a reinforcing agent of Egyptian identification with the Fertile Crescent and the Arabian peninsula. Nasser's involvement in the Yemen was one example. And the very fact that the first experiment of voluntary unification in the Arab world since independence was between Egypt and Syria rather than Egypt and the Sudan or Egypt and Libya is a measure of the pull that the Fertile Crescent has had on Egypt.

Egypt is also the least 'African' of the African countries because of her longer exposure to Western influences. Egypt is in many ways the most Westernized of all African countries apart from South Africa, and her capital city is among the most cosmopolitan.

Yet in spite of being the least African of the Arab countries in the continent, Egypt can still be described as the most Pan-African. As we indicated earlier, the latter policy is substantially due to Nasser's foresight and leadership. In 1870 Egypt's Khedive Ismail asserted that his country 'does not lie in Africa but in Europe'.[2] But by 1952 Nasser was, as we noted, affirming that Egypt could not afford to isolate herself from African affairs because 'We are in Africa'.[3] As L. Carl Brown has put it:

> Abd al Nasir can justly claim credit as the leader of Arab Africa who 'discovered' the dormant political potential lying in the rest of Africa. . . . Before that time the several states of Northern Africa were concerned with their domestic problems, with the colonial or former colonial power, and with their fellow Arab states – more or less in that order.[4]

In concrete terms Nasser's Pan-Africanism has consisted in granting scholarships to African students, in allowing Cairo to become the first major centre of refuge for nationalists from colonial Africa; in converting Cairo Radio into an instrument of anti-colonialism in Africa as well as in the Arab world; in active involvement in the conference diplomacy of African states; in establishing 'cultural links' with Muslims elsewhere in Africa; in undertaking the responsibility of looking after Lumumba's children on his death; and in active participation in the 'struggle against the forces of neo-colonialism in the Congo'.[5]

When Algeria attained independence another militantly Pan-African power emerged from the Arab world. At times Ahmed Ben-Bella seemed prepared to go further in identifying with African causes than Nasser had done – for he seemed prepared to be militarily involved at a significant scale in the remaining liberation movements in Africa. In his short dramatic speech at the Summit Conference at Addis Ababa in May 1963 Ben-Bella said:

There has been talk of a Development Bank. Why have we not talked of setting up a blood bank? A blood bank to help those who are fighting in Angola and all over Africa. . . . Ten thousand Algerian volunteers have been waiting for a chance to go to the assistance of their brothers in arms. . . . A ransom had to be paid for Algeria's liberation. . . . So let us all agree to die a little, or even completely, so that the peoples still under colonial domination may be free and African unity may not be a vain word.[6]

Yet on balance Egypt has done more for Pan-Africanism than Algeria has done – particularly since the Ben-Bella regime was overthrown in Algeria. Nevertheless, the Algerian leadership remains on the whole more Afro-centric than Nasser's regime has been. In the words of L. Carl Brown:

Attraction to Black Africa is perhaps most important in North-west Africa (Algeria, Tunisia and Morocco) for the intellectuals there are more in need of alternative identifications . . . the Maghrib leadership is somewhat dubious about the Eastern Arab performance, less emotionally involved in the Israeli question and – most important – resentful of the East Arab's unconscious air of cultural superiority.[7]

What all this confirms once again is, first, that there are *degrees* of Africanness; and, second, that commitment to Pan-Africanism is not necessarily commensurate with depth of Africanness.

In any case, Arabs might be *natives of Africa* even if they are not fully 'Africans'. Yet by what criterion are they to be regarded as 'natives' of the continent? One answer which I have heard given in Ghana is the following: 'The Arabs by now must be recognized as natives of Africa because they have been in Africa since the seventh century.'[8]

But there are complications in this criterion of length of stay. Supposing we do agree that any group of people that has been in Africa for thirteen hundred years must be regarded as natives of Africa. One question which would now arise is how many of the present-day Egyptians, for example, are descended from the original conquerors? How many, on the other hand, are descended from Syrians and Lebanese who crossed to Egypt only within the last two hundred years? If we said all Egyptians today were natives of Africa, would we not be including fairly recent immigrants into Egypt? What then is our criterion of being 'native to Africa'? Are we not saying in effect that since *some* Arabs in Africa have been on the continent for thirteen hundred years, *all* Arabs now resident in Africa are native to Africa?

Yet if this is our criterion, difficulties would arise in our evaluation of the Arabs of Zanzibar as compared with the status of North Africans. Let us take the example of an Egyptian family today that is descended from the original Arab conquerors of thirteen centuries ago. Let us then compare this family with a Zanzibari Arab family that is descended from someone who immigrated from Oman only *two* centuries ago. Would we really maintain that the Egyptian family, merely by having been in Africa for thirteen hundred years, had become more 'native' than the Zanzibari family? This would be to postulate that to 'go native' has nothing to do with changing one's cultural ways and is merely to be measured by duration of stay. It is arguable that the Arab conquerors in North Africa 'Arabized' their part of Africa, instead of letting *themselves* be 'Africanized'. By the yard-stick of linguistic acculturation this is certainly true. The Arab conquerors of the north turned North Africa into a predomi-nantly Arabic-speaking region – instead of gradually adopting a local language they found among those they conquered.

Yet, by contrast, many of the Arabs of Zanzibar actually ceased to be Arabic-speakers – and became instead native speakers of the basically Bantu language of Swahili. The Arabs of Zanzibar had therefore allowed themselves to become *less* 'Arab' than the Egyptians had done – and yet they were still regarded as less 'native' to their part of Africa than the Egyptians were conceded to be in theirs. As we shall indicate in a later chapter, Arab dominance in Zanzibar before the revolution came to be regarded as a violation of racial sovereignty. Yet the Arab presence in North Africa has seldom been discussed in such terms by Negro nationalists.[9]

What all these complications would suggest is that the distinc-tion between Arabs and Negro Africa is not dichotomous but has the complexity of a continuum. That was one reason why we described the Organization of African Unity as '*multi*-pigmentational' instead of a straight division between black Africa and the so-called 'white Africa of the North'.[10] The Arabs as a race defy straight pigmentational classifications. They vary in colour from the white Arabs of Syria and the Lebanon, the brown Arabs of the Hadhramout to the black Arabs of the Sudan and some of the eastern parts of the Arabian peninsula. Within Africa itself the range of colour among Arabs is also from white to black, though each colour cannot as smoothly be allocated to a specific area. Even within Egypt on its own the range of colour is virtually as wide as it is in the Arab world as a whole.

The crucial point here is that the concept of 'half-caste' is relatively alien to the Arabs. If the father is Arab, the child is Arab without reservations. If we visualized an Arab marrying a Nilotic woman in the fourteenth century and visualized a son being born, the son would be Arab. If we imagined in turn that the son again married a Nilotic woman and got a son – this son too would be an Arab. If we then assumed that the process is repeated, generation after generation, until a child is born in mid-twentieth century with only a drop of his blood still ostensibly of Arab derivation and the rest of his blood indubitably Nilotic, the twentieth century child is still an Arab.

This is the phenomenon which saves the Arab-Negro division in Africa from being a dichotomous gulf – and converts it instead into a racial continuum of merging relationships.

In Pan-African literature it has been more the Afro-Americans than either the Arabs or the black Africans that have grasped this fact of a racial continuum. Edward Blyden, the nineteenth-century Liberian intellectual of West Indian birth, put it in the following terms:

> With every wish, no doubt, to the contrary, the European seldom or never gets over the feeling of distance, if not of repulsion, which he experiences on first seeing the Negro. . . . The Arab missionary, on the other hand, often of the same complexion as his hearer, does not 'require any long habit to reconcile the eye to him'. He takes up his abode in Negroland, often for life, and, mingling his blood with that of the inhabitants, succeeds in the most natural manner, in engrafting Mohammedan religion and learning upon the ignorance and simplicity of the people.[11]

Blyden here captures the paternalism which characterized missionary work both by Arabs and by Europeans. But the essential contrast here is between the 'repulsion' reluctantly felt by even well-meaning Europeans at the time, on the one hand, and the Arab capacity for 'mingling his blood with that of the inhabitants' on the other.

It is true that even in the slave States of America white men 'mingled their blood' with that of their slave girls. But the crucial difference was in attitude to the offspring. Herbert Aptheker, the American Negro historian, has referred to the law in the slave States that in cases in which one of the parents was a slave the offspring would follow the status of the mother rather than the father. Aptheker adds in a footnote that

Generally, of course, where the parents were slave and free, the mother was a slave and the father was a white man, often a slave owner, who, thus, in accordance with law, had both pleasure and profit.[12]

In his book *Black Reconstruction in America* W.E.B.DuBois refers, in parenthesis, to the consequences of that law in more vivid terms:

The law declares that the children of slaves are to follow the fortunes of the mother. Hence the practice of planters selling and bequeathing their own children.[13]

Perhaps because they knew of this rigid prejudice against 'miscegenation' in the Germanic section of the New World, American Negroes who went to Africa were impressed by the Afro-Arab racial continuum. In the United States the divide was between white men and Negroes – and a person could not pass as 'white' if he was mixed enough to be 'brown'. In Africa, however, the division was between Arabs and Negroes – yet there were many Arabs who were as black as the Negroes. And so W.E.B.DuBois could make the following observation:

Anyone who has travelled in the Sudan knows that most of the 'Arabs' he has met are dark-skinned, sometimes practically black, often have Negroid features, and hair that may be almost Negro in quality. It is then obvious that in Africa the term 'Arab' ... is often misleading. The Arabs were too nearly akin to Negroes to draw an absolute color line.[14]

It is perhaps a factor for greater accommodation between peoples in the continent that it is an exogamous race like the

Arabs who inhabit Northern Africa, instead of a more exclusive segment of humanity.

Yet contemporary African nationalism has itself a theme of exclusiveness – the 'exclusive' loyalty to the African continent which is sometimes demanded. In this sense of 'exclusiveness' the Arabs have not been 'exclusive' enough. Speaking of the United Arab Republic before the break with Syria, Awolowo once asserted:

> The United Arab Republic, the pet creature of Nasser, which has one foot in Africa and another in the Middle East, is the very antithesis of a workable African community.[15]

This sort of reasoning is connected with the sentiment which made Nkrumah assert that 'no accident of history . . . can ever succeed in turning an inch of African soil into an extension of any other continent.'[16] Nkrumah had in mind the kind of integrationist claims made by France about Algeria or the claims of Portugal that Angola and Mozambique were part of Portugal. But, as we asked earlier, could not North Africa also be regarded as a westward extension of the Arabian Peninsula?

One possible answer is that it depends upon what proportion of the Arab world is now in Africa and how much of it is still outside. At the time of the Arab conquest in the seventh century it was indeed true that the Arabian peninsula was extending itself into the Fertile Crescent and into Africa. But had not the balance of preponderance now changed as between the different segments of the Arab world? In some ways, is this not the equivalent of the change in relationship between England and the United States? The 'mother country' is now overshadowed by her former imperial extension – and the danger now is of Britain becoming an extension of the United States rather than the other way round.[17]

Does the analogy hold in the relationship between Arab Africa and the rest of the Arab world? It certainly holds as between the old Arabian Peninsula proper on one side and Africa and the Fertile Crescent combined on the other. Countries of the peninsula proper – Saudi Arabia especially from which the Arab invasions of the seventh century originated – is now overshadowed in inter-Arab influence, perhaps by even Iraq and Syria on their own.

But in the context of African exclusiveness we would need to put the Arabian Peninsula and the Fertile Crescent together on one side and distinguish them from Arab Africa on the other side of the Red Sea. Yet even here the balance of preponderance is on Africa's side. As the Egyptian scholar Boutros-Ghali put it in a book published in 1963, 'It must not be forgotten that sixty-six per cent of the Arab community and seventy-two per cent of the Arab lands are in Africa.'[18]

The situation was such that it had become easier to think of the rest of the Arab world as an extension of Arab Africa than the other way round. Certainly Egypt's involvement in Palestine and in Syrian, Iraqi and Yemeni affairs has been one of the persistent themes of Arab politics. Awolowo once conditionally welcomed Egyptian nationalists into his vision of 'the African' community – but he would accept Egyptian nationalist movements only if they were 'separable from those in Syria'.[19] Yet Awolowo himself had elsewhere described Syria as 'a satellite in Egypt's orbit'.[20] If that was the case then even if the Egyptian nationalist movement could not be separated from the Syrian, the danger would still be more a case of 'Africa' interfering in Syrian affairs than the other way round.

But why should Awolowo even conditionally admit Egypt into his 'Community'? Why are the black states of Africa drawn into a diplomatic partnership with the Arab countries at all?

The ultimate reason lies, curiously enough, in the pigmentational homogeneity of *Europe* itself. In no continent are the inhabitants more uniform in colour than they are in Europe. In this sense Europe is *a racial unit* in a sense which is not duplicated in any other continent. This fact is, in the final analysis, the genesis of emotions of continental solidarity in Africa as well.[21]

The connecting link lies in the fact that it was such a racially compact continent as Europe which, in the phrase of DuBois, 'stole the world'.[22] Nowhere else did continental and pigmentational identities coincide so neatly. If history had made India and China the imperial powers in Africa, the phenomenon as a whole could conceivably have been designated as 'Asiatic imperialism'. But there would have been no single colour by which to designate Indians and Chinese together. There could be no Asian equivalent of the 'white man's burden'.

It is even doubtful if Sino-Indian imperialism would have been called 'Asiatic'. After all the consciousness of sharing a continent among Asians resulted from being dominated by Europeans – an 'Asiatic consciousness' might not have grown at all if the imperial powers had themselves come from Asia. Of the three continents of the Old World only Europe had been compact enough to think in continentalistic terms – and then to influence others into similar inclinations.

White men in Africa started by referring to each other as 'white men'. It was probably a growing sense of liberalism which, in time, made the word '*Europeans*' more common. After all, the term 'white man' had been too frank an assertion of the relevance of colour as a basis of classifying people. Increasing liberalism on the issue of race made such a basis of classification unfashionable. The term 'European' was more neutral racially – it could be taken to refer merely to the continent of origin without emphasizing the pigmentational characteristics of its inhabitants.

Yet certain policies were pursued in the colonies which obviously put a 'premium' on colour. In British Africa especially the term 'European' soon acquired all the pigmentational emphasis of the term 'white man'. The discrimination which the 'European' clubs or restaurants practised was regarded not as a 'continental' exclusiveness but as a *colour* bar. The whole experience of living in a European colony made the distinction between 'continent of origin' and 'colour of skin' a difficult one to draw. And so even Asia, with all its vastness and heterogeneity, developed some kind of Pan-continentalism for as long as 'Europe' was ruling large areas of the Asian landmass.

Here we might again reiterate the reasons why this sense of continental identity was sharpened in Africa south of the Sahara. It was not merely a case of white people in, say, Kenya calling themselves 'Europeans'. It was also a case of referring to the black people of Kenya as 'Africans'. So both the white rulers and the black masses in Kenya bore continentalistic labels. This had important consequences for the psychological identification of politically conscious Africans. There can hardly be much doubt that the sense of identity of black nationalists south of the Sahara would have had less of a continental dimension if the race to which they belonged had not been called after a continent.

But complications arose as the colonial era approached its end. It began to be grasped more fully that while an equation between colour and continental origins could be sustained in the case of 'Europeans', such an equation was more vulnerable in the case of 'Africans'. After all, while all inhabitants of the European continent were indeed white,[23] not all inhabitants of the African continent were black.

This is where a curious switch of emphasis began to be discernible in the thinking of some black nationalists. Out of racial pride they had once converted a continent into a mystique. But now they wanted to retain the continental mystique and shed the racial militancy from which it emerged. As Nkrumah said to a group of delegates primarily from Arab countries:

The former imperialist powers were fond of talking about 'Arab Africa' and 'Black Africa'. . . . From now on let us take pride in our continent. Let us tear down any barrier which may contrive to divide us. Of course, we have differences of language, differences of culture and religion, but *our Africanism binds us together*.[24]

It is clear here that the word 'Africanism' is stripped of pigmentational militancy. The ultimate frame of reference is now 'our continent' rather than 'our race'. Five years later, at Addis Ababa, an Organization of African Unity was created on the basis of a continental mystique.

It is out of this mystique that a principle of continental jurisdiction emerged. In some matters it operates *instead* of the principle of racial sovereignty, in other matters it reinforces it further. The principle of continental jurisdiction asserts that there are certain African problems which should only be solved by Africans themselves. And 'Africans' in this instance are definable as members of the Organization of African Unity.

We have already referred to the two-tier structure of African diplomatic activity – the inter-African and the extra-continental. We have also referred to the fact that international law now seems to be intended to govern relations between states in general and makes no distinction as between continental locations of states. But African diplomacy appears to recognize two levels of law. One level is indeed that of international law to govern relations between nations at large. The other level is a kind of Pan-African Law to govern relations between African states themselves. This latter is still much less codified than is traditional international law. And its future is less assured. So far the ultimate documentary expression of Pan-African Law is the Charter of the

Organization of African Unity. Yet, as in the case of traditional international law at large, documents normally emerge essentially as confirmation of some pre-existent consensus on canons of interstate behaviour. Not all rules which are supposed to govern inter-African relations are as yet documented. Nor is the fact that such rules are not always obeyed evidence that they do not 'really' exist. Just as recurrent violations of traditional international law by Western countries did not completely deprive that law of some kind of a role in Western diplomacy, so repeated violations of the Pan-African code of interstate behaviour have not entirely deprived that code of political significance in Africa. Such a code provides African states at least with a frame of reference for their complaints against each other. Sometimes it provides the basis of mediation by other African states towards easing tensions between diplomatic combatants.

The closest analogue of this precept of intra-African continental jurisdiction is the diplomatic system of American states. The latter system has also at times claimed a unique legal personality under international law. In 1917 John Foster Dulles, then a young lawyer, addressed himself to precisely this issue when, at a Pan-American Congress, he discussed the following question: 'Are there specific American problems of international law?' Dulles quoted an eminent Brazilian Ambassador to Washington who had described Pan-Americanism as 'the sentiment of our own separate orbit, of an orbit absolutely detached from the European in which Africa and Asia, not speaking of Australasia, are moving.' Dulles thought that the vigour of this Pan-American sentiment was attested by its persistence for a long time and throughout so great a territory 'in spite of a comparative lack of commercial and social intercourse between many of the American states.'[25]

On the specific issue of the hemisphere's distinct legal personality, Dulles cited the evidence of international conferences in the hemisphere and their distinctive preoccupations. He said:

Consider, on the one hand, the fact that, during the last ninety years, almost a score of . . . international conferences have been held to deal with international problems from the point of view of the American States, and that at no one conference has a non-American nation participated or been invited to participate. Consider, on the other hand, that at none of the international congresses held during the same period at which European nations have participated have the American States generally joined in, except at the Second Hague Conference.[26]

Dulles' conclusion was that such a phenomenon could only be explained by that sentiment of solidarity as phrased by the Brazilian Ambassador, Joaquim Nabuco.

If the number of conferences held within a continental international system, and preoccupied with internal continental matters, is evidence that the system has a legal personality, then the Pan-African international system has been rapidly assuming such a personality. The Pan-African system has, in the few years of its existence, concerned itself with issues like the Congo, border disputes between member-states, mutinies in East Africa, the problem of Angola and Mozambique, the problem of Rhodesia, the issue of *apartheid* in South Africa, subversive activities between African states and a number of lesser problems in the continent.

But the second part of Dulles' statement revelled in the fact that American States had not concerned themselves with conferences outside the Americas. In this respect the American system at that time differed fundamentally from the Pan-African system today. The difference hinges on the fact that Pan-Americanism was not only a desire to keep Europe out of the Americas but also a desire on the part of Americans themselves to keep out of European affairs in turn. Until Woodrow Wilson the Monroe Doctrine was, in other words, as much an assertion of hemispheric *isolation* as it was an assertion of internal hemispheric jurisdiction.

It is this isolation which Pan-*Africanism* rejected from the start. As the former President of the Sudan, General Aboud, put it in regard to the arms race between the great powers:

We, the small nations, cannot stand aloof from this suicidal race . . . of armament. It is our duty to the world to put the Great Powers wise to the dangers of their activities.[27]

The idea of participating in world affairs is a basic component of African nationalism. Unlike the Monroe Doctrine, the African principle of continental jurisdiction has never been isolationist in this sense. There are indeed certain problems of inter-African relations that it thinks only Africans themselves should be permitted to solve. But this limited exclusiveness still leaves room for African participation in problems which are of consequence to the world at large.

This factor is also what distinguishes the old American 'neutrality' from contemporary African nonalignment. As we shall see when we discuss it more fully in later chapters, African nonalignment is not a withdrawal from the affairs of the rest of the world, but an attempt to maximize Africa's impact on those affairs. Nevertheless, the element of 'saving' the African continent from some of the conflicts which rage outside does introduce a limited theme of withdrawal in African nationalistic thought. And just as the principle of majority rule in Africa is, as we have noted, wedded to the principle of racial sovereignty, so also is the doctrine of nonalignment in Africa wedded to the precept of continental jurisdiction. A basic aspect of African nonalignment is, after all, to keep the cold war out of the African continent. Africans have not fully succeeded in preventing the cold war from entering their continent, but it still remains a major nationalistic preoccupation to reduce its impact. There are perhaps certain chilly winds of the cold war against which no wall of African exclusiveness can be effective. But there are aspects of the cold war which can perhaps be avoided. The most widely accepted of such notions is the idea of maintaining Africa as 'a nuclear free zone'.

But within Africa itself the most sensitive implications of continental jurisdiction are not on matters of nuclear survival, but on issues of simple diplomatic recognition between African countries. Under what circumstances does an African government deserve full recognition as a member of the African community? This issue of credentials of legitimacy is one which, by some interpretations, ought to be referred to the inchoate canons of Pan-African Law.

Here again there are analogies with other parts of the world. Whether Fidel Castro's regime in Cuba should be recognized by fellow 'Americans' is a matter which has sometimes 'rocked the boat' of the inter-American system. Which regime of the Dominican Republic should be permitted to be in power was also a matter of hemispheric concern in the course of 1965. But if we go back far enough in history, international law itself would appear to have been analogous to Pan-African Law today. At the time of the French Revolution, for example, international law was still Pan-European Law – intended to regulate affairs within the European community of states. One opponent of the French Revolution used this as a basis for challenging the credentials of the revolutionary government. Edmund Burke felt that European states had a right to decide who was good enough to be recognized as a worthy member of the European community. As Burke put it:

The potentates of Europe have, by that [public law of Europe] a right, an interest, and a duty to know what government they are to treat, and what they are to admit into the federative society – or, in other words, into the diplomatic republic of Europe. This right is clear and indisputable.[28]

Many African states today seem to postulate a kind of 'diplomatic republic of Africa' – for admission into which a regime like that of Moise Tshombe in the first ten months of his Premiership in the Congo did not have adequate credentials.

But by what criteria does African diplomatic thought determine the legitimacy of a government in Africa? Five distinct principles seem to operate, though not all of them at the same time. The most straightforward is that which we earlier attributed to President Bourguiba of Tunisia. This is the principle of *de facto* control – the assertion that that government is legitimate which is effectively in power in a particular country. For that single month between independence and revolution the government of Zanzibar, for example, was regarded by some African states as legitimate merely on the basis of *de facto* control.

The second criterion of legitimacy is, as we indicated, whether a government is *racially* representative – that is to say, whether the people who effectively compose it are 'Africans'. On the basis of this second criterion, the credentials of the Zanzibar government before the revolution were disputed by those who took a more rigorous pigmentational definition of 'Africans' – though no open challenge of the Sultan was made by any African state in a formal diplomatic way until the revolution actually took place.

A third canon of legitimacy is whether the method by which a government assumed power was legitimate. In the case of Zanzibar, the revolutionary method was regarded by some as legitimate because the previous government had 'dubious' pigmentational credentials. A better example of the application of this canon was in regard to the regime which succeeded Sylvanus

Olympio in Togo. The Government of Tanganyika was among several African governments which were suspicious of Olympio's successors. Tanganyika sent the following message to the Secretary-General of the United Nations:

After the brutal murder of President Olympio, the problem of recognition of a successor government has arisen. We urge no recognition of a successor government until satisfied first that the government did not take part in Olympio's murder or second that there is a popularly elected government.[29]

The first condition concerned the issue of whether assumption of power by the new government was by legitimate means. The second opened the possibility of subsequent legitimation of what might have started as illegitimate. An appeal to the country for a mandate through elections could legitimize an assumption of power which was originally made possible by assassination. In either case Olympio's death dramatized for Africa the issue of governmental recognition by reference to the means used to capture power.

A fourth basis of legitimacy is whether the system of government operative in a particular country is itself a legitimate way of governing a people. Questions of elections, and the old constitutional rights of Lumumba as against Kasavubu, do sometimes bring arguments of liberal democracy into African diplomatic utterances on such issues. But in general we can say that the criterion of whether a country's system of government is legitimate, though important in the ideology of the Inter-American system, has had little influence in the Pan-African system.

The basis of denying recognition to Mr Tshombe seemed to be something different. In spite of references to elections and 'the popular will', it was not the system of government which the Congo had which was in question. It was not even how Mr Tshombe came into power. It was how he *maintained* himself in power. And it referred not to whether he tolerated his Congolese opponents, but what *external* help he got in putting them down. In Tshombe's case there was indeed a past record of secessionism and 'collaboration with the imperialists' for him to live down. But Tshombe could have lived down his past fairly quickly had he managed to maintain his position as Prime Minister of the Congo without the use of white mercenaries and aid from Western powers. It is at this level that both racial sovereignty and continental jurisdiction become relevant as a basis of evaluating the credentials of an African regime in power.

Yet it is also at this level that the principle of continental jurisdiction is at its most controversial in internal African politics. By the summer of 1965 the division of opinion as between the supporters and opponents of Moise Tshombe was almost linguistically measurable. On the whole the Arabs and the English-speaking Africans were still against Tshombe, but the French-speaking Africans had actually admitted him into their newly formed Francophone community.[30]

Nevertheless, the very passions which the principle of continental jurisdiction sometimes arouses is a measure of its impact on interstate politics in Africa. That principle gave Algeria, the Sudan and the United Arab Republic the right to take sides in the Congolese civil war at least to the extent of helping to equip the rebels. The reasoning here went thus: If Tshombe was getting aid from non-Africans altogether, Tshombe's opponents were entitled to some help from fellow Africans. By the same token, it was the principle of continental jurisdiction which gave black Africans the right to mediate in the border dispute between Algeria and Morocco.

What has yet to be brought to the test is the right of black Africans to interfere in North Africa in the way that North Africans have sometimes interfered in the affairs of the Congo. This is not to suggest that, given similar situations, Arab Africans will react in a less Pan-African spirit than black Africans have done. If a civil war like that of the Congo were to break out in a North African country, and one side started recruiting white mercenaries from Gibraltar, Portugal or South Africa, black Africans might feel as free to help the other side as Arab Africans have felt in helping Tshombe's opponents. And the broader sense of identity between the two sides of the Sahara could still survive this trans-Saharan intervention. All we know at the moment is that there has not been a North African Congo.

But was this sort of African interference in the Congo in 1964 any different from United States' interference in the Dominican Republic in 1965? In an analysis of the idea of the Western Hemisphere, Arthur P. Whitaker once referred to what he called 'the magic of the American name'.[31] Whatever mutual identification existed between the two Americas owed a good deal to the fact that the two continents shared a name. Yet, in African estimation, the trouble with the Monroe Doctrine was that it was not continental but hemispheric. The Doctrine gave the Colossus of North America a substantial measure of jurisdiction over the affairs of South America. In African diplomatic thought, there is perhaps something rather unnatural in hemispheric jurisdiction. It would have made better sense if the unit of exclusiveness was the continent rather than the hemisphere. The United States and Canada could then constitute one continental system, while South and Central America and the Latin Islands constituted another.

It cannot be stressed too often that the principle of continental jurisdiction is not intended to *replace* the principle of state sovereignty. Like the Monroe Doctrine itself, it again introduces an additional dimension to the doctrine of nonintervention – though with a different unit of exclusiveness. Thus a *Cuban* intervention in the Dominican Republic in 1965 would have been a domestic affair of Latin Americans according to the principle of continental jurisdiction, though still a violation of the rights of the Dominicans according to state sovereignty. But a new level of externality was introduced by the *North* American intervention. In other words, just as Senegal's interference in Morocco's affairs would have been less 'external' than Chinese interference in Morocco, so Cuban interference in the Dominican Republic would have been less 'external' than United States' intervention was deemed to be.

In conclusion, let us reiterate the general African position. African nationalistic thought seems to regard traditional international law as having been naïve when it reduced all tensions to interstate relations. In African estimation, *three* levels of identity are relevant in diplomatic behaviour – a racial identity, a continental identity and the identities of individual sovereign states. But regardless of whether these three classifications of diplomatic identity are recognized in the rest of the world or not, they are implicit in many of the aspects of politics in Africa itself. The 'magic of the American name' resulted in a cumbersome unit of a whole hemisphere. But the mystique of the African name has left behind a more modest legacy of continental consciousness. That consciousness is now struggling not only to transcend the Sahara, but also to give more meaning to the notion of an African jurisdiction over African affairs.

Section II

THE DILEMMAS OF STATEHOOD

CHAPTER EIGHT

PEACE VERSUS HUMAN RIGHTS: A UNITED NATIONS DILEMMA

THE United Nations Organization has played an important role in this movement of ideas leading to African self-government. The very concept of the United Nations is itself part of the body of African political thought. For some nationalists the world body might more appropriately have been christened 'The United *Races* Organization'. It became quite early a symbol more of racial equality than of a search for a harmonious relationship between *states*.

This difference in evaluation has important consequences in the dialogue which goes on in the world body between the new states and the older members. An idiomatic gulf often occurs between the two sets of states. The older members sometimes find it difficult to take the newer ones seriously. In part this is because the language of argument employed by the new states seems to lack immediate relevance to the preoccupations of the world organization as conceived by 'the founders'.

This chapter hopes to demonstrate that the barriers of communication are often just a symptom of a fundamental philosophical clash between the ideal of peace and the ideal of human dignity as it affects politics in the world body. We shall examine this clash first in regard to decolonization, and then relate it to the problem of South Africa. But the clash of these two ideals affects other aspects of international politics as well, especially the issue of the voting system in the United Nations, the policy of nonalignment and the place of poverty in world politics. To these questions too the chapter will address itself.

It may be useful to start with a statement made by a British Colonial Secretary on the eve of the formation of the United Nations. Partly with that impending formation in mind Oliver

Stanley, then Secretary of State for the Colonies, said in March 1945:

I do not believe that any splinterization of the British Colonial Empire would be in the interests of the world. . . . Would the new machinery for world security, which is to be devised at San Francisco next month, be made any stronger by the substitution of these forty [new] states for a cohesive Empire able to act as a strategic whole?[1]

In a sense, Oliver Stanley's question has not yet been answered. At best the syllables which will one day form the complete answer are now being assembled, and it will take a while before the effect is adequately intelligible. But there was one thing which Oliver Stanley did not allow for at the time. One of his fears expressed in the 1945 speech was that a disintegration of the British Empire might, among other things, jeopardize the very existence of the United Nations. In his capacity as Colonial Secretary he should perhaps have been more worried about a reverse possibility – that the existence of the United Nations might itself contribute toward the disintegration of the British Empire. The 'machinery for world security', on whose behalf he seemed concerned, was to become a mechanism for the 'splinterization' of empires.

In principle, this reverse occurrence does not necessarily falsify Stanley's prediction. The United Nations' position as an accomplice in the dismemberment of empires might yet turn out to be a case of 'suicidal murder' – that is, in destroying empires the United Nations was all along involved in a process of long-term self-destruction. All this is, in principle, a *prediction* and may or may not be vindicated. What should concern us here is the underlying theme which is symbolized by Stanley's views on the relationship between 'the new machinery for world security' and the maintenance of 'a cohesive Empire able to act as a strategic whole'. The clash between imperial peace and human rights as conceived by colonial subjects was imminent from the start as a theme in the life which awaited the world organization.

Connected with this dichotomy is the distinction which is sometimes made between the demands of nationalism and of world solidarity. Partly with the experience of the League of Nations in mind, E. H. Carr argued in 1939 in the following vein:

Just as pleas for 'national solidarity' in domestic politics always come from a dominant group which can use this solidarity to strengthen its own control over the nation as a whole, so pleas for international solidarity and world union come from those dominant nations which may hope to exercise control over a unified world.[2]

At first sight this seems to be borne out by the very arguments that a British Colonial Secretary like Stanley found worthy of advancing against a policy of 'splinterizing' the British Empire:

Would it really be an advantage to create another forty independent states, all small? . . . Would the economies of the new world be made any easier by forty more separate divisions, forty more political obstacles; would it free the flow of world trade?[3]

And yet an important distinction exists between international solidarity and imperial cohesiveness. Although an empire may indeed consist of a multiplicity of nationalities, it is not in itself an instance of 'internationalism'. The logical extremity of Stanley's opposition to a multiplication of sovereignties is presumably a complete world union with a world government. And yet even a world government is, strictly speaking, inconsistent with internationalism. Demands for a world government are, in effect, demands that humanity should convert itself into a *single* global state – something quite distinct from the kind of *inter*-state relationships which are normally denoted by the term 'internationalism'. A world state would, in other words, be no more international than the British Empire was when Stanley was defending its unitary cohesion.

And yet Carr argues that 'countries which are struggling to force their way into the dominant group naturally tend to invoke nationalism against the internationalism of the controlling powers.'[4] The history of empires since the United Nations was formed has revealed an oversimplification in Carr's analysis. The whole antithesis between 'nationalism' and 'internationalism' was exposed as decidedly superficial as soon as the Afro-Asian countries began to demand the right of participation in international affairs. For what inspired *nationalism* in those countries was, to a great extent, those very 'universalist and humanitarian doctrines' which Carr identifies with the *internationalist's* stand.[5] It was, in short, the values of internationalism which awakened Afro-Asian national consciousness.

What Carr's analysis tended to obscure was the fact that there are at least three categories of nations and not just two. There are indeed those which are sufficiently strong to stand for internationalism – in the expectation that 'international goodwill' is the best way of stabilizing and perpetuating their dominant position. There may, in addition, be countries which are not yet quite 'dominant' but near enough to dominance to invoke nationalism *instead of* internationalism as the paramount instrument for raising their status. Carr himself cited Germany up to World War II as a country which was at once nationalistic and opposed to internationalism. The category which Carr omitted altogether was that of a country which is quite incapable of attaining world dominance through its own nationalism but which is nevertheless nationalistic. In such a case a country might find itself needing a substantial degree of internationalism in order to start realizing its nationalistic aspirations at all. The best example of this category is that of those countries which based their case for parochial independence upon universal values and now look upon the United Nations as the best hope for some of their national ambitions.

The central universal value in the search for parochial independence has been, of course, the principle of self-determination. An important contributory factor to the popularity of the principle among African nationalists was, as we have noted, the Atlantic Charter which President Franklin Roosevelt and Prime Minister Winston Churchill signed on 14 August 1940. But in the year of 1945 a new Charter was born – and not long after, this new United Nations Charter effectively replaced the Atlantic Charter as the ultimate documentary confirmation of the legitimacy of African aspirations. It is probably safe to say that very few African nationalists had, in fact, read the United Nations Charter. And those who had were less interested in the specific procedures for assuring world peace than in the reaffirmation of 'faith in fundamental human rights, in the dignity and worth of the human person, in the equal rights of men and women and of nations large and small.'[6] But in spite of this limited or selective grasp of what the United Nations Charter was all about, the Charter did become a kind of documentary expression of natural law and a global Bill of Rights. By 1955, when Asia had achieved its independence and Africa was at its most militant in the quest for its own, the nationalists of Asia and Africa were still basing their demands firmly on the Charter. As the final communiqué of the Bandung Conference put it in that year:

The Asian-African Conference declared its full support of the fundamental principles of Human Rights as set forth in the Charter of the United Nations and took note of the Universal Declaration of Human Rights as a common standard of achievement for all peoples and all nations.

The Conference declared its full support for the principles of self-determination of peoples and nations as set forth in the Charter of the United Nations and took note of the United Nations resolutions on the rights of peoples and nations to self-determination, which is a prerequisite of the full enjoyment of all fundamental Human Rights.[7]

The United Nations had by then become a liberating factor in practice as well as in principle. And it was involved in this process in two paradoxical capacities – in the capacity of a collective 'imperialist' with 'trusteeship' responsibilities of its 'own' and in the capacity of the grand critic of imperialism at large. Indeed, as early as 1953 exasperated voices were already complaining that 'perhaps the term "*self*-determination" should be dropped, now that the United Nations is called upon to do the determining'.[8]

But even if the United Nations could 'determine' an end to colonialism, the question which would persist is whether the world body could 'determine' the demise of *apartheid* as well. Could the organization achieve this by helping to isolate South Africa.

The fate of 'isolation' as envisaged for South Africa by the new African states rests on philosophical assumptions which have yet to be adequately analysed. The old hazardous tendency to personify countries and then talk about them almost as if they were individual persons does sometimes affect people's entire attitude toward South Africa. Although it may be hazardous to treat countries as persons, it is nevertheless an exercise which can afford useful insights into the whole phenomenon of passing a moral judgment on another country's 'behaviour'. Let us take the analogy of someone in a town who commits a crime and gets caught. That person may end up in jail. Now, jail is a form of isolation. The criminal behind bars is isolated or at best confined to the company of fellow criminals in a restricted area. Separation from the rest of society is itself seen as part of the pain inflicted upon the criminal.

These same assumptions now appear to be transposed on to the international scene. South Africa is viewed as an offender, if not of the law of nations, certainly of the canons of the new international morality. But the international society – unlike the society of, say, Great Britain or Tanzania – has no jail to which it can send its worst offenders. South Africa may indeed be placed 'before the bar of world opinion', but can she be put behind the bars of a world prison once judgment has been passed? This is where the penalty of isolation suggests itself in a new form – South Africa is to be sentenced not to the literal isolation of a prison cell, but to the limbo of international anomie.[9]

But what is the purpose of this isolation? As in the case of the individual criminal in our home town, three lines of reasoning are discernible. First, you isolate the criminal as retribution for his offence. Secondly, you seek to deter him from repeating the offence or to prevent him from continuing it. And, thirdly, implicit in the very idea of deterring him from doing it again, you attempt to reform the criminal to at least this negative extent.[10] In these attempts to isolate South Africa there lies, then, not only the vengeful aim of punishing her for her offence but also the reformative ambition of preparing her for a resumption on some future date of her place in international society. What the African states are involved in is, in other words, a search for a means of getting beyond a mere verdict of 'guilty' pronounced on South Africa. They are seeking ways to make South Africa as a nation serve the nearest thing to a term of imprisonment – and become a better member of the international community.

But does imprisonment necessarily succeed in reforming an offender? Here again there is a direct analogy between an offending individual and an offending nation. Some individuals become hardened criminals as a result of imprisonment. Others make up their minds never to see the inside of a prison cell again. How can one be sure of the effect isolation would have on South Africa? After all, many would already argue that America's policy to isolate Communist China had aggravated, rather than mitigated, China's sense of grievance and thereby increased her aggressiveness.

This is where the whole issue of isolation touches that of qualifications for membership in the United Nations. If the United Nations is, as most African states continue to regard it, the very centre of the new international society, then exclusion from it is one of the more obvious methods of trying to isolate a country from that society. Communist China is outside the United Nations – should she be in? South Africa is in – should she really be out? These are the twin issues which have sometimes invited the charge of a double standard in the policies of some of the new nations. Madame Pandit, leader of India's delegation to the United Nations at the time, was confronted in September 1963 with such a charge in a television interview at the United Nations. India had suffered direct aggression at the hands of the Chinese and indirect racial humiliation from South Africa. Yet India was in favour of seating Communist China in the United Nations and of unseating South Africa altogether. How could Madame Pandit reconcile the two stands? Her own answer was simply the conviction that South Africa was worse than China.

But on what grounds can this assessment be based? This takes us right back to that Afro-Asian tendency to regard the United Nations not so much as an organization primarily designed to ensure peace and security – as the big powers intended it to be – but as an organization which should be primarily concerned with human rights at large. The actual framers of the Charter in 1945 first declared their determination to 'save succeeding generations from the scourge of war' and then only secondly to

reaffirm faith in fundamental human rights, in the dignity and worth of the human person, in the equal rights of men and women and of nations large and small.[11]

But judging by their policies, attitudes, and stands, the new states of Africa and Asia would have reversed the order of affirmation; they would have affirmed, first, 'faith in fundamental human rights [and] in the dignity and worth of the human person' and only secondly their determination 'to save succeeding generations from the scourge of war'.

This has an important bearing on qualifications for membership in the United Nations as viewed by, on the one hand, countries like the United States which are opposed to the 'admission' of Communist China and, on the other, countries like Tanzania which has sought South Africa's expulsion from the world Organization. Those who are opposed to Communist China's 'admission' have interpreted Article 4 of the United

Nations Charter as restricting membership to those countries which are 'peace-loving'. This whole emphasis on peace is more characteristic of the big powers' conception of the United Nations role than it is of the new, smaller powers' view.

This is not to deny the importance which some of the major powers attach to human rights. Historically, American foreign policy has been known to err on the side of 'excessive' attachment to moral principles of this kind. And even today American pronouncements and rationalizations of political stands are often singularly humanistic and moralistic in tone.

On the other hand, it must not be assumed either that the new states are so preoccupied with demands for basic human rights that they have no time to worry about the problem of peace. On the contrary, these states revel in seeing themselves as peacemakers in the disputes of the giants.

Nevertheless, there does remain a significant difference in scale of values between the newer and older states. With regard to India's annexation of Goa, for example, a major power may have argued that the very enjoyment of human rights presupposed a peaceful settlement of disputes. In a sense this line of reasoning makes peace more fundamental than those rights – at least to the extent that it makes it fundamental *to* those rights. But with that Goan experience in mind, the same great power may have become concerned that peace in western Africa would also be seriously disturbed if human rights were not extended to Angolans. In this second case it would at first appear that the major power was making human rights fundamental to peace rather than vice versa. And yet a good deal would depend upon whether this was an *ad hoc* calculation by the big power in regard to the particular situation or whether it was a basic, general postulate of its diplomatic reasoning at large. If, as is likely in this case, the calculation was *ad hoc*, then peace was still being deemed more fundamental than human rights – since the granting of human rights by Portugal in Angola was here regarded as *instrumental* in the promotion of peace. In general, it was more the new states than the older ones which supported India over Goa.[12] And it tends to be more the new than the old which are concerned about the rights of Angolans irrespective of the effect of such reforms on peace at large.

At times it is almost as if the new arrivals in international politics were reminding the older participants of the simple proposition that the importance of peace is, in the ultimate analysis, *derivative*. Taken to its deepest human roots, peace is important because 'the dignity and worth of the human person' are important.

Once humanity is accepted in this way as a more fundamental moral concept than peace, membership in the United Nations might then be based not so much upon a test of being peace-loving as upon a test of being respectful of that 'dignity and worth of the human person'. And in African estimation – as in the estimation of India's Madame Pandit – *apartheid* is a more flagrant failure of that test than territorial aggrandizement by the Chinese. This is not necessarily a mitigation of the gravity of Mao Tse-tung's aggression; it is just a heightened condemnation of Verwoerd's arrogance. On this rests the determination of African states to sentence, if possible, Verwoerd's republic to something approaching solitary confinement.

In some ways this is a highly moralistic stand to take in international relations. And some African countries have yet to translate their moral indignation into specific policies of boycotting South Africa.[13] And yet, if moralism is irrelevant in international relations, emotionalism is not. And *apartheid* remains the most emotionally charged single issue in the politics of the United Nations and perhaps of the world at large.

But should these small countries be allowed to reverse the order of importance between peace and human dignity? This brings us to the whole issue of the voting system in the United Nations and to the significance of the growing power of a General Assembly based on a system of one state, one vote. On 1 August 1957, Sir Winston Churchill addressed the American Bar Association on the dangers arising from the new responsibilities which the General Assembly sought to assume. He said:

> We wish these new nations well . . . but it is anomalous that the vote or prejudice of any small country should affect events involving populations many times exceeding their own numbers, and affect them as momentary self-advantage may direct.[14]

In his preface to the 1957 edition of *War and Peace*, John Foster Dulles emphasized that the increase of United Nations membership since 1950 had accentuated the need for a reformed system of voting.[15] In 1962 Lord Home, then British Foreign

Secretary, was exasperated enough with the militancy of the small powers in the United Nations to talk about a 'crisis of confidence' as regards the future of the world Organization.[16]

It is safe to assume that these leaders were more polite in their public complaints than they might have been in their private thoughts. At any rate, certain sections of opinion in their countries have discerned a touch of absurdity in a situation in which little 'tribes' have 'the same say' or the same voting weight in the United Nations as some of the older giants have in international politics.

An African might retort that this whole way of thinking stems from the premise that the more powerful a country is, the greater should be not only its capacity but also its *right* to determine what ought to happen in the world. Its vote in the United Nations should count for more than the vote of a small country. This conclusion would certainly follow if the purpose of the United Nations were to make the powerful even more powerful. Any attempt to make the balance of influence in the United Nations commensurate with the ratio of strength outside the UN is not merely to make the Organization reflect the realities of the outside world but is to give the big powers an *extra* arena of power. It is to *add* to the diplomatic influence which size and strength have already conferred upon them.

The argument continues that it would surely not serve the purposes of the United Nations to do this. The purpose of the UN should not be to make the powerful a little more influential; on the contrary, the United Nations should be concerned with moderating the immense capacity for independent initiative which power gives to the powerful. And in this task of moderation, a distortion of the vote in the UN to favour the smaller countries might be precisely what is needed. The distorted vote is certainly consistent with Dag Hammarskjöld's conception of the United Nations as, in the ultimate analysis, the hope of the small and weak countries.

But is this distorted vote consistent with a scale of values which puts the 'dignity and worth of the human person' first and peace only second? Ambivalence is certainly involved in all this. In his fight for self-determination in his own country the African had declared his allegiance to the principle of 'One Man, One Vote'. In his fight for international participation through the United Nations he seems to stand for the principle of 'One State, One Vote'. And yet the premises on which the two principles stand are not always mutually consistent. The principle of 'One Man, One Vote' seems to rest on the moral premise that no individual human being is to count for more than another human being. But the principle of 'One State, One Vote' seems indifferent to equality as between *individual* human beings. A vote which represents less than four hundred thousand Gabonese is put on a par with a vote representing over two hundred million Russians. As between the Gabonese and the Russian in the General Assembly, there can be no doubt that it is the Russian who is underprivileged. A remark of E. H. Carr's in 1939 has indeed now found a paradoxical substantiation – the claim that 'the equality of man is the ideology of the underprivileged seeking to raise themselves to the level of the privileged.'[17] In his nationalism, when contending with, say, British settlers, the African militant had been underprivileged and had stood for 'One Man, One Vote'. In his internationalism at the United Nations, he was later to leave the belief in numbers to people like Sir Winston Churchill, John Foster Dulles, and Lord Home since these leaders lamented the anomaly by which – to put it in Churchillian terms – 'the vote or prejudice of any small country should affect events involving populations many times exceeding their own numbers.'[18]

And yet, if this is a cry for the democratic principle of representation according to population size, the African might well wonder why the cry was not raised from the very inception of the United Nations, considering that nearly twenty of the original signatories of the UN Declaration were Latin American countries, including Panama with its population of less than a million. But then most of the Latin American votes were predictably Western. An African would be justified in wondering whether this was the factor which stilled the voices of the Churchillian prophets of proportional representation. In any case, even conceding that Africa is over-represented in the United Nations, it is easily established that Asia is *under*-represented. And if population were the criterion, many is an African who might in 1962 have settled for eight UN votes answerable to Mr Nehru on the Katanga issue for every vote answerable to Lord Home. A few might even settle for, as it were, two Sukarnos for every de Gaulle on almost every issue discussed at the United Nations since 1960.

All the same, it remains true that in the United Nations, if nowhere else, the African prefers 'sovereign equality' (as between states) to 'human equality' (as between men). And if the rationale for this preference is that sovereign equality helps to moderate the power of the big states and to keep the peace, this is certainly one area of African ideology where peace is put first and the dignity and equal worth of the human person is put second.

But how is nonalignment itself related to these two ideals: peace on the one hand and equal dignity on the other? At first glance it would appear that the ultimate rationale for nonalignment must be the extent to which it promotes peace. The whole policy seems actually to *mean* a disengagement from the cold war itself, though not from attempts to *end* the cold war or to prevent its warming up. So important has this peace-keeping or mediating side of nonalignment been that even such a sincere friend of the nonaligned as Sir Hugh Foot has warned the non-aligned to beware lest they be accused of waiting first until the two blocs have expressed their opinions and then seeking a position in between, expressed as the opinion of the nonaligned.[19]

In defence of the nonaligned, it can indeed be said that it is sometimes less important to have an independent categorical opinion than to remain sufficiently ambiguous to be acceptable to both sides as a potential mediator. In his famous rebuke of British aid to India, for example, Nkrumah must have felt that if everyone were to commit himself strongly on the rights and wrongs of the Sino-Indian conflict, the chances of impartial mediation would diminish further. Nkrumah's position in that instance consisted in giving his opinion not on who was right in the dispute, but on what was best from the point of view of settling it.[20]

But what was left of nonalignment in the face of that very conflict between China and India? Could it still be maintained that nonalignment as a disengagement from the cold war was a practical proposition? Until the autumn of 1962 there was no ring of obsolescence in the idea of nonalignment. It was indeed often attacked in the West but on the mutually contradictory grounds that it was both 'meaningless' and 'untenable'. With the Sino-Indian conflict the policy itself became exposed to the additional charge of sheer obsolescence – of being a myth of the past already exploded along the Sino-Indian frontier.

In the next chapter we shall examine more closely the assumptions made in this kind of judgment. But even if the Africans conceded that the Indian predicament was a case where non-alignment had not paid, they would have to see the Cuban predicament as a case where outright alignment had not paid either. When all is said and done the humiliation of Cuba in the autumn of 1962 arose out of permitting a foreign nuclear base on Cuban soil – a contravention of one of the basic tenets of Afro-Asian neutralism.

But was not the Cuban confrontation of the giants itself evidence of the futility of nonalignment in the sense of mediation by small countries? When it comes to the test, can either Russia or the United States be expected to pay the slightest attention to the protesting voices of little neutrals? In answer to this question, it might be pointed out that in the Cuban confrontation neither giant paid much attention to the little allies either. If, then, an African voice is going to be at best marginal within an alliance with either bloc, it might as well be marginal outside the blocs altogether – or perhaps marginal in influencing *both* blocs instead of only one.

And yet, important as these peace-keeping aspirations of non-alignment might be, it would be a mistake to assume that they constitute the ultimate reason for the existence of nonalignment. The attraction of nonalignment for the small countries does not rest primarily on the ideal of peace; it rests, in fact, on that other ideal of equal dignity. To be part of an alliance led by massive powers is to be overshadowed by those powers. An alliance involves an element of self-denial and self-discipline, but if you are a very small member of an alliance led by giants the 'self-denial' and 'self-discipline' might not be so self-imposed after all. In any event one thing surely holds – nonalignment gives small powers at least the *appearance* of independent initiative. To the extent that it involves fewer formal ties with big powers, nonalignment becomes the external extension of domestic self-government. It becomes, at any rate, an additional badge of independent status.

What makes such 'independence' possible for countries which *are*, in some cases, absurdly small? Never in history have the voices of the weak been so strong in the councils of the world. How has this happened?

Of late the big powers have become more 'enlightened' and tolerant in some respects. But this has not always been so. Afro-Asian neutrals sometimes speak as if they must be nonaligned in order to prevent the big powers from going to war. What is nearer to the truth is that the small powers can afford to be nonaligned precisely because the big powers are already afraid of going to war. It is not a case of nonalignment making peace possible – it is more a case of the fear of war making nonalignment possible. The voices of the weak have become strong because the strong are already afraid of one another. At any rate this is how it started. But although indulgence toward the weak may be the child of a mutual fear between the strong, that indulgence may already be changing into genuine respect. This respect would in turn make nonalignment more effective as a moderating influence on the big powers. The whole process has aspects of sheer circularity; fear of war among the big powers leads to toleration of presumptuous small powers; that toleration makes nonalignment possible; habit turns that toleration into a genuine respect; genuine respect makes the powers more responsive to the opinion of the nonaligned on at least some marginal issues; and nonalignment thus at last vindicates the peace-seeking side of its existence.

But there is yet another variable in relations between bigger and smaller states which must now be examined – the issue of distribution of wealth in the world. We have already discussed this matter in relation to fears of neo-dependence. What might now be analysed is the relevance of poverty to human dignity and to prospects for peace.

To a large extent, the nonaligned have been a community of Afro-Asian nations. But this whole idea of a community of Afro-Asian states is a fellowship as much of 'underdevelopment' and poverty as it is of shared colonial experience. And the sensitivity which new states sometimes show when they are described as 'underdeveloped' underlines the connection between indignity and indigence. Julius Nyerere articulated a widely-shared view when he said in September 1963 that although Tanganyikans had won the right to international equality when the country became independent, yet a man who was ignorant, who could not produce enough food for himself, or who suffered from disfiguring diseases could not really stand on terms of equality with all others.[21]

Two years earlier Nyerere had linked the international distribution of wealth to a Marxist analysis of class. He had argued in these terms:

Karl Marx felt there was an inevitable clash between the rich of one society and the poor of that society. In that, I believe, Karl Marx was right. But today it is the international scene which is going to have a greater impact on the lives of individuals. . . . And when you look at the international scene, you must admit that the world is divided between the 'Haves' and the 'Have-nots'. . . . And don't forget the rich countries of the world today may be found on both sides of the division between 'Capitalist' and 'Socialist' countries.[22]

A few years later Arnold Smith, the Canadian diplomat who became the first Secretary-General of the Commonwealth, saw in this latter division a global danger. His misgivings were along the lines we discussed when we analysed the implications of the European Economic Community. Smith said:

The division of humanity between the white and the other races, which coincides too closely for comfort with the division between the affluent industrialized peoples and the poor underdeveloped peoples is, I think, the most difficult and potentially dangerous problem in the world.[23]

Those who analyse this problem further sometimes discuss it on an assumption similar to that made by Hans Morgenthau in his concept of 'a status quo power'.[24] The assumption is that a vested interest in the international status quo is a child of satisfied needs. It is therefore to be expected that developed states, to the extent that they have satisfied many of their domestic needs, would be reluctant to risk a change in the prevailing situation. On the other hand, the very concept of a 'revolution of rising expectations' in the underdeveloped countries implies that those countries are keenly dissatisfied with matters as they stand – since they have numerous new expectations which are still far from being met.

From this kind of reasoning it is an easy transition to the belief that rich countries are more concerned about peace than poor ones. To a certain extent this belief is vindicated by the very dichotomy in scale of values which we attributed to politics in the

United Nations. The prevailing view of the purpose of the United Nations among the richer countries is, as we argued, the maintenance of peace; the prevailing view among poorer countries, especially the new states of Asia and Africa, is of the UN as a global ombudsman, protective of the rights of man at large. And, as we have noted, many nationalist leaders feel that the very poverty of their countries is not adequately consistent with human dignity. All these factors would therefore seem to suggest that the fear of war is more characteristic of developed than of under-developed states. And this suggestion in turn has sometimes led to the conclusion in the West that China was so poor that she would have nothing to lose by engaging in a major military conflict.

In rebutting this kind of reasoning Edgar Snow has first admitted that 'It is true that individual Chinese have nothing much to lose but their lives.' He has then gone on to ask 'Is fear of losing the wealth in private property of some of us in the West a greater deterrent against war than fear of losing all our lives?'[25]

To a certain extent Snow is unfair to the view he is combating. It is true that poor people still have their lives to lose in a war – and the fear of losing one's life can be at least as effective a deterrent as the fear of losing one's wealth.

But the point here is that the rich countries have *both* fears operating instead of only one. Nor is the meaning of 'losing one's life' necessarily the same as between the rich and the poor. Cultural factors, frequency of death in the family, general life expectancy in the society, as well as the degree of ease or hardship encountered in the course of being alive should all have a bearing on a people's attitude to death.

Nevertheless, there remains a serious fallacy in the argument that rich countries value peace more than do poor ones. The argument takes for granted that to have a vested interest in the status quo is the same thing as to have a vested interest in peace. That does not follow. Having a vested interest in the status quo can sometimes impel a nation to *disturb* the peace – in a bid to prevent change. Students of international politics see this easily enough when they are looking at events within the conceptual framework of 'balance of power' theories. They can interpret the action of President Kennedy over Cuba in the autumn of 1962 as a case of risking war in a bid to *prevent* a major change in the status quo. But some of the same students of international politics might then proceed to take it for granted that a 'status quo power' necessarily has a greater interest in peace than a country which has yet to 'arrive'.

But perhaps a more serious fallacy in this theory lies in the psychological hypothesis which underlies it. The theory assumes that the acquisitive instinct in man is more violent than the protective one; that the 'Have-nots' in their bid to *acquire* would be more reckless than the 'Haves' in their bid to *protect* what they already possess.

And yet this psychological theory is contrary to all human experience at the level of the individual. Readiness to use force in order to protect one's property is, almost *a priori*, more widespread than readiness to use force in order to acquire *new* property. To put it in another way, there are more people who would use violence to avert losing what is already theirs than there are people who would use it to acquire new possessions.

If the same tendency is to be expected of human behaviour at the international level the theory that the poor are more likely to risk war than the rich would need serious reconsideration. Indeed, the reverse would now be implied. The potential for violence would be greater in the wealthy who were insecure than in the poor who were ambitious. Either might indeed precipitate conflict but the balance of risk would now be seen to be leaning the other way.

But where would this leave our previous argument that in the politics of the United Nations it is the established powers rather than the new states which put peace above human rights in importance? No contradiction need, in fact, be involved. The great powers could care more for peace than for, say, self-determination – and still be no more peace-loving than the small powers. The two sets of countries might have the same amount of love for peace – the difference between them being solely in their attitude to self-determination. That alone might vary from one member of the United Nations to the next – the value of peace, were it measurable, remaining constant.

An alternative but more modest claim is to say that what is in question is not the relative value which different sets of countries in the United Nations might attach to peace and human rights, but merely their conceptions of the role of the world body itself. Hypothetically all members of the United Nations might be equal in their concern for both peace and human rights, and still vary in their notions of the proper functions of the world body. One set of nations might say that given the state of the world and the limitations of the Organization the United Nations should put this ideal first as a *function*, and the other ideal only second. Another set of nations might reverse the order of propriety of functions for the world body.

But the balance of evidence continues to indicate that this is more than a matter of varying conceptions of the role of the United Nations. There is a more substantive difference in scale of values between newer and older members. Given the difference in historical experience, it remains true that the older powers of Europe and the Americas have been less concerned about problems of racial equality and self-determination than have the countries of Asia and Africa. Their respective conceptions of the purposes of the world organization, as indeed their views on a variety of other matters in international politics, are conditioned by this initial divergence. So are the idioms in which they conduct diplomatic discourse at large.

CHAPTER NINE

NONALIGNMENT AND THE RESIDUUM
OF 'PAX BRITANNICA':
A COMMONWEALTH DILEMMA

OLIVER STANLEY'S statement cited in the previous chapter had asserted that a disintegration of the Empire would imperil the effectiveness of 'the new machinery for world security'. Stanley was formulating in a variant form a dictum which had for a long time been an integral part of the imperial ideology – the dictum that the Empire was an umbrella of peace. The whole vocabulary of colonial legitimation abounds in references to the 'order', 'law' and 'peace' which the imperial umbrella had afforded the areas it covered. The idea of *Pax Britannica*, verbalized in those terms or merely taken for granted within the complex of imperial assumptions, was central to the frame of reference of Greater Britain.

Here again the dichotomy which we traced in the politics of the United Nations finds a historic root. It is not merely with peace that a concept of *Pax Britannica* has been associated. It is also part of the history of race arrogance and of the struggle for equal dignity between peoples. The most extreme development of this idea came to be *Pax Germanica*. As Hitler put it:

Who really would desire the victory of pacifism in this world, must work with all his power for the conquest of the world by the Germans. . . . Actually the pacifist humanitarian idea will perhaps be quite good, when once the master man has conquered and subjected the world to a degree that makes him the only master of this earth.[1]

The British ambition of global pacification was more modest than this. And where British rule was established it was, of course, more humane than *Pax Germanica* threatened to be. But the idea of the British people as a pre-eminent 'governing race' was implicit in the vision of *Pax Britannica* too. As one imperial patriot, Joseph Chamberlain, put it in 1897:

In carrying out this work of civilization we are fulfilling what I believe to be our national mission, and we are finding scope for the exercise of those faculties and qualities which have made us a great governing race. . . . In almost every instance in which the rule of the Queen has been established and the great *Pax Britannica* has been enforced, there has come with it greater security to life and property, and a material improvement in the condition of the bulk of the population.[2]

If the concept of *Pax Britannica* was so central to the imperial ideology it could not but be connected with other important notions about the Empire. And here it might be useful to juxtapose another statement by Joseph Chamberlain. In March 1896, in a speech at the Canada Club in London, Chamberlain asked and answered an important question: 'What is the greatest of our common obligations? It is Imperial defence.'[3]

For the purposes of our analysis in this chapter, we could ourselves ask one further question. What historically was the relationship between this latter idea of Imperial defence and the more rhetorical but influential notion of *Pax Britannica*? By the notion of *Pax Britannica* British imperial patriots like Chamberlain were, as we indicated, asserting Britain's right to pacify the less advanced parts of the world. By the notion of 'Imperial defence', on the other hand, Britain was asserting both an obligation to protect the Empire from other covetous eyes, and a right to receive help from the Empire should Britain herself be in military need.

Out of the overlap between the vision of *Pax Britannica* and the policy of joint Imperial defence grew concepts like that of a 'protectorate' as distinct from 'colony'. A colony was a territory ostensibly in a state of pacification under the terms of *Pax Britannica*. A protectorate, on the other hand, was ostensibly being shielded from the ambitions of other major powers under a special arrangement within the terms of Imperial defence. Both the notion of internal British pacification in Africa, and the notion of defence against an external threat persisted at least until the army mutinies which took place in independent East Africa in January 1964. By that time the residuum of *Pax Britannica* was coming into conflict with the new policy of 'nonalignment' which the former British subjects now espoused in their foreign relations.

But the historical picture would not be complete if we did not examine a major postulate of both the vision of *Pax Britannica* and the policy of Imperial defence. They both rested on the myth of identity of interest between the colonial power and her dependencies. Lord Lugard's ideas on Africa typify this mode of imperial thinking. Britain and her colonies were to him mutually dependent both militarily and economically. He even believed that the defence of British freedom was *ipso facto* a defence of the *freedom* of her colonies as well.

In the First World War, when he was in office in Nigeria, Lugard felt that 'defence was a common interest between Nigeria and Britain, for which it was fair that as a wartime measure, Nigeria should bear some sacrifice.'[4] A few years after the war his book, *The Dual Mandate in British Tropical Africa*, was arguing the thesis that the 'liberties' of the African peoples had been 'at stake no less than our own in the recent war'. He then went on to ask whether 'the native of the tropics' was to bear no share in the cost of defence 'for the future'. Was there not a case for 'some reciprocity . . . in the cost of defence'? He himself was convinced that the African was not 'by nature ungrateful, and would not shirk his share of the burden.'[5]

In the course of the Second World War nothing happened to shake Lugard's belief in the 'gratitude' of the African peoples in the matter of common defence. It was all part of the total imperial myth of protective reciprocity. In 1943, when Britain had survived the most critical stage of the war, Winston Churchill made the following gratified observation:

Three years ago, all over the world, friend and foe alike – everyone who had not the eye of faith – might well have deemed our speedy ruin at hand. Against the triumphant might of Hitler, with the greedy Italians at his tail, we stood alone with resources so slender that one shudders to enumerate them now.

Then, surely, was the moment for the Empire to break up, for each of its widely-dispersed communities to seek safety on the winning side, for those who thought themselves oppressed to throw off their yoke and make better terms betimes with the all-conquering Nazi and Fascist power. Then was the time. But what happened?[6]

In so far as Africa was concerned, the answer had already come from Lugard two years before. In 1941 Lugard was already in a position to praise Africans for

the loyalty they have shown in this, and in the last war, by readiness to serve in the field, and by gifts often pathetic in their simplicity towards the cost of the war or to Red Cross funds.[7]

Africa had indeed responded to what Churchill described as 'the trumpet-call of a supreme crisis'.[8] The Commonwealth and Empire were above all a matter of common defence – or so it continued to be believed.

And then in 1962, for the first time since World War II, a member of the Commonwealth was attacked by an outsider. China invaded Indian territory, and Britain granted military aid to Nehru's Government. President Nkrumah immediately wrote to Mr Macmillan in the following terms:

Are you sure that by giving support, whatever this is, to one side against the other, you will be able to increase the chances of bringing an end to hostilities? Assistance by way of arms and equipment to any country engaged in a conflict with another, in my view, is likely merely to occasion a counter offer of assistance to the other party to the dispute. The balance of military strength therefore remains the same but the dispute is made much more difficult of solution through the involvement of outside powers.[9]

In his reply Mr Macmillan said that he found it difficult to understand Dr Nkrumah's objection to British sympathy and support for India. Mr Macmillan argued that when the territory of a Commonwealth people was invaded, it was surely right and natural that Britain should be sympathetic and helpful. Mr Macmillan was here virtually suggesting that Britain had a duty to help India militarily because India was a fellow-member of the Commonwealth. The logic of Macmillan's stand implied that the Commonwealth was a kind of *de facto* military alliance. This it was when the *independent* Commonwealth consisted of Britain and the older Dominions only. Indeed, until the Statute of Westminster of 1931 the Commonwealth was a military alliance both *de facto* and *de jure*. After that Statute it remained an alliance in fact, though no longer in strict law in so far as the independent members were concerned. This was the case until, paradoxically, India acceded to independence – and turned the independent sector of the Commonwealth not only multi-racial but also 'multi-ideological' in its foreign policies. The question which arose when India was invaded in 1962 was whether this new Commonwealth had truly ceased to have a military side to it following India's invention of 'nonalignment' a decade earlier. The Chinese invasion of India was, in other words, a test case. Mr Macmillan's interpretation of Commonwealth 'ties' seemed to imply an almost automatic rallying to India's defence. But Dr Nkrumah's view was perhaps more representative of the Afro-Asian conception of it:

The Commonwealth is not a military alliance and it would be most detrimental to its progress if the impression were created that Commonwealth members did not judge each issue independently on its merits, but instead automatically sided with a fellow Commonwealth country when that country was engaged in a dispute with an outside power.[10]

In fact, a Macmillan interpretation of Commonwealth ties amounted to a distinct moral judgment on the presuppositions of India's foreign policy up to the time of the Chinese invasion. India had for years been criticized by many Westerners for her policy of nonalignment; but the usual criticism was that it was naïve to be nonaligned. The new judgment which Mr Macmillan was, by implication, now passing was that India had been naïve in imagining that she was nonaligned at all – when all the time she had a *de facto* military alliance behind her in the form of the Commonwealth.

What have emerged out of the moral judgments which have been passed on India are two views of what would constitute an abandonment or violation of nonalignment. According to one view, a basic presupposition of nonalignment is that it is possible for a country to be left alone militarily by *both* blocs. In order to invalidate nonalignment all you therefore need is an invasion of a nonaligned country by a member of one of the blocs. Mao Tse-tung fulfilled this condition when he attacked neutralist India. In other words, Mao succeeded where Dulles failed – in murdering nonalignment. Or so concluded a large number of people in the Western world. *The Times* of London had a curt editorial to celebrate the explosion of the myth of neutralism.[11] On 11 November 1962 the *New York Times* even managed to collect quotations from unobtrusive Africans allegedly disillusioned with nonalignment. On the night of 3 December 1962, a professor from the London School of Economics commented over the BBC upon the end of the neutralist myth. This interpretation of the significance of the Chinese invasion of India was fairly representative of Western opinion at large.

But what was wrong with the inference that the mere fact of being attacked by a member of one of the blocs invalidated nonalignment? The weakness of the argument lay in the fact that India was not the first nonaligned country to be attacked by a member of one of the blocs in the cold war. Nonalignment was first tested not on the Asian continent, but on the African. And the first threat to nonalignment came not from China but from Britain herself, in collusion with France. In other words, if it was really true that the mere fact of being attacked by a member of one of the blocs invalidated nonalignment, Egyptian nonalignment would never have survived the Anglo-French invasion of 1956. And yet, in spite of all the predictions that the attack would tip Nasser into the communist camp, that remarkable Egyptian remains as remarkably independent as ever.

If we accept Egypt as an African country, we can proceed to say that the first major British threat to the nonalignment of independent Africa took the form of a direct attack against an African country. African nonalignment survived this kind of threat. But the next major British threat to the viability of African neutralism came in January 1964 – and it took the form not of a British attack against an African country, but of British military *protection* for the governments of three East African countries. Where British aggression in 1956 failed in neutralizing the efficacy of neutralism, did British protection succeed in 1964?

Here we are back to the problem of criteria as to what would constitute being 'aligned'. A mutual defence pact between, say, Kenya and Ethiopia is obviously not the sort of alignment which is meant here. The most obvious form of alignment is a formal alliance against 'the other side in the cold war'. Now that the Cold War is no longer as neatly polarized as it was before Mao and De Gaulle started asserting themselves, the whole idea of 'the other side in the cold war' is not quite as readily meaningful as it once was. All the same, it is still safe to say that an African or Asian country that is in an alliance specifically aimed against, say, 'the communist threat' cannot convincingly claim to be 'nonaligned'.

Another criterion of alignment is more subtle. It does not insist that the alignment be directed against 'the other camp in the cold war'. It would be enough if the alliance is with a country which, in another context, is allied with *others* against a side in the cold war. Thus Somalia would be compromising her nonalignment if, hypothetically, she entered into a formal military pact with the Soviet Union against *Ethiopia*. Obviously this is different from having a pact with the Soviet Union against the *United States* or against *Britain*. In the latter instance of alignment the very 'enemy' against whom the pact is intended is an 'enemy' in terms of the cold war. But in the former instance of alignment, it is not Somalia's 'enemy' (Ethiopia) but Somalia's 'ally' (the Soviet Union) that belongs to a cold war camp.

It is by this second criterion that Tanganyika felt she was in danger of compromising her nonalignment when she found herself needing the help of British troops in January 1964 when her own troops mutinied. As Nyerere confessed to the Organization of African Unity following his call for British military help, the success of the policy of nonalignment 'may depend not only on remaining outside such [East/West] conflicts but also on being seen to remain outside them.'[12] How could the East African Governments convince others that they had no alliance with a big power when they were prepared to call in British troops?

The obvious retort was that a military alliance between, say, Tanganyika and Britain would have postulated a third power against which Tanganyika would be seeking British protection. And yet Nyerere himself had insisted that there was 'no evidence whatsoever to suggest that the mutinies in Tanganyika were inspired by outside forces – either Communist or imperialist.'[13] So how could Tanganyika's use of British troops be counted as 'alignment' in the absence of an external enemy?

The argument was not without a logic of its own. But the next question which arose was whether Tanganyika would have refrained from calling in British troops if the danger was indeed external. If the Tanganyika Government were to answer 'yes', we could only infer that the government was prepared to call in British troops to protect Tanganyika from its own troops but was not willing to call in British troops to protect Tanganyika from hypothetical Russian ones. A related implication was that the

Tanganyika government was prepared to risk a situation where British troops might conceivably have had to kill or wound African soldiers but the same government was reluctant to see British troops kill or wound hypothetical Russian antagonists on its behalf. This was the dilemma of those who, on the one hand, would sanction the use of British military aid to quell mutinies internally but would disapprove of British military aid against external enemies. They were prepared to see a residual *Pax Britannica*, but could not bear a remnant of 'imperial defence'.

As it happened, the British Government itself made no sharp distinction between the two. Sir Alec Douglas-Home interpreted the internal East African mutinies as evidence of a grand design by some external enemy. We have already mentioned that the first serious test that Afro-Asian nonalignment was put to was when nonaligned Egypt was a victim of, *inter alia*, British aggression. We might also concede that the second major test was when non-aligned India was a victim of Chinese aggression in the autumn of 1962. The third major test were the events in East Africa – and this time the test first took the form of British protection. Yet, by a curious coincidence, Chou En-Lai was expected to arrive in East Africa at just about the time when Britain was called upon to 'protect' the area. And Sir Alec Douglas-Home was soon to justify British military aid to East Africa partly by citing Chou En-Lai's remark that revolutionary prospects were excellent in Africa.[14] Sir Alec was probably misreading the events on the East African mainland when he detected a communist design behind the mutinies. And yet even a misreading of the situation in those terms was enough to convert East Africa into an area where Britain and China were once again participating in another crisis for nonalignment. This time they were participating in the same crisis. And in the background of it all was the Zanzibar revolution and its aftermath.

It will be a while yet before East Africa becomes 'frank' enough for anything approaching a definitive analysis of the events of that period. But indications so far would suggest that nonalignment in East Africa was at the time tested from two sides. The revolution in Zanzibar sparked off, by its example, army mutinies in Tanganyika, Uganda and Kenya. The question which arose was whether that use of British troops to subdue the mutineers had cost East Africa its stature among the nonaligned.

But meanwhile the communists within Zanzibar's revolutionary regime seemed to be consolidating their position. And technicians and advisers from communist countries abroad were soon conspicuous on the island. Again East African nonalignment seemed to be facing the beginnings of a crisis – but this time arising from an apparently growing involvement with the *other* camp in the Cold War. It took a swift Pan-Africanist move by Nyerere of Tanganyika and Karume of Zanzibar to earn a reprieve for nonalignment from this second crisis – for the time being.[15]

The United Republic of Tanzania as a whole later proceeded to strengthen relations with Communist China, but by then the aim was to make the republic's nonalignment more 'genuine'. Behind this latter aim was perhaps the conviction that while Zanzibar on her own could 'flirt with Communist countries' only at the risk of becoming a satellite, Zanzibar and Tanganyika together were capable of strengthening ties with communist countries and still be more nonaligned than ever.

The impact of Communist China on the whole doctrine of nonalignment will be discussed in further detail in a later chapter. But for the moment our preoccupation must revert to Anglo-African relations. In justifying British military aid to East Africa partly on the grounds of Chou En-Lai's interest in Africa was Sir Alec putting forward a Macmillan interpretation of the demands of Commonwealth ties? Was the British Government once again treating the Commonwealth as a *de facto* military alliance?

There were indeed occasions early in 1964 when the rationale advanced by the British for their military response implicitly asserted some kind of military understanding between Commonwealth countries. Even in East Africa itself it was possible for the leading English language newspaper to argue in terms like these: 'If Britain is asked to give active help in an emergency, undoubtedly the request will be considered, *as of one Commonwealth country to another*.'[16]

And yet no one in authority, either in Britain or in Africa, seemed enthusiastic about the idea of a 'Commonwealth Army'. Mr Kenyatta, when asked what he thought of the idea, virtually said 'No comment'.[17] One would have thought that a composite 'Fire-Brigade' Army, drawn from the Commonwealth at large, would be less of an embarrassment to a nonaligned country than British troops were. But, when all is said and done, British troops were less 'alien' in East Africa than even Indian troops would have been. And once again multilateral Commonwealth ties were exposed as being a little less real than bilateral ties with Britain on her own.

But how permanent are even the bilateral ties in the military field? Here again one must examine the presuppositions and implications of nonalignment itself in relation to what has been happening in the countries concerned. Of the East African states Kenya is the only one which devised military arrangements with Britain of a genuinely *reciprocal* kind. But the rules of nonalignment continue to be such that while a country might be forgiven for *receiving* military aid from a big power in an emergency, it is less readily forgiven if it *gives* some form of military assistance to such a power. It might, for example, be all right for India to get Anglo-American aid in her conflict with China, but India's nonalignment could not survive if India reciprocated by granting Britain or the United States a base against China in return. By the same token Kenya's reputation probably suffered more when Kenyatta decided to help Britain with over-flying and staging facilities for the Royal Air Force than it did when Kenya was on the *receiving* end of military assistance in the crisis of her mutiny.

And yet these complex and reciprocal arrangements which Kenya made with Britain were deemed to be only temporary. When we turn to Tanganyika we find that she was more impatient to disengage herself from military relations with Britain once the immediate crisis was over. She was also unenthusiastic about British help even in the *training* of the new Tanganyika army.

But how genuine is the distinction between getting *military* aid from Britain and getting other forms of British aid? Obviously this is an issue which goes far beyond the dilemmas of the East African states alone. Almost exactly two years before Tanganyika appealed for British troops, a report in the *New York Times* was describing the Ivory Coast in the following terms:

The most striking anachronism to the radical African nationalists is that M. Houphouet-Boigny has practically abdicated sovereignty in the military field. The Ivory Coast has only a small force for internal security. And even this force has French officers. The French army assures the external defence of the country. It has been asked to do so,

M. Houphouet-Boigny says, because 'we wish to devote our modest means to economic and social development.'[18]

How fundamental was the difference between, on the one hand, an Ivory Coast which got French military assistance and used her own resources for economic development and, on the other, a Ghana which used her own resources for military expenditure, and asked for British aid in economic development? Of course aid and internal resources are not neatly divided in their purposes in this way. But it remains pertinent to ask nevertheless whether economic aid which enables a country to use her own resources on military expenditure is not, in its effect, military aid.

Let us test this equation of military and economic aid against the case of that first country in Africa to have had her nonalignment threatened – the case of Egypt. At about the same time that the Sino-Indian conflict was supposed to be in the process of invalidating nonalignment, increased American aid to Egypt was supposed to be due to the fact that Nasser had proved himself 'a genuine neutralist'.[19] In other words, if Chinese hostility to India had deflated nonalignment, American generosity to Egypt was vindicating it at about the same time.

But one of the six principles of the Egyptian Revolution still remained what Aly Sabry once briefly described as 'setting up a strong national army'.[20] If we accepted the argument that greater economic aid from the United States made it possible for Egypt to divert her own resources to that particular military principle of the revolution, the implication would be that the United States was helping to build up Egypt's military capacity. And if we further postulated that getting military aid from the United States compromised nonalignment, the logical consequence of it all would be a massive case of irony. We would, on the one hand, be saying that increased American generosity to Egypt was in recognition of Egypt's genuine neutralism. We would, on the other hand, be implying that to the extent that the generosity amounted to military assistance to Egypt, it made 'Egypt's genuine neutralism' no longer genuine.

The moral of this irony is that a complete equation between economic and military aid is difficult to sustain. If a country uses her *own* resources for military expenditure, she has a wider area of initiative than she would otherwise have. She has, for example, greater freedom in deciding where this or that item of armament is to be bought from. John Foster Dulles did embark on a policy of trying to restrict a small country's *military* initiative through *economic* aid. The United States' offer of assistance to Egypt at the time for the construction of the Aswan Dam was virtually made conditional upon a military self-denial by Egypt – especially a self-denial of arms from Czechoslovakia. But Dulles' whole policy was later reversed under the Kennedy Administration. Even before Kennedy changes were already emerging. Though Western economic aid did help this or that nonaligned country to use other resources for military purposes, the Dulles formula of trying to establish a more direct connection between economic assistance and military commitment was significantly revised. By 1962 American aid to Egypt was not a measure of Egypt's commitment, but a measure of her 'genuine neutralism'.

Having now made the point that no complete equation is tenable between economic and military assistance, we ought now to take a few steps back – and reassert some kind of connection between the two all the same. The connection is particularly clear in those countries whose armed forces are more modest than Egyptian armed forces are. There is a degree of economic weakness which is indistinguishable from military vulnerability. And some of the black African states are better illustrations of this principle than Egypt is. None of the East African countries can afford many more battalions than what few they had when the mutinies broke out. How sovereign then is East Africa? And how meaningful is a policy of nonalignment when it is floating on a pool of diluted sovereignty?

This takes us back to our previous discussion on the distinction between state sovereignty and racial sovereignty. And it also links up with the point raised earlier in this chapter that concepts like that of *Pax Britannica* and *Pax Germanica* have implications for race relations at large.

The case of Zanzibar itself just before the revolution presented a good illustration of our two levels of sovereignty. According to state sovereignty, Zanzibar was a free and sovereign state if it was established that the rulers were *Zanzibaris*. But according to the implications of racial sovereignty, the island could only become 'free and sovereign' if the rulers were essentially *African* by race. Nor was this a simple case of defining 'freedom' in terms of majority rule. The new revolutionary Zanzibar could still be ruled by a minority. It could even be a smaller and more ruthless minority. But the demands of racial sovereignty were satisfied if the rulers were a special kind of minority – if, in other words, they were a minority of the majority *race*.[21]

By the criterion of state sovereignty, Tanganyika at the end of December 1963 was a foreign power from Zanzibar's point of view. A member of Zanzibar's Afro-Shirazi Party before the revolution would therefore have been committing 'treason' if, hypothetically, he conspired with a foreign power like Tanganyika to overthrow the government of his own state. But according to racial sovereignty such a conspiracy – far from being treasonable – was to be regarded as commendably 'patriotic', assuming that Zanzibar was indeed being ruled by Zanzibaris of a minority race before the revolution.

Let us now use this principle of dual sovereignty to examine events on the East African mainland itself. Dependence on troops of another race would seem to detract from racial sovereignty. And yet this might well have been a case of detracting from racial sovereignty in order to consolidate state sovereignty. What ought to be remembered, however, is that in the military field there had been a dilution of racial sovereignty in East Africa all along. British officers continued to be in command in some West African Commonwealth countries. And when Tanganyika was negotiating for the loan of Nigerian troops to replace British troops in the country, one of the possibilities which had to be borne in mind was that Nigerian troops might arrive in Tanganyika under British officers. In short, a nationalism which, in several Commonwealth African countries, had refused to tolerate for very long 'expatriates' in top administrative jobs was nevertheless pragmatic enough to continue to use expatriates in top military jobs.[22]

In Tanganyika there was, indeed, a change following the first mutiny. The government capitulated to the demand of the First Battalion that British officers be replaced. And yet one of the minor ironies of the events which followed was that a British commander who was expelled by the Tanganyika Government in response to the demands of the mutineers later came back at the head of British troops to subdue the mutineers. The important point to remember is that this use of British troops to make African troops behave themselves was not quite as 'revolutionary' as it might have appeared. In a sense, it was merely an extension of the previous use of British officers to make African troops behave like good soldiers. *Pax Britannica* had now temporarily assumed something of its former thoroughness, but it had in any case been present in the supervisory role of an officer corps.

But under what conditions can the state sovereignty of an African country be maintained without violating its racial sovereignty in this way?

There is a sense in which the concept of *nationhood* might be regarded as the ultimate meeting point between state-sovereignty and ethnic or racial sovereignty. In imperial history capacity for sovereign statehood was at times judged according to whether the peoples of a particular dependency had as yet been moulded into 'a single nation'. Whether a country was so moulded needed in turn a yardstick of its own. And the logic of imperial reasoning was soon to include the following postulate – that capacity for sovereign statehood, or for the obligations of nationhood, presupposed a capacity for self-defence. There was, for example, an echo of this postulate in Sir Michael Hicks-Beach's speech on imperial defence in June 1897:

The other day Canada was spoken of with just pride by its Premier as a nation. That is true. Canada is a nation . . . but what does Canada pay for her Navy? How many sailors does Canada send to the Imperial Navy?[23]

On the other hand, H. M. Stanley was quite impressed by the Buganda of Mutesa before British annexation. 'I saw about 3,000 soldiers of Mutesa nearly civilized', he said in great admiration.[24] Mutesa's army was not indeed strong enough to prevent British annexation but one measure of Buganda's nearness to the 'dignity' of statehood was that she 'had an army and a navy'. Indeed, one criterion which emerged during the scramble for Africa was that a country or tribe which could least 'resist encroachment' was one which most deserved it.[25] Capacity for self-rule was again almost equated with capacity for self-defence.

Among the prerequisites for self-defence was one which could be all too easily overlooked – the loyalty or commitment of the 'warriors'. With this loyalty in mind, Sir Alec Douglas-Home invoked even in 1964 the old equation between capacity for self-rule and capacity for self-defence. Commenting on events in East

Africa in a television interview following the mutinies, Sir Alec said:

I have always pleaded with our African and Asian friends that they should not push their requests for independence too soon because I was afraid – and this has been proved, of course, beyond doubt now – I was afraid that they would get their independence before they had the two essential things that are necessary if you are to run a country. One is a police force, loyal to the Government; and another is armed forces, loyal to the elected government of the day.[26]

By the very definition of the word 'mutiny', the most direct revelation of the events in East Africa at the time was indeed the fact that the loyalty of the armed forces to the new independent governments had yet to be well-established. The soldiers turned out to be less reliable than they had been under the colonial regime. As Jomo Kenyatta said following the suppression of the Kenya mutiny:

During the colonial days the men of the King's African Rifles served the British Government loyally. Now that we have our own African government, the world and our own people are justified in expecting even greater loyalty from the Kenya Army.[27]

But the soldiers concerned had failed to come up to those expectations. A tradition of loyalty to Kenya or Tanganyika as national units had yet to be adequately developed. The soldiers had obeyed colonial masters, but had yet to learn obedience to nationalist governments.

And yet there is a certain irony in the very fact that soldiers in Africa should seem to betray governments which came into power on the wave of African nationalism. The irony arises because of the role that African ex-servicemen are supposed to have played in the very creation of nationalism in Africa. As we mentioned in another context, even before the last world war ended, a Colonial Office Advisory Committee on Education in the Colonies was already observing that Africans

who have seen active service and been on foreign service in Ceylon and Madagascar, Abyssinia and the Middle East, have been educated in an additional sense by travel, by contact with other nationalities, and most of all by a dawning realization of themselves as Africans, even as 'nationals' of a territory like Northern Rhodesia, playing a part in world affairs.[28]

By 1956 Thomas Hodgkin could describe 'the experience of African servicemen in the various theatres of the war' as a factor of political transformation in West Africa 'too familiar to require detailed repetition'.[29] All the same Dennis Austin reminded us the following year that the hundred and fifty thousand ex-servicemen throughout British West Africa 'contributed to the general feeling of unrest, which remained unassuaged, if it was not stimulated, by the mild constitutional reforms of the mid-1940's.'[30] In short, African military experience abroad in the 1940's contributed to the birth of African nationalism at home. It is this which introduces an element of irony in a situation two decades later in which the military in parts of independent Africa threatened new nationalist governments – and were thwarted by troops borrowed from the former colonial power.

But then, irony is often the fundamental law of historical development at large. If it is true that the Second World War was a factor of great importance in the development of African nationalism, and if this importance is partly derived from the fact that Africans actually participated in the war on the same side as the colonial rulers, then we can say that African nationalism in Commonwealth Africa arose partly out of an alliance with Britain. In the words of Margery Perham:

Even in the First World War Britain had been forced to call upon African, as upon Indian troops. On the whole she had obtained, both in Africa and Asia, such support as she needed. But the Second World War was different. When Britain stood alone she was forced to ask from her African colonies not only soldiers to fight far beyond Africa but more, and sometimes different, production in return for a diminishing supply of the imported goods they wanted in return. She had, therefore, to appeal for co-operation and understanding in terms never used before.[31]

To a very large extent Britain did get the co-operation and understanding she asked for. For Africa at that time there was *no* 'nonalignment' – not even at the level of passive resistance against being drawn into the war by Britain. There was, instead, an African *commitment* in the fight against Germany, Italy and even Japan. Out of that commitment and its varied implications Africa's own self-consciousness was sharpened. But out of the sharpened self-consciousness in turn African *neutralism* emerged.

And yet, was that 'neutralism' prematurely born? Ultimately it is perhaps with this question that East Africa confronted

African nonalignment at large early in 1964. Capacity for self-defence may or may not be an essential part of capacity for sovereign statehood. But that same capacity for self-defence might well be a prerequisite of meaningful nonalignment when a major crisis faces a minor country. There is, in short, such a thing as capacity for nonalignment. And it is something which varies in magnitude from country to country. In a later chapter we shall discuss the implications of the Sino-Russian dispute. But for the moment it remains true that the two super powers – the United States and the Soviet Union – cannot be nonaligned in the 'neutralist' sense for the simple reason that to be 'neutral' is to be neutral between *them* and between what each is supposed to represent. But while the super powers are thus 'incapable' of nonalignment only as a matter of definitional logic, all other powers vary in their capacity for nonalignment according to the size of military crisis with which they can cope on their own. East Africa's crisis in January 1964 was at once trivial and fundamental. It was trivial because what it involved was not a major external military threat, but the misbehaviour of some soldiers at home. It was fundamental because ability to cope with an external military threat should one occur itself presupposes a reliable soldiery at home.

It is not easy to find a scale to measure a country's ability to fulfil its own foreign policy. What we might say about the East African countries is what Robert Browning said about the phenomenon of human ambition generally – 'A man's reach should exceed his grasp, or what's a heaven for?' In the final analysis, 'heaven' for the nationalist should be, quite simply, a capacity for consistent nationalism once independence has been achieved. But given the demands of running a state, capacity for consistent nationalism is often an elusive ambition. Compromises have to be made – and those who reach for neutralism sometimes find themselves grasping *neo*-alignment at best.

This state of affairs is perhaps a temporary inadequacy. But while it lasts an implicit Anglo-African *neo-alignment* is persisting as a defiantly enduring vestige of *Pax Britannica*.

CHAPTER TEN

PAN-AFRICANISM VERSUS
NONALIGNMENT:
AN AFRICAN DILEMMA

IN THE previous chapter we discussed the difficulties of maintaining consistency in the policy of nonalignment. We pointed out how easily the policy could become a kind of 'neo-alignment' between an African country and the former colonial power. The fact nevertheless remains that the language of African nationalism reflects a profound desire to be genuinely 'nonaligned'. Nor is the profundity of this desire surprising. There is a sense in which formal diplomacy is the most distinctive thing about African independence. After all, independence in essence is the attainment of statehood, and the ultimate characteristic of statehood is the right to conduct one's own foreign relations. One could almost say that the most tangible difference between a colony and a sovereign state is the foreign embassy – the embassy which the sovereign state established abroad or allows to be established in its own capital. It is essentially because formal diplomatic activity is, in this way, the ultimate expression of sovereignty that control over defence and foreign relations became characteristically the last powers to be handed over by the imperial country.

But the nature of African nationalism had been such that on attainment of sovereign status African countries started devising a two-tier structure of diplomatic activity. As we indicated in our discussion of continental jurisdiction, one tier of African diplomatic activity concerned relations between African countries themselves; the other tier concerned relations with the outside world.

In the idiom of inter-African relations the most pervasive concept is that of 'Pan-Africanism'. In the idiom of African policies

164

in world politics at large the most recurrent notion is that of nonalignment. What this chapter hopes to analyse is the complex of interrelationships between Pan-Africanism and the doctrine of nonalignment.

There is a sense in which this whole complex of interrelationships could be reduced to a single simple proposition – the proposition that *unity is power and neutrality is freedom*. While the ultimate inspiration behind Pan-Africanism is a desire to see Africa become more powerful in the world, the ultimate ambition of nonalignment is to reconcile Africa's weakness today with a certain degree of diplomatic freedom. As we indicated when we discussed the relationship between peace and human rights in world politics, the basic psychological desire behind nonalignment is not a desire to end the cold war, but a desire for a sense of independence in spite of being a small country.

The connection between the concept of power and the concept of freedom has therefore some relevance in an analysis of Pan-Africanism and nonalignment. Perhaps we can best link the different factors together by asking three questions on this issue of interrelationships. Firstly, to what extent can we regard Pan-Africanism and nonalignment as different expressions of the same psychological longing? Secondly, to what extent can we say that Pan-Africanism and nonalignment are not only different expressions of the same thing, but actually help to make each other feasible? And thirdly, to what extent can we ever say that Pan-Africanism and nonalignment are incompatible?

This is where the concept of power (in Pan-Africanism) and the concept of freedom (in nonalignment) come into relevance. The desire for power and the desire for freedom together amount to an African quest for significance. It is a desire to assert what in a more straightforward idiom would be the proposition that 'Africa matters in the world'. Pending the formation of a continental or sub-continental African federation nothing has contributed more to the feeling that 'Africa matters in the world' than the part which African states have been able to play in the cold war and as a result of the cold war.

There are different ways of securing a sense of self-significance. One is to become part of something 'big'. Membership of the United Nations or of the Commonwealth, or signing a nuclear test ban treaty, can be a way of becoming important by joining something bigger than oneself. But another method of securing a sense of significance is almost the opposite of the first one. This second way of feeling important is by asserting one's *independence* of those who are 'big' rather than by joining them. A European example of the first method is the example of Britain when she seeks to assert a special relationship with the United States. On such occasions Britain might be seeking a sense of importance by attaching herself to a giant. The example of De Gaulle's France, on the other hand, is of seeking importance by *detaching* herself from the American giant.

In their policy of nonalignment the new countries are essentially 'Gaullist' – though they were 'Gaullist' before Charles de Gaulle himself started asserting his independence in the cold war. It is this aspect of the question which links nonalignment to the whole issue of sensitivity to 'neo-colonialism'. As we indicated earlier neo-colonialism arises out of a feeling of vulnerability to external manipulation. The vulnerability itself arises out of needing others. Dependence on others is a measure of relative difference in *power*; external manipulation a measure of balance of initiative and dilution of *freedom*. To the extent that nonalignment is an attempt to avert external manipulation by the bigger powers, it is an attempt to avert neo-colonialism.

How does this relate to Pan-Africanism? In so far as both nonalignment and Pan-Africanism are inspired by a desire to be convinced that 'Africa matters in the world', they are a response to the same psychological longing. In foreign affairs the common question they face is how the African voice might be better respected in the councils of the world. Refusal to be tied to any of the giants in the cold war is the method which nonalignment prescribes. An African determination to become a giant in her own right is the method prescribed by Pan-Africanism. The two policies might in this respect be deemed to be mutually reinforcing.

Another point of contact between Pan-Africanism and nonalignment is in regard to their attitude to factionalism. To the extent that nonalignment is an attempt to be outside the cold war as a contestant, nonalignment is a retreat from the divisions of others. Pan-Africanism is, on the other hand, horrified by Africa's own divisions – and aspires to put an end to them. But both doctrines imply an anti-factionalism. This is certainly true when nonalignment assumes its peace-seeking function. It joins Pan-Africanism in being a declaration of war against the forces of division in Africa and the world at large. In this instance nonalignment and Pan-Africanism are different aspects of the same ethical orientation, but they are not necessarily mutually reinforcing in practice.

As regards the mechanics of conduct in international affairs, there have been three lines of policy which the nonaligned could take in regard to the cold war – and still remain out of it. First, the nonaligned could play the role of peace-makers between the two camps. Second, they could be *passively* neutral in the cold war – not wishing to influence relations between the big powers one way or the other. Third, they could try to perpetuate or prolong the cold war.

In terms of narrow self-interest as small powers, the best policy for the nonaligned is to do what they can to perpetuate or prolong the cold war. But it is perhaps to the credit of the small powers that they have seldom even *tried* to do this. Instead they have tended to alternate between those two other policies – that is, *either* refrained from trying to influence relations between the two camps one way or the other, *or* tried to influence those relations in the direction of lesser tension. In both these alternatives they have in part responded to the dictates of anti-factionalism as a diplomatic ethic.

But can nonalignment ever be in conflict with Pan-Africanism? In trying to answer the question let us make the observation that nonalignment is essentially a peace-time form of neutrality. It makes sense only as long as the great powers do not declare war on each other. Nonalignment is therefore at best a neutrality of trying to prevent war rather than of keeping out of it – the idea of a 'cold war' being essentially a figurative way of expressing an unsettled and perhaps dangerous peace.

To describe nonalignment as a peace-time form of neutrality is not to denigrate it. On the contrary it is this fact which helps to make nonalignment a *positive* form of neutrality. The neutrality of trying to *prevent* a war has greater creative potential than the neutrality of keeping *out* of a war.

If then we do accept non-alignment as a neutrality of war-prevention its influence should not be measured in the conventional terms of military capability or economic power. In 1964 Adoko Nekyon, Uganda's Minister of Planning and Community

Development, displayed a diplomatic insight of some interest in the course of theorizing about the failure of negotiations on the formation of an East African federation. Nekyon said to the Uganda Parliament that in a world of nuclear armaments even the combined armies of Africa would be an ineffectual force. The East African countries needed *individual voices* – for if a country did not possess military strength 'it has to make a noise'. The Minister asserted that Uganda did not intend to give up her voice in the United Nations for the sake of an East African federation.[1]

It is considerations such as these which link Pan-Africanism as well as nonalignment to the United Nations. As we indicated in a previous chapter the most important arena of articulation for nonalignment is, in fact, the United Nations. One measure of the policy's impact there is the degree to which the big powers are prepared to respond to the arguments of the nonaligned. In positive terms this is the most important measure. But another indication of the influence of nonalignment is the number of UN members who are, in fact, nonaligned. And this takes us right back to the voting system of the General Assembly and the multiplicity of small powers within it. What needs to be examined now is something which can well too easily be overlooked – the extent to which the voting system of the United Nations encourages some of the small powers to *remain* small. In the African context this links the voting system of the United Nations not only to the effectiveness of nonalignment but also to the prospects for regional or even continental unification in Africa. Given the voting system of the United Nations and given that the influence of nonalignment is to be measured partly by the number of countries which are nonaligned in the General Assembly, nonalignment would stand to suffer if its adherents *ceased* to be small. This is to postulate that ceasing to be small is to integrate with others into bigger territorial units. It is to postulate a situation where two or more members of the United Nations unite to form a new *single*, if bigger, member.

There are indeed forms of regional grouping which fall short of total political integration. The East African common market and common services organization still left mainland East Africa with three seats in the UN instead of one. But assuming that East Africans are concerned with the effectiveness of nonalignment in the United Nations, future voting power is an important factor to take cautiously into account every time they talk about forming one bigger state. And that was precisely what Adoko Nekyon did in his analysis of the importance of *individual* voices for the cause of peace.

Yet, given our old premise that nonalignment is essentially an extra badge of independent status and of the dignity of independent initiative, Africans would, in fact, be generally less worried by the future of nonalignment itself than by the future of the status of Africa in the United Nations. Bigger African states would mean *fewer* African states and therefore fewer African votes in the United Nations. Symbols of sovereignty are important to countries which are newly sovereign. And a seat in the United Nations is sometimes regarded as the ultimate symbol of at least formal independence. A *collection* of seats becomes a symbol not just of sovereignty but also of influence; and the voting system of the United Nations is such that by this measurement Africa's influence would decline should Africa become stronger by uniting. Pan-Africanists often advocate full political integration between African states on the ground that this would among other things raise Africa's stature in the world. But the United Nations – which is so important as a means of giving the African a sense of stature since Africa is now weak and divided – is so constituted that it tends to lure some Africans away from the Pan-Africanist's goal. In short, raising Africa's world stature by reducing the African vote in the United Nations is a paradox of realism which has yet to be squarely faced.

When put in its historical context this factor has a touch of irony. The Rt Hon. Oliver Stanley, in that speech in 1945, sought to protect the United Nations from a 'splinterization' of the British Empire. Through its role in decolonization, the United Nations then helped to bring about that 'splinterization' of empires. The irony of the present day is that the UN has temptations for small countries which may encourage them – however marginally – to *remain* in that state of splinterization. The idea of a multiplicity of African states in the General Assembly is, in fact, only one such temptation. The United Nations may also – with the best will in the world – help to mitigate difficulties which, if left unsolved by the Organization, might compel Africans to greater exertions toward unity.

Nations already sovereign will give up their sovereignty only if there are compelling needs which only such renunciation would meet. These needs may range from military insecurity to economic problems.

In spite of the events in East Africa in 1964, it is still true that the most important instance of military insecurity experienced so far by independent Africa revolved around the Congo situation. But the role of the UN in the Congo cannot be described as having been hostile to African unity. On the contrary, the Congo itself could hardly have been maintained as one country without UN exertion.[2]

It is, paradoxically, the less involved economic activities of the world Organization which could inadvertently militate against greater union in Africa. This follows if we start from the premise that there are two possible unifying factors at stake in any significant programme of foreign aid to Africa. One factor which might induce Africans to federate is their own poverty – and the hope that union would solve their economic inadequacies. To the extent that foreign aid helps to mitigate the inadequacies, does it make this particular federative inducement less and less compelling? Presumably this would partly depend upon the volume and kind of aid given. There may be some forms of economic aid which, while meeting some inadequacies, generate new demands – and perhaps spell out an even better case for federation. For example, even if it is accepted that foreign aid weakens the need for union, it may be argued that foreign *investment* strengthens it – at least to the extent that private investment often prefers larger markets. In spite of these qualifications, it remains true that some forms of aid militate against joint effort by Africans themselves. A country which can secure aid to establish and support its own university, for example, would be less inclined to seek ways and means of pooling resources with neighbouring countries – and establishing a *joint* institution of higher learning in the area. What applies to joint or federal universities might apply to federalism at large.

Another potentially unifying factor at stake in foreign aid is related not to aid itself, but to the *source* of the aid. In his list of reasons for which people seek federal unity, K. C. Wheare included 'a desire to be independent of foreign powers'.[3] Few will doubt that this is a desire of considerable persuasive force for many African countries. Indeed, now that most of Africa is *formally* independent, the Charter of the United Nations has become a Charter of neo-decolonization almost as much as it is a Charter of self-determination. At any rate, the term 'neo-colonialism' has become a major debating concept in the General Assembly. We have already noted that in spite of the complaints of people like Mr Spaak, the term 'neo-colonialism', though vague, is certainly not meaningless.[4] Very often it signifies a condition of being so dependent on other powers as to become vulnerable to political manipulation by the benefactors. The fear of being in such a condition is perhaps precisely what Wheare meant by 'a desire to be independent of foreign powers'. In order for this desire to lead to federation, Wheare himself postulated something else – 'a realization that *only* through union could independence be secured.'[5] It is the applicability of this 'only' which the United Nations could so easily put in doubt – particularly should the UN serve as the channel through which all aid, say, to Africa were extended. This would thereby reduce the threat of the 'neo-colonialist' benefactor and, correspondingly, the impetus to union.

About three years before the United Nations was born E. H. Carr argued that the threat of military power to national self-determination and to the independence of small states was recognized by the peacemakers of 1919 – and came to underlie the aspirations of the Covenant of the League of Nations.

But wedded as the peacemakers were to nineteenth-century conceptions of *laissez-faire* and of the divorce between economics and politics, they failed to detect the more recent and more insidious threat of economic power.[6]

The question which now arises is whether, firstly, the great powers would allow the UN to mitigate threats of economic as well as military power; and, secondly, whether such mitigation of the economic threat to self-determination is wholly desirable. Carr himself made a distinction between the principle of self-determination and the principle of nationality. The principle of nationality tended to be 'one of disintegration' whereas self-determination did not necessarily entail that. 'Men may "determine" themselves into larger as readily as into smaller units', Carr said.[7] It is difficult to talk of the principle of 'nationality' in the African context. But if we substitute for that the principle of territorial independence, we can almost say that the United Nations' role in Africa so far has promoted self-determination only in the sense of determining territorial independence. The point at issue now is what type of UN activities would increase or reduce the chances of a more integrative form of self-determination. We have analysed in other contexts the two fundamental elements of African nationalism. We have noted that one concerns the relations of Africans with the outside world; the other pertains to the relations of Africans with each other. The former includes the fear of being manipulated by non-Africans; the latter comprehends the desire for greater unity among Africans. If the United Nations were to be the clearing house for all forms of aid to Africa, it might satisfy that element of African nationalism which fears foreign manipulation. But at the same time it might hamper that element of African nationalism which longs for greater unity in the continent. This is assuming that one factor which would encourage Africans to unite is precisely the fear of being externally manipulated if they remain divided. The UN would in this case be neutralizing that fear. In other words, if the most effective way of stripping foreign aid of the aura of 'neo-colonialism' is to channel it through the United Nations, then the United Nations might also be the most effective instrument for depriving the cause of African federalism of the unifying services of neo-colonial fears.

What all this means in turn is that the United Nations is not a unifying factor in African politics but is at best a liberating one. It has been valuable as a major arena for nonalignment and a possible shield against neo-colonial manipulation by the big powers. But the world body has also remained a possible indirect obstruction to Pan-Africanism.

Another instance of a possible conflict between nonalignment and Pan-Africanism was dramatized at the time that Britain was applying for entry into the European Economic Community. We have already discussed the issue of African neo-dependency which arose in the course of the general discussion of Britain's application. What we might examine now is the related issue of nonalignment in regard to the European Community.

The question arose at the time whether African association with the Community was compatible with the African policy of nonalignment. But why should the issue of compatability have arisen at all given the 'neutral' tone of Part IV of the Treaty of Rome on such association? One possible answer is that just as one could not judge the politics of France merely by consulting the French Constitution, one could not judge the politics of the European Community merely by going through the clauses of the Rome document. Cases of stretching the letter of the Treaty of Rome or discreetly ignoring it had already emerged. On the desirable side, such cases had included the obliteration in practice of the legal distinction between the former Italian part of Somalia, entitled to EEC Development aid, and the former British part, legally ineligible for such aid pending British entry.[8] Also desirable were the bilateral West German credits and grants to ex-British territories 'despite [West Germany's] obligations to the European Development Fund.'[9]

More ominous, however, were West Germany's intrigues in November 1962 to get the EEC Development Fund used as a method of deterring African associates from recognizing East Germany.[10] This would have been a case of basing eligibility for the Community's aid on the *extra* treaty undertaking by associates not to recognize East Germany.

Also important as a factor which an African neutral might have weighed was the attitude of the European Economic Community to *European* neutrals. On the one hand the Community offered association to Africans with the assurance that it would not compromise their neutrality. On the other hand, the Community hesitated to grant association to Sweden precisely because she was neutral. What were involved were, of course, different forms of association. But if the association which was offered to the Africans was the more generous of the two, the greater was the mystery of not demanding a cold war price for it. What *was* the Community up to? – such a question might have worried many an English-speaking neutralist in Africa.

But French-speaking Africa was already associated with the European Community. Had those African states then allowed themselves to be tied to an economic alliance within the cold war? In a sense Francophone Africa had, in fact, decided to compromise a little of its nonalignment for the sake of economic advantage. English-speaking Africa on the other hand decided to put nonalignment first and possible economic advantage second.

But was this also a case of putting nonalignment first and Pan-Africanism second? Such a case was arguable. A joint association with the EEC by Africa as a whole *could* have been positively unifying. Associates were, for example, required to extend the most favoured nation treatment to each other – a possible 'nucleus' of an African Common Market. Secondly, a joint African participation in decisions on trade and development might have increased the habit of inter-African co-operation. And thirdly, since Francophone Africa was already associated with the EEC, the association of Commonwealth Africa as well would have eliminated a possible area of trade friction between them.[11]

Yet these inducements to Pan-African co-operation were renounced by Commonwealth Africa for the sake of nonaligned respectability. Since then Nigeria and the East African countries have shown greater interest in association with the European Economic Community. They have, however, asked for terms specifically different from those which govern relations between the EEC and the original African associates. In other words, Nigeria and East Africa, while interested in association with the European Community, have rejected precisely those elements of association which might have served as inducements to greater Pan-African co-operation between them and the original French-speaking associates. Nigeria and East Africa asked for an arrangement designed to distinguish them significantly from the original eighteen.[12] Nigeria has since succeeded in getting such terms.

And yet of all the countries concerned here – East Africa, Nigeria as well as the original eighteen associates of the EEC – are members of the Organization of African Unity. And Article III of the Charter of the Organization includes an 'affirmation of a policy of nonalignment with regard to all blocs'. Is not this common allegiance to the principle of nonalignment, however varying in shade of commitment, itself a positive contribution to Pan-Africanism?

This is an argument of some persuasiveness. A common approach to foreign affairs is indeed itself a form of unity, even when it is not institutionalized. Alternatively we could view a common approach to foreign affairs not so much as a form of unity, but as a basis for future unity. Again the experience of the European Economic Community has some value for the insights it affords. Why does the Community still consist of only six members? There are of course a number of reasons for that, the most important of which being that Britain was kept out of the Community and, with her, Britain's 'allies' in the European Free Trade Area. But even if Britain had gone into the Community some of her EFTA partners would not have been able to follow her into the Market – precisely for reasons of foreign policy. Sweden, Switzerland and Austria are still unable to join their fellow Europeans in the Market because they themselves are neutrals. The possibility of some kind of *association* has been explored, especially with Austria's delicate position as an involuntary neutral in mind. But full membership of the Community is not open to any of the European neutrals. Here then is a case of Pan-Europeanism being narrowed in its scope because of fundamental differences in approaches to foreign affairs.

On the other hand, the fact that nonalignment is so widespread in Africa is a contribution to harmonious relationships between African states in at least this area of attitude to the cold war.

And yet, of all common approaches to foreign relations, nonalignment is by definition the least unifying. We have already argued that both Pan-Africanism and nonalignment are *anti-factionalist* in orientation. But they differ in their anti-factionalism in an important way. Pan-Africanism is, at its most ambitious, a desire for a deeply unified African community. Should such a community fall short of federation it would at least become, to all intents and purposes, a *bloc* of like-minded African states. Non-alignment, on the other hand, is a diplomatic ethic which is *opposed* to blocs. As the Declaration of the Non-Aligned Conference held in Belgrade in September 1961 put it, 'the non-aligned countries represented at this Conference do not wish to form a new bloc and cannot be a bloc.'[13]

We can, therefore, say that the type of anti-factionalism which underlies nonalignment is not easily compatible with that which activates Pan-Africanism.

A related characteristic of nonalignment is that it is an assertion of everyone's right to be *different* should one wish to be. The Belgrade Declaration emphasized that:

all peoples and nations have to solve the problems of their own political, economic, social and cultural systems in accordance with their own conditions, needs and potentialities.[14]

Indeed, nonalignment has sometimes been interpreted to mean the right of a country to be 'neither Western nor Eastern' even in the system of government which it has at home. It is these considerations that make nonalignment the least unifying of all possible *common* approaches to political problems. This is because it is 'common' only as an insistence on national *individuality* in world affairs.

If one were grading the unifying potential of the three major stands in the cold war, one would have to say that Africa would best have achieved unity if it all went communist. Second as a unifying factor would have been a united African allegiance with the West *against* communism. The first cause implies a greater degree of commitment and common ground than the second, in spite of the split between China and the Soviet Union in recent times. But a common commitment *against* communism would still have been more unifying than the loose diversity of nonalignment.

But should a Pan-Africanist therefore proceed to align himself in order to realize his Pan-African ambitions? This conclusion might follow if he was assured that other Pan-Africanists would join him in his choice of alignment. But it is easier to get Africa to agree on 'nonalignment', loosely defined, than to get all of it united as a communist or anti-communist force. Pan-Africanism has therefore to settle for the more modest agreement in international affairs signified by nonalignment. It has to do this in spite of the inner logical and sometimes practical tension between the demands of African unity and the dictates of a neutralist ethic in world affairs.

CHAPTER ELEVEN

PAN-AFRICANISM IN THE COLD WAR

To THE extent that it examined the relationship between non-alignment and Pan-Africanism, the previous chapter was itself a study of the effect of certain cold war considerations on the fortunes of Pan-Africanism. That was one approach to the subject. Another approach is to examine Africa's relations with the major participants in the cold war. Selectivity is essential in this instance. A defensible line of analysis is to concentrate on the leaders of the two camps, the United States and the Soviet Union. But in view of the Sino-Soviet dispute, and of the impact of Communist China on Afro-Asian politics, an estimate of the significance of China in this regard also needs to be attempted.

This chapter will therefore first relate the cold war to the historic links which Africa has had with the United States, and proceed to examine the place of anti-Americanism in African nationalistic thought. We shall then assess the general ideological influence of the Soviet Union on Africa, and go on to hypothesize on the relationship between African unity and Russia's national interest. The third part of the chapter will be the discussion of China's impact on the doctrine of nonalignment and on inter-African relations.

As might be inferred from previous discussions, the connection which Pan-Africanism has with America is of longer standing than its connection with either the Soviet Union or Communist China. Pan-Africanism was intimately linked with America when it was intimately linked with Pan-Negroism. We have already mentioned the divorce which took place between Pan-Africanism and Pan-Negroism.

An additional factor which emphasized that divorce came to be the cold war itself. As citizens of the leading nation in the Western alliance, the issue of disengagement from the cold war never fired the imagination of American Negroes. American Marxists did try to capture the movement for civil rights, but even a Marxist-led Negro movement in America would have remained fundamentally different from the ideology of positive neutralism which emerged in Africa.[1] Pan-Negroism had been a movement of peoples and not of governments; but Pan-Africanism, once independence was achieved, came to be both. The interest of Pan-Negroism had been inter-racial relations; the interest of Pan-Africanism came to include international relations. And it is in the context of international relations that nonalignment operated. This alone would have been enough of a difference between the ultimate concerns of Pan-Africanism and the concerns of Pan-Negroism. The difference became all the greater because of the essential Americanness of American Negroes and their inner commitment to the Western side in the cold war. 'I oppose communism's political totalitarianism', Dr Martin Luther King has declared.[2] It is an attitude which goes on to colour American Negro conceptions of 'international communism' at large.

A more enduring relevance of America for Pan-Africanism lies in the image of the United States as a model for continental unification. Many is an African nationalist who has looked at the United States with its wealth and power – and then dreamt of a 'United States of Africa'.[3] The very name 'United States of Africa' is often consciously intended to echo the name of the American union – and to conjure up an image of global stature and strength.

As for African discussions and arguments on the form which African unity should take, these are often soaked in the language of federalism which is perhaps America's most distinctive contribution to political and constitutional thought.[4]

How relevant is the principle of federalism to that aspect of the cold war which is concerned with ideological competition? In its genesis federalism was intimately related to the values of liberalism at large. The liberal commitment to diversity, to limited government and – especially in America – to the device of 'checks and balances' found comfortable accommodation in federalist assumptions and aspirations. But for Africa outside Nigeria the liberal postulates of federalism are not even remembered. Few Africans have bothered to ask themselves whether the idea of a one-party state is compatible with federalism. Could East Africa operate a federal system if each of the constituent parts is a one-party state *by law*? Or could it do so if Uganda and Kenya continued to have fluid party systems while Tanganyika remained a *de jure* one-party state. If these were some of the questions asked, the principle of federalism itself would have been a matter of ideological disputations of the cold war kind. But African nationalists have admired the American union not for the extent to which the federal government was weakened in a system of checks and balances, but for the extent to which the sub-continent was strengthened for having united in the first place.

What of the new relevance of the United States for Pan-Africanism? A contrast with the original past should be illuminating. Historically, what was relevant for African nationalism at one time was the interest which American Negroes took in Africa. Of far more importance today is the interest which the American government takes in the continent. And since Africa now has African governments, relations between the United States and Pan-Africanism are now partly at the institutionalized level of inter-governmental relations, and relations with the OAU. There are occasions when the United States is almost an ally of Pan-Africanism on some policy-issue – as on the issue of selling arms to South Africa. There are other occasions when policy-conflicts are recurrent – as in the long story of the Congo problem. All that one can say with conviction is that the history of Pan-Africanism – as the history of so much else in the contemporary world – has important points of contact ahead with the history of the United States.

Partly arising out of this omnipresence of America as a power in the world is the whole phenomenon of anti-Americanism as a factor in international politics. For our purposes what we need to inquire into is the place of anti-Americanism in African nationalistic thought.

A good approach for the inquiry is to look at the latest region to show signs of anti-Americanism – East Africa. Anti-Americanism in East Africa is, in some ways, an old phenomenon and in others a new one. The first proponents of anti-Americanism in East Africa were white settlers. They often accused the United States of stabbing Britain's imperial back. Those accusing fingers could always turn to point at West Africa. In that part of the continent American-educated leaders had, as we have noted, tended to be more militant in their nationalism than their British-educated counterparts. In East Africa there were, it is true, few major nationalistic figures who had been American-trained. In fact, there were few leaders in East Africa for quite a while who were educated abroad at all – and what few there were were British-trained. The first African member of the Kenya Legislative Council, Eliud Mathu, was a product of the Oxbridge tradition. Kenyatta had a British background, complete with a British wife. But his radicalism often tended to be blamed on his brief visit to Stalin's Russia. There later emerged Julius Nyerere on the East African political horizon. He was educated in Britain, and for a while many discerned in him a British gradualist, a believer in compromise and phased-out change.

If then there were hardly any living militants in East Africa who were American-educated, why was there so much anti-Americanism among white settlers there? Partly because of the conviction that there *would* be such militants if many young Africans found their way to the United States. But this conviction in turn arose out of a general belief that the United States was essentially anti-empires in her national temperament. In 1961 it fell upon G. Menen Williams to trigger off once again the latent anti-Americanism in white settlers. Mr Williams, while on a visit to East Africa, had affirmed that 'Africa was for the Africans'. There was immediate settler indignation from the Limpopo to the source of the Nile.

But among Africans in East Africa there was still no significant anti-Americanism. On the contrary, many was an African nationalist who found support and encouragement when touring the United States. Why has there now intruded an anti-American bias in the nationalism of some Africans?

Before attempting to answer the question let us first have a note of caution. Uganda was the first African country to join the communist 'bloc' in publicly denouncing American 'aggression' in Vietnam. But in reality anti-Americanism in Uganda is still more a posture than a genuine emotion. The chances are you will find more anti-Americanism in Britain, let alone France, than you will find among ordinary people in Uganda.

But it still remains true that there is now in East Africa less hostility towards the former colonial power, Britain, than there was before and more hostility towards the United States than there was before. Part of the explanation is perhaps not peculiarly East African. Anti-Americanism all over the world has been developing into a sub-ideology. There is cultural anti-Americanism, especially in Europe – the reaction against the American brand of modernity, its mass culture and its neo-Texan cult of 'bigger and better'. But then there is also political anti-Americanism. The great majority of left-wing radicals in the world – including American radicals – have in their temperament an inherent anti-American bias. There is a sense in which it is almost a logical contradiction to be left-wing and pro-American at the same time. Part of radical disapproval of the United States is concerned with the image of America – erroneous in important ways – as a bastion of *laissez-faire* capitalism and a centre of plutocratic arrogance and racial bigotry. The other aspect of radical disapproval concerns the nature of America's omnipresence in the world as a whole and the foreign policies involved in that presence.

If then that is the connection between radicalism and anti-Americanism, it was only a matter of time before African radicals displayed the same bias as fellow radicals elsewhere. It can almost be said that the colonial situation had suppressed a latent anti-Americanism in African radical thought – that situation having centred radical attention on the imperial culprit himself, the British or French ruler. But once colonialism retreated it was inevitable that sooner or later radicalism in Africa should take the same anti-Yankee turn that it had taken elsewhere.

Related to this is America's increasing presence in Africa following Africa's independence. An aspect of this is *economic* presence. Few Africans are, in fact, Leninists, but one part of Lenin's thought has been greatly influential in Africa, his economic interpretation of imperialism. We will remember that Lenin had described imperialism as the highest stage of capitalism. It might be true that America had not been a leader in imperialism; but by being a leader in capitalism she could so easily become an imperial suspect as well.

The Leninist view had been more an economic interpretation of imperialism than a theory of economic imperialism. Lenin had tried to explain full political annexation in economic terms – rather than to show how there could be economic exploitation

N

without territorial annexation. But Leninist views are now echoed by the concept of 'neo-colonialism' in Africa – and the phenomenon denoted by this concept is economic domination rather than territorial annexation. It therefore makes sense that anti-Americanism in Africa should essentially be a post-independence phenomenon.[5] After all, for as long as Africa was directly colonized, the major enemies were the colonial powers who had actually annexed Africa. But since economic imperialism does not presuppose annexation, the greatest suspect might well be the richest country in the world – particularly since the United States is not only a leader in wealth, but also a leader in capitalistic methods.

Where this issue links with legitimacy is in the Congo situation. America has already established a reputation elsewhere of readiness to maintain in power regimes which might not survive otherwise. In Latin America the United States had exercised that prerogative on a monopolistic basis for a long time now. In Asia the American presence began to have this effect not long after Asia was decolonized. And now there is genuine fear among many Africans that Africa, too, will soon be converted into an American sphere of influence. And the United States might play the role of king-maker and even king-breaker in defiance of the wishes of the rest of the continent. That is perhaps why Prime Minister Obote compared the Congo to Vietnam.[6] And that is why the American presence in Africa is, in some respects, deemed to be in conflict with the African postulate of continental jurisdiction.

There is perhaps a historical dialectic involved in all this. The principle of continental jurisdiction is an aspect of Pan-Africanism. Pan-Africanism was born out of Pan-Negroism, the unity of black peoples in both Africa and the Americas. When independence came to Ghana, Nkrumah expressed Africa's gratitude to the new world by converting Ghana into a home for two of the most distinguished founding fathers of Pan-Africanism, George Padmore (a West Indian) and W.E.B. DuBois (an American by birth). We can therefore say that the origins of Pan-Africanism were inter-continental, involving participation by both Africa and the New World. But out of this inter-continentalism has now emerged a doctrine of continental exclusiveness implicit in the very composition of the Organization

of African Unity. Once again America is challenging this exclusiveness, but this time it is by the actions of the State Department
rather than the old dedication of disgruntled Afro-Americans like
DuBois. Many African nationalists are apprehensive about this
new American participation in African affairs.

In any case, the American presence in Africa is providing a
meeting point between the diplomacy of inter-African relations
and the diplomacy of African dealings with the outside world.
Uganda's relations with the Congo can become intimately connected with her relations with the United States. Perhaps there is
a brighter side to this. Perhaps there is an educative purpose to
be served by a fusion of the two parts of African diplomatic
experience on at least some issues. The problem is to determine
which are the best areas for this exercise in diplomatic
miscegenation.

What of Russia's role in the history of Pan-Africanism? The
most radical Pan-Africanist among African leaders was Kwame
Nkrumah. And Kwame Nkrumah was an American-educated
Marxist. Not all African leaders admit to being 'Marxian-
socialists'. But we could nonetheless seek information as to
how much of the socialistic thought of contemporary Africa
must be traced to Marxism. What is the relevance of this for
Pan-Africanism and the cold war? And where does the Soviet
Union come in?

Here, as in so many other matters, we need to draw a distinction between the experience of French-speaking Africa and the
experience of English-speaking Africa. The main point to grasp
is that the leadership of French-speaking Africa was more directly
exposed to Marxism in the colonial period than British Africa
ever was. Whereas the Communist Party of Great Britain has, on
the whole, always been a negligible force, the Communist Party
of France has been a major aspect of the French political scene.

It is true that even among English-speaking Africans there had
been some contact with communists, and even with the Soviet
Union from fairly early days. George Padmore (though not
strictly an African) and Jomo Kenyatta were among the pioneers
of Negro contacts with the Soviet Union. In 1930 Padmore was
studying colonial problems in Moscow at the University of
Workingmen of the East and became a member of the Moscow
Town Soviet.[7] Also in the 1930's Jomo Kenyatta spent a short

period in Stalin's Russia. But these were relatively limited contacts between Soviet communism and English-speaking Africans. It was French-speaking Africa which Moscow could really touch by proxy – using the hand of the French Communist Party. For a while the French Communists managed to establish a direct alliance with the parent mass party of Francophone African nationalism, though the alliance did not last long.[8]

Another difference of importance between French Africa and British Africa was the fact that a few of the Francophone African leaders were deputies in the French parliament itself and were therefore direct participants in the politics of metropolitan France.[9] The Soviet Union was bound to be a more relevant issue for reflection if an African was listening to policy-speeches in the French National Assembly than if he was demanding 'Uhuru na Kazi' in Pumwani, Nairobi.

A third point of difference is the difference in educational emphasis between the policy of France in her colonies and the policy of Britain. French colonial policy in the field of education was tied to assimilationist principles – and the same philosophical-orientation which one found in the metropolitan educational system found its way into schools in French colonies as well. This philosophical-orientation aroused interest in Marxism at the intellectual level among the elite of French-speaking Africa.

But although French-speaking Africans had thus been more exposed to Marxism than their English-speaking counterparts had been, the Francophone foreign policy orientation on attainment of independence was more pro-West. Guinea and Mali were the exceptions. But in general it would be true to say that Francophone nonalignment has tended to be more forgiving towards the West than towards the East.

This difference of orientation in foreign policy as between French speakers and others was an important factor in the original division of Africa into a Brazzaville group and a Casablanca one. The divisions were not, of course, along neat linguistic lines. The Casablanca group was linguistically mixed. The Brazzaville group was neatly Francophone, but the Monrovia group encompassed the Brazzaville states and some others. All the same the relative Western orientation of Francophone nonalignment was unmistakable.

And yet, in another sense, Francophone African nonalignment is a purer form of nonalignment than the Anglophone version is. This is to assume that nonalignment is purer if it is more exclusively concerned with the cold war as such. For Francophone Africa, nonalignment does not necessarily mean having no military pact with France. It all depends upon the purposes of the pact and the enemy at whom it is directed. If the pact is specifically aimed at the Eastern bloc, nonalignment has been compromised. But if French military aid is for internal security in an African country against, say, mutineers, or the aid is for 'defence' in very general terms without reference to any cold war strategy, then nonalignment is not an issue at all. Admittedly, France is a member of the Western alliance. But France can have relations with her former colonies as France and not as a member of the Western bloc – just as Senegal can in turn have relations with others in her capacity as Senegal and not as a member of the Organization of African Unity. Francophone African nonalignment has tended to recognize the fact that countries have multiple roles to play – and a 'Western power' can have an interest in an African country independently of cold war considerations.

Shifting the discussion now from specific foreign policies to ideology at large in Africa, we can first begin by affirming that all schools of socialism among African leaders today owe something to Marx – but not all the African leaders are even aware of their debt. One must go on to add that virtually none of the African leaders are Marxist enough to renounce Pan-Africanism. On the contrary, a good many Africans are too Pan-African to be happy about Marxism. George Padmore, a founding father of Pan-Africanism and a former convert to communism, actually saw the two ideologies as alternatives for Africa. As he put it in his book *Pan-Africanism or Communism? The Coming Struggle for Africa*, 'in our struggle for national freedom, human dignity and social redemption, Pan-Africanism offers an ideological alternative to Communism. . . . Pan-Africanism looks above the narrow confines of class, race, tribe and religion.'[10]

But the Soviet Union itself has not been convinced that Pan-Africanism looked 'above the narrow confines of *race*', whatever else it might do. The Soviet Union has preferred the wider concept of 'Afro-Asian solidarity'. But in general Dr I. I. Potekhin, the late Soviet Africanist, was fairly representative of

Soviet attitudes to Pan-Africanism when he gave it a qualified general approval in 1959. He said:

Pan-Africanism as an ideology contains much that is alien to our [Soviet] ideology. But Pan-Africanism aims at uniting all the peoples of Africa for the struggle against colonialism and imperialism, and for their national liberation. And from this point of view Pan-Africanism deserves the support of all people of good will who are striving for the ideals of progress and democracy.

But Potekhin went on to lament that Pan-Africanism was a little too Gandhian in its non-revolutionary methods – 'The spirit of nonresistance to coercion which permeates the speeches of many of the leaders of this [Pan-African] movement cannot command respect and sympathy.'[11] Since that time in 1959 Pan-Africanism has become less Gandhian in those aspects of its activities which are concerned with anti-colonial resistance. The Committee of Nine in Dar-es-Salaam operates under the umbrella of the Organization of African Unity. The Committee is in turn an umbrella for movements of violent resistance to the remaining cases of colonialism.

What kind of model does the Soviet Union itself present for Pan-African emulation? In a sense the Soviet example of 'continental unification' is of greater relevance to the African situation than the example of the American union. The cultural and linguistic pluralism of the Soviet landmass is more analogous to the situation of the African continent than the American experience can ever be. And yet in practice few African nationalists have been interested in the Soviet Union as a case of 'continental unification'. On this particular issue of continentalism it is the United States that has stolen the show. The image which the Soviet Union has managed to sell is not of successful unification in spite of size but of rapid industrial development in spite of initial backwardness.

But of what relevance to the Russian national interest has been the Pan-African movement? For a long time it used to be taken completely for granted by many observers that the more communist countries there were in the world the better was the Russian national interest served. The neatly polarized cold war situation of up to three years ago lent itself to such presumptions. But now it is becoming less and less self-evident that a mere multiplication of communist regimes in the world is necessarily in the Russian interest. A number of qualifications now need to be made. And one of the qualifications must be the size and potential power of any new convert to communism.

Here then we can pose the hypothesis mentioned earlier of the whole of Africa being converted to communism. If the Africa which is so converted still consists of small countries, then their conversion to communism would be a definite advantage to the Soviet Union. For the countries would be too small to be serious rivals to the Soviet Union as regards leadership in the communist world. Small communist African countries would, in the normal event, be *followers* rather than leaders within the communist camp. The only question would be whether they would follow Communist China or the Soviet Union. The chances are that, in spite of the racial issue, the Soviet Union would have at least half of Africa on her side.

But let us now hypothesize that, instead of an Africa consisting of small communist states, Nkrumah's brand of Pan-Africanism had succeeded and given us one massive African state, at least south of the Sahara. Let us further assume that such a Pan-African state is converted to communism. It would still be too underdeveloped to be an equal even of Communist China, let alone the Soviet Union. But its size might give it stature and influence, and its potential might make it more influential by anticipation. Such a Pan-African state would *not* be in the national interest of the Soviet Union. Unlike a multiplicity of small African states, this united one could not be *shared* as between the Soviet Union and Communist China. Assuming the rivalry between Russia and China still existed, a massive Pan-African state would be either on China's side, or on Russia's side or holding the balance between the two. From Russia's point of view, none of these three possibilities would be an improvement on the prospect of leading even half of an Africa consisting of small communist states. A unified Africa on the side of China would be disastrous from the point of view of Russian leadership in the communist world. A Pan-African federation holding the balance between Russia and China could stifle Soviet initiative even more effectively than if Africa was definitely on the side of China. For an Africa which is neutral as between Russia and China, but capable of taking sides if pushed too far by either side, would be an Africa that might greatly tax Soviet wooing resources. But what if the Pan-African state were definitely on Russia's side in the hypothetical continuation of the rivalry with China? Even this would not be an improvement on the alternative of leading half of a balkanized Africa. A multiplicity of small communist African states would *follow* the Soviet Union – but a major Pan-African federal state would be nearer a *partner* for Russia than a follower. And a partner that might need to be amused if it is to remain a partner.

In practice these are calculations which do not seem to have influenced Soviet attitudes to the different schools of Pan-Africanism. The calculations are 'hypothetical' because of the relative remoteness of their two basic hypotheses – the conversion of Africa to communism and the unification of African countries into a massive federal state. Should the situation change in respect of these hypotheses, Soviet attitudes to the different schools of Pan-Africanism would affect Soviet policy more directly.

But in the meantime the ideological dispute between the Soviet Union and Communist China has persisted. And it is to its implications that we should now turn our attention.

In 1923, writing on his death bed, Lenin linked three populous countries together and assessed their impact on the world. Lenin said:

> In the last analysis the outcome of the struggle will be determined by the fact that Russia, India, China, etc., account for the overwhelming population of the globe. And it is precisely that majority that, during the past few years, has been drawn into the struggle for emancipation with extraordinary rapidity.[12]

Lenin saw in this fact an assurance for the complete victory of Socialism. For a while in the 1950's it did seem that the three most populous countries in the world intended to remain on sufficiently friendly terms to exert a shared influence on the rest of the world. But then alternative possibilities began to be discernible. If China and Russia remained together communism would retain a powerful alliance on its side. If India and China remained together something approaching 'Pan-Asianism' would continue to exert a shared influence on diplomatic events in the world – and could constitute a collective leadership of the coloured nations of Asia and Africa at large.

Yet for a while it was India rather than China which was the effective leader of the new states. And one factor which helped

India to retain this leadership for a decade was the general diplomatic isolation of Communist China, including her exclusion from the United Nations. In the meantime India bequeathed to the new states the doctrine of nonalignment. As Milton Obote said in his tribute to Nehru when he died: 'Nehru will be remembered as a founder of nonalignment. . . . The new nations of the world owe him a debt of gratitude in this respect.'[13]

But even as Obote said that nonalignment in the *old* sense had already been rendered impossible by Communist China. The two biggest members of the old community of Afro-Asian states had each played a crucial role in the history of nonalignment – one, India, had virtually invented it; the other, China, had virtually destroyed it in its original form.

But, as we have already noted, it was not the Chinese invasion of India which killed nonalignment. At the most what the Chinese invasion imperilled was *India's* nonalignment. And even if that invasion had eliminated nonalignment from the rest of Asia as well, it could, as we said, still have left Africa and the Middle East as the last bastions of nonalignment in the world.

What killed nonalignment of the old sense was then not China's conflict with India, but China's dispute with the Soviet Union. The old nonalignment which Nehru had bequeathed to fellow Afro-Asians had taken for granted a bi-polarized cold war. Its whole conceptual framework postulated a dichotomy between 'East and West' – and sometimes between 'communism' and 'capitalism'. China's dispute with Russia suddenly rendered such dichotomies a little too simple. Reluctantly, but with increasing tempo, African states saw themselves having to cope not only with 'old-fashioned' contests between Russians and Westerners, but also with competition between the Russians and the Chinese.

The intrigues of the different embassies and their readiness at times to take sides in internal disputes between Africans have been known to exasperate African governments. In September 1964 Mr Grace Ibingira, then Secretary General of the Uganda People's Congress and Minister of State in Premier Obote's government, warned such embassies in strong terms. It had been brought to Mr Ibingira's notice that some foreign embassies were trying to influence political opinion in Uganda. Ibingira said:

I wish to give public warning that if such activities continue I personally will investigate expulsion from this country of such officials of foreign embassies, and this is no idle threat.[14]

Not long afterwards a Kenya Minister expressed the concern of his Government about the activities of some foreign embassies in Nairobi. There was reference to an occasion when a high-ranking Communist diplomatist had shared a political platform with Mr Oginga Odinga, then Kenya's Minister of Home Affairs.[15]

Since then ideological disagreements between Oginga Odinga and his colleagues in the Kenya Government have become more open. Bitter public arguments were carried on during the months of April and May 1965. The question of varying shades of non-alignment had by then become a major *domestic* issue in the politics of an African country. The formation of a new opposition party under Odinga confirmed the ideological split in Kenya.

But these are instances in which the dispute between Russia and China, superimposed on the old division between the Soviet bloc and the West, is disturbing political alignments within *individual* African countries. What we might now look at more closely is the place of China in the Pan-African movement as a whole.

We mentioned earlier that the links which Pan-Africanism has with the United States are older than its links with either China or Russia. This is true. But in another sense it can be argued that China as a major sector of the coloured population of the world was in the background of Pan-Negroism from the start. The feeling of 'Negroism' among the Negroes of the New World has not always made a distinction between *black* people and *coloured* people. Among the latest manifestations of militancy in 'Pan-Negroism' in the United States has been the ideology of the followers of Elijah Muhammad, the 'Black Muslims'. But their very acceptance of the original Arab prophet of Islam as 'a fellow black man' is a measure of their flexibility in defining 'black'.[16]

A precursor of the Black Muslim movement was the movement which was headed by Marcus Garvey in the 1920's. Garvey's ideology was, as Nkrumah has pointed out, 'concerned with *black* nationalism'.[17] And yet Garvey retained a sense of identification with coloured races which were not black. Roi Ottley tells us how Garvey sent a goodwill greeting to Abd-el-Karim, a rebel leader in Spanish Morocco – 'and advocated unity with all darker peoples – in the Caribbean, Africa, India, China and Japan.'[18]

Another founding father of Pan-Africanism, W. E. B. DuBois, was even more convinced of the bonds of fellowship in adversity between coloured peoples in different parts of the world. He discerned inter-connections between the subjugation of the coloured races, their poverty, and the enrichment of the white races. As DuBois put it in a grotesque but poetic way in 1935:

Immediately in Africa a black back runs red with the blood of the lash; in India, a brown girl is raped; in China a coolie starves; in Alabama seven darkies are more than lynched; while in London the white limbs of a prostitute are hung with jewels and silk.[19]

In regard to the Chinese the analogy with Negroes even included a shared experience of 'diaspora'. Though much fewer in numbers there were Chinese 'in exile' in the Americas as there were Negroes. George Padmore tells us of his 'distinguished countryman, Eugene Chen (Chen Yujen), who was born in Trinidad'. Like Padmore's own role in Africa's 'renascence', Chen returned to his ancestral land to play a part in *China's* 'renascence'. With a sense of pride which is almost patriotic Padmore recounts how Sun Yat-sen invited Eugene Chen back to China and how Chen served in three Chinese Governments as Foreign Minister – 'but never in the national government since the Kuomintang turned right'.[20]

The migration of the Chinese to other parts of the world was not quite as involuntary as the method by which Negroes came to be in the Americas. But China as a source of cheap labour is part of the history of Western dominance in the world. In Africa the Chinese were sometimes considered by the imperial powers as possible supplementary labour to native labour. In an article in *Foreign Affairs* in October 1926 Lugard discussed the relative merits of importing Indian and Chinese labour into Africa. He said:

... there is the question of supplementing African labour by importing workers from overseas. The two sources of supply in the past have been India and China. . . . The Indian Emigration Act of 1922 has prohibited the indenture of Indian coolie labour. There remains China. . . . The Chinese refuse to bring their wives with them . . . and there is the serious question of racial miscegenation. On the other hand, if the strict supervision exercised by a special official, which is adopted in Malaya, is enforced, there are no grounds for humanitarian objections as far as the Chinese themselves are concerned.[21]

The idea of using the Chinese, Indians and Africans as – to use a Kantian formulation – 'means rather than ends' is here implicit in Lugard's whole approach to imported and native labour. But for barriers of language and culture Pan-Africanism's links with China might indeed have been almost as meaningful and as old as its bonds with the United States. For DuBois perhaps they were. In December 1958 at the All Africa People's Conference held in a Ghana which was now independent, this father of Pan-Africanism was still reminding his fellow African nationalists of their ties with China and other coloured races. He said to them:

Your nearest friends and neighbours are the coloured peoples of China and India, the rest of Asia, the Middle East and the Sea Isles, once close bound to the heart of Africa and now long severed by the greed of Europe. Your bond is not mere colour of skin, but the deeper experience of wage slavery and contempt.[22]

This child of the American racial experience continued to let the distinction be blurred between those who were 'Negro' and those who were merely 'coloured'. But even as he spoke a new China was on the world scene – and her role in Afro-Asian politics was undergoing successive changes. There was once the bond of a shared humiliation by the white races. Out of this there later grew 'the spirit of Bandung' and later conferences on the theme of Afro-Asian solidarity. By 1962 China was, as we have noted, in open conflict with India. And shortly afterwards she had become a diplomatic factor of some significance in the politics of Pan-Africanism.

In the Congo China had been playing a modest part among the factions almost from the beginning of the crisis.[23] Even earlier were the contacts which the Chinese established with people like Felix Moumie, the late rebel of the Cameroun, and Abdulrahman Babu of Zanzibar.[24] A matter of more direct Pan-African repercussions was the claim made by Dr Hastings Banda in September 1964 that the Embassy of Communist China in Dar-es-Salaam had been trying to buy Malawi's diplomatic recognition – and attempting to exert pressure on the Malawi Government through some members of the Government. In a sense, the accusation marked the beginning of a rapid deterioration of relations between Malawi and Tanzania, soon aggravated by the Pan-African consequences of Dr Banda's treatment of his dissident Ministers at home. In the meantime, old myths about oriental politeness were in danger of being exploded by Chinese diplomacy in East Africa. For the Chinese Embassy in Dar-es-Salaam it was not enough to describe Banda's accusations in the usual platitude of being 'without foundation'. Dar-es-Salaam heard a Chinese spokesman attack the head of a neighbouring African government in terms like: 'It is a big lie.'[25]

Within the same general period the Embassy of the Chinese People's Republic in Nairobi issued two long statements strongly denouncing the Congolese Prime Minister, Moise Tshombe, and attacking American intervention in the Congo. The Chinese statement from Nairobi said that 'the reactionary rule of the US–Kasavubu–Tshombe puppet clique' was on the verge of disintegration – while the 'patriotic Congolese armed forces' were carrying forth the revolution vigorously.[26] It is true that Tshombe's government was hardly the most popular in Africa. Nevertheless, this was a case of a non-African Embassy in an African capital being openly abusive about the government of another African country – as well as using the occasion for anti-American denunciations of the cold war style. A few days later Jomo Kenyatta was appointed Chairman of the OAU reconciliation committee on the Congo. It was fortunate that the Chinese Embassy in Mr Kenyatta's own capital had by then stopped denouncing the 'fellow African' with whom Kenyatta was now called upon to negotiate.

All these verbal outbursts from African capitals were only the latest manifestations of a Chinese tendency to use almost every available platform in the general war of words. Among the countries which gave Chou En-Lai the warmest welcome on his trip to different African countries in 1964 was Guinea. But, as Robert Scalapino has pointed out, even in Guinea Chou's success was qualified by 'African resentment against his attack on US policy toward Panama, a breach of a previously agreed rule against criticism of third parties.'[27] Yet the distinctive thing about the Chinese denunciation of Tshombe from Nairobi and their denunciation of Banda from Dar-es-Salaam was that in these particular cases the Chinese had used African capitals to attack heads of other African governments.

Communist China became a more direct divisive factor within East Africa itself when Chou En-Lai visited Tanzania in June 1965. The Kenya Government took public exception to Chou

En-Lai's prediction of revolutions in Africa. A correspondent of the *New York Times* went on to forecast at the time that China's *commercial* relations with Tanzania, too, would militate against East African unity. Referring to the working sessions that Chou En-Lai and Nyerere had been having, Lawrence Fellows asserted:

It now seems almost certain that Tanzania is ready to impose almost a complete ban on imports from her neighbour [Kenya] to the north. . . . The Chinese have already begun to transport clothing, bicycles, sewing machines, canned goods, radios, toys and other items to Dar-es-Salaam for sale so as to raise funds to pay for development programmes.[28]

Fellows exaggerated the divisive impact of China on East Africa, but the general disruptive tendency he discerned was not entirely mythical. As some African governments established closer links with China, others worried about China's readiness to establish strong ties with dissident groups as well as with governments. As Colin Legum has put it, the Chinese

offer themselves as the allies of oppositionists, rebels and power-seekers. In this field, they have virtually no competition – neither the West nor the Russians will openly support movements against the *status quo*.[29]

Among French-speaking Africans Communist China's activities had also become a matter of some concern. The question of China's presence in Africa and its implications was reportedly one of the two most sensitive issues discussed at the conference of Francophone African states at Nouakchott in February 1965.[30]

But, when all is said and done, it is still too early to grasp the full meaning of China's diplomatic and political entry into the new Africa. It is true that the Chinese Government, unlike the Governments of the United States and the Soviet Union, does not consist of white men. But, as an editorial in a British newspaper once put it, 'Africans can be relied upon to notice that the Chinese are not black either.'[31]

In the romance of shared humiliation the Chinese had once touched the history of Pan-Negroism and been at times almost identified with it. But the future of Sino-Negro relations promises to be different in important ways. Latter-day Garveyites might never again find it easy to confuse or equate the concept of 'the Negro race' with that of 'the coloured people'.

CHAPTER TWELVE

TOWARDS A CONCEPT OF
'PAX AFRICANA'

LINKED with these themes of alignment and military stability after independence is the closely related theme of disarmament. In its modern guise disarmament is either what the Great Powers ask each other to agree to, or what the smaller powers demand of the bigger powers. The summit conference of independent African states which created the Organization of African Unity included in its preoccupations the question of disarmament – and then appealed to the Great Powers to reduce conventional weapons, put an end to the arms race and sign a general and complete disarmament agreement under strict and effective international control.[1]

But disarmament is not necessarily something negotiated and agreed upon between equals. It can be something imposed by the mighty on the weak. In this latter sense 'disarmament' of a kind was part of the rationale of imperialism. What this chapter hopes to demonstrate are some of the long-term ideological repercussions in Africa of this aspect of the imperial experience.

Disarmament is normally associated with the ideal of peace. But it has important implications for that other ideal of human dignity. Historically dignity has been more often served by the bearing of arms than by their renunciation. For many societies there was something rather effeminate or infantile in being 'defenceless'. Manliness postulated a capacity to defend oneself physically. On this point the Constitution of the United States and the tribal ways of the Kikuyu people have been in accord. The Second Amendment of the American Constitution guarantees 'the right of the people to keep and bear arms'. And Jomo Kenyatta tells us of the paramount resolution of young Kikuyu boys on being initiated by ancient custom – 'We brandish our spear, which is the symbol of our courageous and fighting spirit, never to retreat or abandon our hope, or run away from our comrades.'[2]

But imperial rule then came to Africa – and with it came, as we have noted, concepts like that of *Pax Britannica*. V. I. Lenin was later to argue that imperialism was 'the monopoly stage of capitalism'. What was perhaps more defensible was the thesis that imperialism was a monopoly stage of *warfare*. Nor is this a mere witticism. Implicit in concepts like that of *Pax Britannica* was the idea that the white races had a duty to disarm the rest of mankind. And so when the champions of imperial rule were at their most articulate in its defence, one argument they advanced was that imperialism had given the African, for example, a chance to know what life was like without violence. In 1938 Jomo Kenyatta could therefore complain bitterly in the following terms:

> The European prides himself on having done a great service to the Africans by stopping the 'tribal warfares', and says that the Africans ought to thank the strong power that has liberated them from their 'constant fear' of being attacked by the neighbouring warlike tribes. But consider the difference between the method and motive employed in the so-called savage tribal warfares and those employed in the modern warfare waged by the 'civilized' tribes of Europe, and in which the Africans who have no part in the quarrels are forced to defend so-called democracy.[3]

It is to be remembered that this complaint was made about a year *before* World War II. The preceding world war had been enough to demonstrate Europe's capacity for self-mutilation while still asserting the right to disarm the coloured races except for purposes of fighting Europe's wars. The Third Pan-African Congress held in Lisbon in 1923 was already challenging this doctrine of the white man's exclusive right to initiate war. The Congress first argued the link between Negro dignity and world peace. 'In fine, we ask in all the world that black folk be treated as men. We can see no other road to Peace and Progress', the meeting affirmed. It also asserted a connection between Negro dignity and the right to bear arms, though it linked this second assertion with a demand for general disarmament. The reasoning implicit in the demands of the Congress was that if the white man was going to insist that everyone else should be disarmed the white man must also renounce his own weapons. And so this Third Pan-African Congress called for

World disarmament and the abolition of war; but failing this, and as long as white folk bear arms against black folk, the right of blacks to bear arms in their own defence.[4]

In each colony the imperial doctrine of monopoly of warfare merged with a more familiar doctrine in political analysis – the idea that in a political community only the rulers ever have a right to use violence in dealing with citizens. Indeed, political analysts since Weber have sometimes *defined* the state in terms of its 'monopoly of the legitimate use of physical force within a given territory'.[5]

A variant formulation of this same idea in the West is the ethic that no citizen should 'take the law into his own hands'. This again is an assertion of state-monopoly in certain forms of coercion.

When the colonial power became, to all intents and purposes, 'the State' in many parts of Asia and Africa, a doctrinal merger took place between this principle of state-monopoly in physical coercion and the imperial claim of monopoly in warfare. In the total ideology of imperialism the right to *initiate* violence became a prerogative which only civilization and statehood could bestow.[6]

It was in the context of these assumptions that a new doctrine was later born to challenge imperial rule. This is the doctrine of passive resistance which Gandhi came to symbolize. Passive resistance fought against imperialism without challenging either the State's exclusive right to physical coercion or the imperial doctrine of monopoly of warfare. It sought to fight the imposition of *Pax Britannica* on India without violating the principle of peace.

A new conception of the coloured man's dignity grew out of the principle of passive resistance – a dignity not of the soldier and the right to bear arms but a dignity of the martyr and his resistance to the violence of others. The martyrdom of Jesus Christ himself became the martyrdom of a coloured man. Gandhi, for one, preferred to think of Jesus as a fellow Asian and therefore a man of colour like himself. Not long before he died, Gandhi had occasion to quote once again the Golden Rule, 'Do unto others as you would that they should do unto you.' He then went on to ask:

Or do [the white men] take in vain the name of Him who said this? Have they banished from their hearts the great coloured Asiatic who gave the world the above message? Do they forget that the greatest of the teachers of mankind were all Asiatics and did not possess a white face? These, if descended on earth and went to South Africa, will have to live in segregated areas . . . unfit by law to be equals of whites.[7]

Gandhi did not include himself among those great teachers of mankind but Kwame Nkrumah of Ghana was later to pay tribute to him in these terms: 'We salute Mahatma Gandhi and we remember, in tribute to him, that it was in South Africa that his method of nonviolence and nonco-operation was first practised'.[8]

But Gandhi became more than just the Jesus of Afro-Asian nationalism. In some ways he became almost an antidote to Jesus Christ. Just as Augustine had allied Christianity with a concept of *Pax Romana*, so did Christianity later come to be linked to the whole vision of *Pax Britannica*. In Africa Christianity came to be particularly associated with colonization. In one of his early speeches twenty years ago, Jomo Kenyatta is said to have compressed into a witticism a feeling of disaffection shared by many other nationalists: 'The white man came and asked us to shut our eyes and pray. When we opened our eyes it was too late – our land was gone.'[9]

Much later Albert Luthuli, himself a devout Christian, came to feel keenly the handicap which the religion had come to experience in the age of nationalism in Africa. Luthuli lamented:

The average African says the white man is the cause of all his troubles. He does not discriminate between white men and see that some come here for material gain and others come with the message of God.[10]

It was in contexts of this kind of reasoning that Mahatma Gandhi sometimes became a nationalistic antidote to Jesus Christ. The message of Jesus had been used to encourage submission from the natives. That message had not been presented as a call for 'non-violent *resistance*' but at best a call for 'non-violence'. Christianity could even be interpreted to mean 'non-resistance' – a coming to terms with the kind of rule God had put the natives under. 'My Kingdom is not of this earth' – this declaration came to imply what E. H. Carr called 'a boycott of politics'.

But Carr was wrong in bracketing Gandhism and Christianity together as 'doctrines of non-resistance'.[11] What Gandhi provided to Negro nationalism was the element of resistance to the passivity of imperial Christianity. Carr was certainly wrong in extending the description of 'boycott of politics' to Gandhism as well as to Christianity. If politics is an activity between groups rather than between individuals, then Gandhism was almost a politicization of Christian doctrine. As Martin Luther King, Jr., the American Negro leader, put it:

Prior to reading Gandhi I had about concluded that the ethics of Jesus were only effective in individual relationship. The 'turn the other cheek' philosophy and the 'love your enemies' philosophy were only valid, I felt, when individuals were in conflict with other individuals . . . Gandhi was probably the first person in history to lift the love ethic of Jesus above mere interaction between individuals to a powerful and effective social force on a large scale. . . .[12]

The Reverend Dr King came to feel that Gandhism was 'the only morally and practically sound method open to oppressed people in their struggle for freedom.'[13]

It is, in fact, one of the curious things of history that, outside India itself, the torch of Gandhism came to be passed not to his fellow Asians, but to Negroes both in the New World and in Africa. It is not without significance that the first non-white winners of the Nobel Prize for Peace were Ralph Bunche, Chief Albert Luthuli and Martin Luther King.

Perhaps Gandhi himself would not have been surprised. Quite early in his life he saw non-violent resistance as a method which would be well-suited for the Negro as well as the Indian. In 1924 Gandhi said that if the black people 'caught the spirit of the Indian movement their progress must be rapid'.[14]

In 1936 Gandhi went even further. And to understand his claim one should perhaps link it up with something which was later said by his disciple, Jawaharlal Nehru. Nehru said: 'Reading through history I think the agony of the African continent . . . has not been equalled anywhere.'[15]

To the extent then that the black man had more to be angry about than other men, he would need greater self-discipline than others to be 'passive' in his resistance. But by the same token, to the extent that the black man had suffered more than any other, passive but purposeful self-sacrifice for the cause should come easier to him. And to the extent that the black man had more to forgive the rest of the world for, that forgiveness when it came should be all the more weighty. Perhaps in response to adding up these considerations, Gandhi came to the conclusion by 1936 that it was 'maybe through the Negroes that the unadulterated message of non-violence will be delivered to the world.'[16]

And so it was that in America the torch came to be passed to King. And in South Africa, where Gandhi first experimented with his methods, it passed to Luthuli. In Northern Rhodesia Kenneth Kaunda became a vigorous Gandhian – 'I reject absolutely violence in any of its forms as a solution to our problems.'[17]

In the Gold Coast Nkrumah had translated *Satyagraha* into a programme of 'Positive Action', a programme which he himself defined as 'nonco-operation based on the principle of absolute non-violence, as used by Gandhi in India.'[18] In 1949 *The Morning Telegraph* of Accra went as far as to call Nkrumah the 'Gandhi of Ghana'.[19]

African conceptions of dignity now seemed very different from what was implied by that old ceremonial affirmation of young Kikuyu initiates which Kenyatta once told us about – the glorification of the spear as 'the symbol of our courageous and fighting spirit'. But these new conceptions of dignity could now also be differentiated from the submissive virtues of early missionary teachings.

Yet one question remained to be answered: could passive resistance survive the attainment of independence? Would Gandhism retain political relevance once its immediate objective of liberation from colonialism was achieved?

It is perhaps not entirely accidental that the two most important Indian contributions to African political thought were the doctrines of non-violence and nonalignment. In a sense they are almost twin-doctrines. Gandhi contributed passive resistance to one school of African thought; Nehru contributed nonalignment to almost all African countries. We have noted how Uganda's President Milton Obote put it in his tribute to Nehru on his death. Obote said: 'Nehru will be remembered as a founder of nonalignment. . . . The new nations of the world owe him a debt of gratitude in this respect.'[20]

But how related are the two doctrines in their assumptions? For India itself Gandhi's non-violence was a method of seeking freedom, while Nehru's nonalignment came to be a method of seeking peace. And yet nonalignment was, in some ways, a translation into foreign policy of some of the moral assumptions which underlay passive resistance in the domestic struggle for India's independence. Gandhi himself once said:

> Free India can have no enemy. . . . For India to enter into the race for armaments is to court suicide. . . . The world is looking for something new and unique from India. . . . With the loss of India to non-violence the last hope of the world will be gone. . . .[21]

In spite of Gandhi's vision, independent India did not practise abstinence. Gandhian non-violence was not fully translated into a foreign policy. Suspicion of Pakistan in particular was too strong to permit that. And yet of all the countries in the world, India under Nehru came nearest to symbolizing the search for peace. For a crucial decade in the history of Africa and Asia, India was the diplomatic leader of both continents. And in the doctrine of nonalignment she bequeathed to many of the new states a provisional foreign policy for the first few experimental years of their sovereign statehood.

With that policy the wheel of global pacification had come full circle. Asia and Africa had once been colonized partly with a view to imposing peace upon them. But now nonalignment had turned the tables on old concepts like *Pax Britannica*. It was now those who were once colonized that were preaching peace to their former imperial tutors.

As we have noted, the shrine within which this message is preached is now primarily the United Nations. There are many aspects of peace with which the United Nations has tried to grapple. The most idealistic of these is the quest for disarmament. Many of the most important aspects of disarmament are discussed outside the United Nations, though often with its blessing. The eighteen-member Geneva negotiations on disarmament are a case in point. But for Africa it is not the idea of disarming nuclear giants which is of immediate import; it is more modest ventures in military abstinence. And modest issues of disarmament remain directly linked to the work and aspirations of the United Nations.

But what role is envisaged for the UN in this regard? Broadly, two conceptions of the role of the UN in disarmament have been discernible among Africans. The United Nations is conceived either as an instrument for bringing about disarmament or as an additional armed entity capable of forcing combatants apart.

Sometimes the old idea of monopoly of violence which imperial-ism once claimed has, somewhat unrealistically, been urged on to the world body today – a call to the United Nations to become something like *Pax Humana*. On the eve of their independence Tanganyikans discussed precisely such a concept as one hypo-thetical solution to the new nation's military needs. Joseph Nyerere, brother of the leader of Tanganyika's ruling party, proposed in the National Assembly in November 1961 that the new independent Tanganyika should consider placing her armies under the United Nations. After all, Tanganyika could not defend herself against a major power. Joseph Nyerere therefore urged that

as far as military operations against any other country is [*sic*] concerned we would have no right to use our forces at all, except under the orders of a United Nations' command.[22]

Joseph's brother, Julius Nyerere, shared some of the premises but drew a different conclusion. In a speech addressed to a seminar of the World Assembly of Youth in August 1961 Tanganyika's national leader criticized the whole concept of each state in Africa arming itself separately. Given discrepancies in power, it was unlikely that an African state's motive for arming itself was to protect itself against an attack by one of the Great Powers of the world. 'If an African state is armed then, realisti-cally, it can only be armed against another African state', Julius Nyerere asserted.[23]

Nyerere might have been overstating his case. But the experience of Somalia's dispute with Ethiopia, Algeria with Morocco, Rwanda with Burundi, Gabon with Congo-Brazzaville, Tshombe's Congo with her neighbours, and even the accusations between Malawi and Tanzania in 1964–5, were soon to lend credi-bility to that analysis of Julius Nyerere's at the seminar in 1961.[24]

But was Nyerere suggesting that newly-sovereign African states should renounce armaments? His answer for Tanganyika was:

All that we need within our national boundaries are sufficient police forces for the purposes of maintaining law and order within those boundaries; as far as larger commitments are concerned, these should be on an African basis.[25]

This introduces us to that concept in the rhetoric of general pacification which, to establish historical continuity, we have called *Pax Africana*. But the political ambition implied by this concept is not to impose an African peace on *others* – that would indeed be ambitious. The word 'Africana' in this concept describes both the nationality of the peace-makers and the continental limits of their jurisdiction. For *Pax Africana* asserts that the peace of *Africa* is to be assured by the exertions of *Africans* themselves. The idea of a 'Pax Africana' is the specifically military aspect of the principle of continental jurisdiction.

For Tanganyika itself the problem was dramatized not at the time that Tanganyika attained her independence, but two years later. On achieving independence Tanganyika did not, after all, renounce armaments for herself. She succumbed to what Janowitz describes as 'a universal political conception that a new state requires an army.'[26]

But, as we have noted, in January 1964 the army of independent Tanganyika mutinied. And in order to subdue the mutinous soldiers we know that the Tanganyika Government had to ask for the help of British troops. So had the Governments of Kenya and Uganda. For at least a few weeks the old slogan of *Pax Britannica* received a new lease of life. And British patriotism found a new feeling of global purpose. The British Prime Minister could even afford to indulge in a few benign, I-told-you-so remarks addressed to leaders of former British colonies at large. We might here repeat Sir Alec Douglas-Home's remark at the time:

I have always pleaded with our African and Asian friends not to push their requests for independence too soon. . . . I was afraid that they would get their independence before they had the two essential things that are necessary if you are to run a country. One is a police force, loyal to the Government; and another is armed forces, loyal to the elected government of the day. . . . This has been proved, of course, beyond doubt now.[27]

But for Tanganyika at any rate reliance on *Pax Britannica* was short-lived. President Nyerere called an emergency meeting of the Organization of African Unity and appealed for help to replace the British troops in Tanganyika with African ones as soon as possible. In effect he was invoking the doctrine of *Pax Africana* as defined above. Nyerere's fellow Africans responded – and it was not long before Nigerian troops replaced British troops in the barracks of Tanganyika. In the meantime Tanganyika set out to create a new and more reliable army for herself.[28]

But it has been in regard to the Congo that the ideal of *Pax Africana* has had a particularly direct political relevance. Let us remind ourselves of the continental context of the Congo's independence. 1960 was the year in which more than fifteen African countries became independent. Never before had so many states become independent in a single year. Nor is that phenomenon ever likely to be repeated in any other year in the future. Among the countries which became independent in that year was, as we know, the Congo. But it was not long before law and order broke down in that country. And so the Congo situation articulated in a particularly eloquent way a question which many others had already asked about the continent as a whole – who was going to keep the peace in Africa now that the imperial powers were withdrawing?

Belgian troops moved into the Congo when law and order broke down. Was there no alternative to imperial peace? Africa was as yet not equipped to assert a *Pax Africana* over itself. Lumumba invited the United Nations – and the rest of Africa was soon to approve of this move for the time being. Better a collective police action by the world body than a return to imperial pacification. And so in August 1960, at an All-Africa Conference held in Leopoldville at the behest of Lumumba, a resolution was passed commending the United Nations 'for the work it is doing for peace in the Congo by effecting a withdrawal of the Belgian troops of aggression from the entire territory of the Republic of the Congo.'[29]

As between the old idea of imperial pacification and the new ambition of *Pax Africana* the United Nations temporarily provided a third alternative. And yet it was soon clear that the United Nations as an alternative could never be as self-sufficient as imperial pacification had been and as African self-policing aspired to be. Among the first to insist on some kind of accountability by the United Nations to Africa as a whole was Kwame Nkrumah. In March 1961 Nkrumah argued that

unless at this juncture the United Nations acts in full consultation with the African States and in accordance with the needs of Africa, the same results will flow from the United Nations' intervention in the Congo as flowed from the intervention of the great powers in African affairs.[30]

Nkrumah discerned a parallel between big power competition in 1960–1 for the control of the Congo and the colonial rivalry which led to the Berlin Conference of 1885. That colonial rivalry of the late nineteenth century was to Nkrumah 'the cold war of those days' – and at the Berlin Conference 'the only interested parties not represented were the inhabitants of Africa'. Nkrumah warned lest the United Nations should now be converted into a similar 'conference', designed to settle the rivalry of the Big Powers of today at the expense of the racial sovereignty of others. What the Ghanaian President was asserting was the dictum that peace in any part of Africa could now only be assured under the supervising eye of the rest of the continent.[31]

The United Nations did try to pacify the Congo under the critical eye not only of Africans but also of others. By the end of 1963 it was clear that the United Nations did not have either the resources or the independence to be an effective substitute for the old Imperial Peace. Towards the middle of 1964 the United Nations therefore withdrew from the Congo.

And yet pacification of the Congo by Africans themselves from internal continental resources was as yet not a practical proposition. It was within this context that the employment of mercenaries by Moise Tshombe became a major issue in inter-African politics.

But what indeed are the implications of white mercenaries for the whole ideal of *Pax Africana*?

From one point of view the employment of mercenaries by an African government should be more consistent with the country's sovereignty than a request to another country, or even to the United Nations, for a loan of troops. By *buying* foreign soldiers for his own use, Tshombe showed, in one sense, greater independence than Lumumba had done when he invited the United Nations to help him out. After all, while Tshombe's mercenaries were presumably answerable to Tshombe who paid them, the troops of the United Nations were never accountable to Patrice Lumumba.

If, then, the purchase of soldiers of fortune by an African government is more of an exercise in sovereignty than the loan of troops answerable to someone else, it should follow that the employment of white mercenaries by Tshombe was more in keeping with *Pax Africana* than either Lumumba's request in

1960 for UN troops or the request of Uganda, Kenya and Tanganyika in 1964 for the loan of British troops.

It could further be argued that the purchase of soldiers from outside was comparable to the purchase of arms and ammunition. Both mercenaries and guns were instruments of warfare. It might be true that Tshombe could only remain in power with the backing of foreign soldiers. But none of the other African governments manufactured their own military equipments either. In any case, one government might remain in power by equipping its *native* army with *foreign* guns. Another might hypothetically have its own 'home-made' guns but used by soldiers externally recruited. A third might survive by employing both foreign soldiers and foreign guns. Why, it might be asked, should any one of these be less of a distortion of the balance of forces in a divided country than any of the others?[32]

Considerations of nonalignment might preclude certain forms of military aid. But the purchase of soldiers is more analogous to military *trade*. And the buying of arms, for example, had never been regarded as a compromise of nonalignment.

There was another way in which the ideal of *Pax Africana* might be said to be served by the use of white mercenaries. Future peace in Africa partly depends on minimizing the chances of continuing feuds. Sometimes Tshombe's critics in 1964 seemed to take it for granted that it was better for the Congolese to be killed by fellow Congolese than to be killed by white mercenaries. But it was at least as convincingly arguable that if there was any killing to be done, it was better for the Congo's future that it should be done by foreigners. For this must mean that the Congolese themselves would have fewer atrocities to *forgive each other for*. Tshombe himself might never be forgiven. But from the point of view of the country's future, it might indeed have been a good thing if his *entire* army had consisted of white mercenaries. The Civil War in the Congo would then have been less of a *civil* war. And there would have been fewer Congolese among the casualties of at least the Government side of the war.[33]

By minimizing reasons for future revenge between Congolese themselves, the use of foreigners to commit some of the atrocities might, cynically but truly, be a positive contribution to the realization of future peace.

But there is another side to the issue of mercenaries from the point of view of *Pax Africana*. What mattered about the mercenaries was not simply that they were non-Africans but that there was good reason to suspect them of being fundamentally *anti*-African. Even in the days when Tshombe was employing mercenaries to help detach Katanga from the rest of the Congo, his chosen fields of recruitment were singularly 'anti-African' in their reputation. As Nkrumah said to Tshombe in a letter dated as far back as 12 August 1960, 'you have assembled in your support . . . the most determined opponents of African freedom. How can you, as an African, do this?'[34]

Perhaps it was inevitable in the circumstances that Tshombe's most promising field of recruitment of mercenaries should have been the Republic of South Africa. But the participation of white South Africans in an African Civil War had immense symbolic implications for African nationalism at large. Very soon the Congo became the first battleground between Afrikaners and troops from or supported by independent African states. It is true that the Afrikaners were not part of a regular South African army. Nor were they all trained for military service. But if, in spite of that, they could tip the scales in an African civil war, Africa's military vulnerability when confronted with South Africa had wider implications than had originally been supposed. *Pax Africana* was a remote ideal if a few South African adventurers could determine which faction in an African country remained in power.

The symbolic implications of the situation were aggravated by one further consideration. Of all the countries in Africa south of the Sahara, the only one which had the potential to rival South Africa in wealth, and in the power which came with wealth, was in fact the Congo itself. Only the Congo had the requisite combination of territorial size, population and mineral resources to be a possible serious rival to South Africa before the end of the century. And yet here were the fortunes of the Congo being determined by the intervention of amateur soldiers from the land of *apartheid*.

Associated with the problem of *apartheid* is the problem of the remaining colonies in Africa, with particular reference to the lingering Portuguese presence. On the question of methods of liberation a major change has taken place in the ethic of African nationalism. When Ghana attained independence in 1957 without resort to an armed insurrection, Gandhism appeared to have once again been vindicated. Nkrumah, as we have noted, had been a disciple of Gandhi in his methods – and now his country was the first black colony to win independence from Britain. The following year Ghana's capital was the scene of the first All-African Peoples Conference, the Accra conference of December 1958. At that conference one of the major areas of debate was the issue of whether violence should be recognized by the conference as a legitimate instrument of African nationalism. The Algerians – then struggling with the French – put up a spirited case in defence of armed insurrection, but black Africa was not fully in agreement. In the end a compromise resolution was agreed on:

That the All-African Peoples Conference in Accra declares its full support to all fighters for freedom in Africa, to all those who resort to peaceful means of nonviolence and civil disobedience as well as to all those who are compelled to retaliate against violence to attain national independence and freedom for the people. Where such retaliation becomes necessary, the Conference condemns all legislations which consider those who fight for their independence and freedom as ordinary criminals.[35]

The resolution was a compromise in that it legitimated insurrection only when the colonial regime had become 'violent' in its methods. On balance, however, the prevalent mood of the conference was what its Chairman, Tom Mboya, described it – 'the December, 1958, Accra Conference resolves to use non-violent positive actions', Mboya observed.[36]

But by the time of the conference at Addis Ababa which set up the Organization of African Unity, Africa's mood regarding violence in the colonies had changed. The Heads of State at the Conference had received a joint memorandum from national liberation movements in the remaining territories. The memorandum had urged the formation of an 'African Liberation Bureau' whose functions were to include the following basic ones:

a. To co-ordinate the struggle for African liberation in all non-independent territories.

b. To receive, distribute and transport funds and other forms of aid, *including military equipment and personnel*, on behalf of the African liberation movements.[37]

The Heads of the independent States responded with suitable

resolutions. Resolution 10 of the conference started by urging the liberation movements themselves to co-ordinate their efforts in a way which would result in a 'rational use of the concerted assistance given to them'. Resolution 11 established a co-ordinating committee of the Organization of African Unity itself. The committee, which later became known as 'the Liberation Committee' or 'the Committee of Nine', was made 'responsible for harmonizing the assistance from African States and for managing the Special Fund to be set up for that purpose.'[38]

Resolution 14 granted refuge on the territories of independent states to nationalists from liberation movements 'in order to give them training in all sectors'. Finally, there was Resolution 15 which was a decision

to promote in each State the transit of all material aid and the establishment of a body of volunteers in various fields, with a view to providing the various African national liberation movements with the assistance they need in the various sectors.[39]

But what had happened to the Gandhism which had once animated and inspired many an African nationalist? There were a number of reasons for the greater militancy which the ethic of African nationalism had now assumed. But one important factor in the transformation of Africa's mood was the action taken by India herself over Goa. This was the first instance of a former colony taking direct military action to eject an imperial power from the neighbourhood. It is true that China's role in the old French Indo-China contributed to the humiliation of the French at Dien Bien Phu. But China was never a colony in quite the same sense as India and Africa had been. And the victory of the Vietnamese at Dien Bien Phu was in any case substantially a victory of the Vietnamese themselves – much as Algerian independence came to be ultimately attributable to the Algerians themselves. India's military action against the Portuguese regime in Goa was, however, in a class by itself. It was accomplished with ease and confidence. It was a display of Asiatic power against the imperial arrogance of a European country. It was the first case of a former colony appearing to 'bully' magnificently one of the oldest Empires that European expansionism had created.

The impact of this event on Africa was greatly accentuated by the fact that Portugal's last Empire was now in Africa itself. Tom

Mboya was soon saying in Kenya that he was 'strongly in favour' of India's action over Goa. He went on to say that it was disturbing that some Goans in Kenya should still owe allegiance to Portugal. Mr Mboya was emphatic in his assertion that: 'No African in Kenya will tolerate any Goan who supports Salazar.'[40]

And on the West coast of Africa the man who had once been described as the 'Gandhi of Ghana' was, as we have noted, now declaring: 'I am most happy about India's annexation of Goa, which I consider long overdue.'[41]

This then was the great paradox of India's ideological impact on African nationalism. The same country which had once made African nationalists subscribe to the Gandhian approach to liberation had now set a grand military precedent of armed ejection.

The United Nations in turn was soon to feel the effects of this new militancy in anti-colonialism. There were pressures on the world organization for some kind of military sanctions against Portugal. By the middle of 1965 Tanzania's Second Vice-President, Rashidi Kawawa, was telling a United Nations committee that its functions were the same as those of the Liberation Committee of the Organization of African Unity. It was the twenty-four nation UN Committee on Decolonization that Kawawa bracketed together with the OAU Committee of Nine – and called them 'two liberation committees of historic importance in the struggle against colonialism.'

The Chairman of the UN Committee, M. Coulibaly of Mali, appeared reluctant to see a UN Committee identified with a neo-military regional body. Mr Coulibaly therefore said that he had always advocated peaceful means – and, with a shrewd diplomatic touch, he went on to praise President Nyerere of Tanzania for supporting 'the peaceful achievement of independence in colonial territories'.[42]

But by the end of that conference in Dar-es-Salaam Chairman Coulibaly's tone was different. His Committee adopted a resolution on Portuguese territories on 10 June 1965. Commenting on the resolution the following day, Chairman Coulibaly said it would be legitimate for other states to give every form of aid to nationalist movements in Portuguese African countries. Force could legitimately be used in those territories to prevent the Portuguese from using force to suppress nationalist movements.

M. Coulibaly added that this was the first time that a UN Committee had directly called for such military support for the African people.[43]

Was the world body, which was originally intended for peace, now being perverted to serve nationalistic ends? It all depended upon the point of departure of one's reasoning. The world as a whole could perhaps best be shielded from the consequences of breaches of the peace in Africa when those breaches were dealt with by Africans themselves. But for as long as a colonial presence lingered on in Africa, such a principle of *Pax Africana* could not encompass the whole continent. For that very reason, nationalists might assume the principle would fall short of complete effectiveness. A *Pax Africana* postulated a triumph of continental jurisdiction, and perhaps of racial sovereignty. The Portuguese presence violated both those principles. A breach of the peace of the kind sanctioned by the UN Committee on Decolonization might therefore be inevitable before a concept of *Pax Africana* could at last assume some meaning. In short, the old idea of imperial pacification had to end before a new African peace could assert itself. It was therefore arguable that the United Nations, if involved in such an undertaking, might conceivably fulfil both the ultimate goal of peace and the immediate cause of African dignity.

A more difficult problem for *Pax Africana* concerns the behaviour of its own instruments of enforcement *internally*. The ultimate instruments of self-pacification in Africa are Africa's own police and armed forces. If the peace is disturbed by a tribal insurrection or by corrupt politicians, Africa's armed forces might be called upon to re-establish authority. But what if the peace is disturbed by those armed forces themselves?

As we have noted, East Africa in 1964 had to invite back a *Pax Britannica* in order to cope with her own mutinous troops. There have been other examples since then of military insubordination in Africa, sometimes directed against military regimes themselves. The painful search for a *Pax Africana* therefore continues. Decolonization might be a necessary condition for it. But it is far from being a sufficient one.

CONCLUSION

EVERY major historical phenomenon is as much a slice of the history of ideas as it is of events. Indeed, ideas are themselves a category of events. What we have attempted in this study is an outline of the main features of this category in Africa's experience.

We have noted that out of a new African self-consciousness grew a body of ideas which came to influence African political behaviour at large. There was first the excitement of finding out that one was 'an African'. This was the self-recognition which led to the affirmation of the Pan-African tautology that all Africans are, in the final analysis, 'fellow Africans'. But the temper of African politics has sometimes been affected by the distinction between the *continental* definition of 'an African' – which would include a Tunisian or Egyptian – and the more narrowly *pigmentational* definition. On balance, however, African nationalism is at its most radical when, like Nkrumah's nationalism, it is trans-Saharan.

Yet in this lies one of the curious features of nationalism in English-speaking Africa. Essentially it is a race-conscious nationalism – but it becomes less racially exclusive as it assumes greater militancy. On the whole it is perhaps the mystique of the *continent*, rather than of the Negro race, which inspires Pan-African *radicalism*. And so hostility to North Africans tends to be discernible more among the 'conservative' Negro Africans – especially within the Brazzaville group – than among radicals like Sekou Touré, Kwame Nkrumah and Modibo Keita.

The principle of an 'indivisible Africa' is reinforced by the general fear of factionalism which one recurrently discerns in African political attitudes. The dogma that imperial powers once divided in order to rule has affected several aspects of African thought. It has given Pan-Africanism itself an additional rationale – as a defence against the divisive tactics of colonialism. The ethic of the one-party state also includes within it the general principle of anti-factionalism. The mystique of a classless Africa, as well as the denigration of 'tribalism', are further manifestations of the same principle of 'African oneness'. So is the choice of 'socialism', presumed to be a centralizing ideology suitable for national integration.

The relevance of this principle of anti-factionalism for the whole ambition of *Pax Africana* is evident. Political disorder is the ultimate excuse for external intervention in Africa. Such disorder in individual African countries arises not simply because Africans fail to agree between themselves but because their disagreement takes the form of passionate and sometimes armed factionalism. Peace between Africans and freedom for Africa are therefore deemed to be intimately related – for peace between Africans themselves is one prerequisite for the exclusion of external powers from African affairs.

This general ethic of anti-factionalism is connected with but distinct from Africa's aspiration to be its own policeman. The connection lies in the fact that both are apprehensive lest conflict between Africans should expose the continent to external manipulation. But whereas the ethic of anti-factionalism seeks to avert external interference by averting internal divisions, Africa's ambition to be its own policeman is seeking a different safeguard. It is seeking a capacity to avert external interference even in the event of internal conflict. It would like Africa to have a military capability great enough to enforce a domestic continental jurisdiction over Africa's own quarrels.

In relations between African states a modest step towards *Pax Africana* was taken when the Organization of African Unity set up its Commission of Mediation, Conciliation and Arbitration. The machinery was used in the border conflicts between Algeria and Morocco and Ethiopia and Somalia. The Commission did not succeed in resolving the issues involved in the disputes. What it succeeded in providing was what has been called 'a *modus vivendi* for avoiding the settlement of the disputes by force'.

Another OAU Commission of relevance for *Pax Africana* is the Defence Commission. But the Defence Commission has so far been among the least effective of Pan-African institutions. Africa might indeed aspire to be her own policeman, but she does not seem ready as yet to pay the price for it. The OAU Defence Commission decided to give priority to exploring the possibility of creating a joint military command. Such a priority was evidence of a desire to give African continental jurisdiction some military effectiveness. Yet the ambition of a joint military command turned out to require more consensus than the members of the Commission could command. The Commission consisted of the Defence Ministers of African States and their chiefs of staff. They failed to rise above their immediate obligations to their own countries on this vital matter.

We have already discussed in the last chapter the relevance of th OAU National Liberation Committee for the principle of *Pax Africana*. This Committee has functioned with some effectiveness in its task to aid national liberation movements in those parts of Africa which are still under alien rule. The Committee's relations with individual movements have not, however, always been smooth. A contributory factor to the Committee's difficulties has been the fact that the nationalist movements of both Angola and Rhodesia have been bitterly divided against themselves.

But, when all is said and done, it is not merely by how Africans behave towards each other that peace and freedom in Africa can be secured. It is also by how they behave in international politics at large and by how other powers respond to that behaviour. The doctrine of nonalignment is therefore closely related to the ambition of *Pax Africana*. A basic aspect of African nonalignment is the aspiration to keep the cold war out of the African continent. Africans have not, of course, fully succeeded in preventing the entry of the cold war into their continent, but it remains a preoccupation of theirs to reduce its impact. As we have noted, there are indeed certain chilly winds of the cold war against which no wall of African exclusiveness can be effective – they blow into the continent inevitably. But there are other aspects of the cold war which can be avoided, pre-eminent among which being military bases or quasi-military entanglement with either the United States, the Soviet Union, or Communist China each on its own. To have a pact with one of these is to give one or both of the others the excuse of denying Africa the tranquillity she aspires to.

In analysing these different African political ideas we have drawn from the utterances and writings of African political leaders, as well as from African political behaviour at large. How defensible was it to have relied so much on the ideas of individual African leaders?

This is where a distinction needs to be made between the concept of 'political thought' as understood in well-established countries like Britain and the United States, and that same concept as applied to new states. When one talks of 'American political thought' one is not likely to be referring to the thinking of Presidents Johnson, Kennedy, Eisenhower or Truman. One is more likely to be referring to the ideas of towering American political *philosophers*.

Yet when we refer to 'African political thought' what we are likely to have in mind are the ideas of Leopold Senghor, Kwame Nkrumah, Julius Nyerere and other African men of affairs. One reason for this is that contemporary Africa has no background of written philosophical works on the nature of politics. If, in spite of this, we are interested in finding out the kind of ideas which form the basis of African political evaluations, we have to look for them in sources other than formal exercises in political theory. Among other places, we have to look at the ideas of those who claim to speak for the African masses.

But there is a more positive reason than that for paying special attention to those first heads of the new African states. And the reason is precisely because they *are* the first heads. Many of them are 'founding fathers' in a meaningful sense. The concept of 'American political thought' might not normally denote the ideas of Eisenhower or Johnson but it does include the ideas of Jefferson and Madison. There might have been later American Presidents who were more original in their ideas than some of the founding fathers had been, but their impact on American intellectual history could not be as great. Even George Washington left an inaugural address which remains more famous than the great majority of addresses which have been delivered after him. At least some of the ideas of a founding father become part of the very foundation which he lays for the nation.

A similar phenomenon is discernible in the Russian experience. The ideas of Lenin, even when they are subsequently rejected or modified, are likely to remain in a class by themselves regardless of any greater intellectual originality which some future Russian leader might have. The ideas of Stalin, in spite of the present eclipse of his name, may also retain significance in the history of ideology in Russia because of the position he held as one of the founders of the new order.

In the Middle East Turkish political thought continues to give a place of eminence to the ideas of Ataturk. In India the thoughts of Gandhi, and now of Nehru, seem destined to form part of the total intellectual heritage of independent India.

But why are the thoughts of those who have led revolutions given such eminence? One reason is perhaps because the persons themselves are of unique historical interest because of the role they played. But another reason is the presumption that the first holders of authority in a new order play a uniquely decisive part in shaping that order even if they themselves are later rejected or overthrown. This presumption is not always vindicated, but the myth could persist in spite of evidence to the contrary. And for certain purposes the myth could be more important than the evidence.

This then is part of our case for treating with seriousness the ideas of at least some of the founders of the new African states. Yet the primary purpose of this book has not been to analyse the political thought of specific leaders as such. If what we were interested in was the political thought of, say, Kwame Nkrumah as a specific figure in Africa's history, there might have been a case for postponing the evaluation until the dust had settled on Nkrumah's career. But our interest was not in Nkrumah or Nyerere as such, but in them as part of the ferment of ideas which have resulted in major political changes in the continent.

In the meantime conflict between such leaders themselves, or between them and the military, or between one soldier and another, remains an aspect of the African political scene. So does the risk of foreign intrusion. The quest therefore continues for an African tranquillity capable of being protected and maintained by Africa herself.

Section III

APPENDICES

THE CHARTER OF THE ORGANIZATION
OF AFRICAN UNITY

We, the Heads of African States and Governments assembled in the City of Addis Ababa, Ethiopia;

CONVINCED that it is the inalienable right of all people to control their own destiny;

CONSCIOUS of the fact that freedom, equality, justice and dignity are essential objectives for the achievement of the legitimate aspirations of the African peoples;

CONSCIOUS of our responsibility to harness the natural and human resources of our continent for the total advancement of our peoples in spheres of human endeavour;

INSPIRED by a common determination to promote understanding among our peoples and co-operation among our States in response to the aspirations of our peoples for brotherhood and solidarity, in a larger unity transcending ethnic and national differences;

CONVINCED that, in order to translate this determination into a dynamic force in the cause of human progress, conditions for peace and security must be established and maintained;

DETERMINED to safeguard and consolidate the hard-won independence as well as the sovereignty and territorial integrity of our States, and to fight against neo-colonialism in all its forms;

DEDICATED to the general progress of Africa;

PERSUADED that the Charter of the United Nations and the Universal Declaration of Human Rights, to the principles of which we reaffirm our adherence, provide a solid foundation for peaceful and positive co-operation among States;

DESIROUS that all African States should henceforth unite so that the welfare and well-being of their peoples can be assured;

RESOLVED to reinforce the links between our states by establishing and strengthening common institutions;

HAVE agreed to the present Charter.

ESTABLISHMENT

Article I

1. The High Contracting Parties do by the present Charter establish an Organization to be known as the ORGANIZATION OF AFRICAN UNITY.
2. The Organization shall include the Continental African States, Madagascar and other Islands surrounding Africa.

PURPOSES

Article II

1. The Organization shall have the following purposes:
   a. to promote the unity and solidarity of the African States;
   b. to co-ordinate and intensify their co-operation and efforts to achieve a better life for the peoples of Africa;
   c. to defend their sovereignty, their territorial integrity and independence;
   d. to eradicate all forms of colonialism from Africa; and
   e. to promote international co-operation, having due regard to the Charter of the United Nations and the Universal Declaration of Human Rights.
2. To these ends, the Member States shall co-ordinate and harmonize their general policies, especially in the following fields;

a. political and diplomatic co-operation;
b. economic co-operation, including transport and communications;
c. educational and cultural co-operation;
d. health, sanitation, and nutritional co-operation;
e. scientific and technical co-operation; and
f. co-operation for defence and security.

PRINCIPLES

Article III

The Member States, in pursuit of the purposes stated in Article II, solemnly affirm and declare their adherence to the following principles:

1. the sovereign equality of all Member States;
2. non-interference in the internal affairs of States;
3. respect for the sovereignty and territorial integrity of each State and for its inalienable right to independent existence;
4. peaceful settlement of disputes by negotiation, mediation, conciliation or arbitration;
5. unreserved condemnation, in all its forms, of political assassination as well as of subversive activities on the part of neighbouring States or any other State;
6. absolute dedication to the total emancipation of the African territories which are still dependent;
7. affirmation of a policy of non-alignment with regard to all blocs.

MEMBERSHIP

Article IV

Each independent sovereign African State shall be entitled to become a Member of the Organization.

RIGHTS AND DUTIES OF MEMBER STATES

Article V

All Member States shall enjoy equal rights and have equal duties.

Article VI

The Member States pledge themselves to observe scrupulously the principles enumerated in Article III of the present Charter.

INSTITUTIONS

Article VII

The Organization shall accomplish its purposes through the following principal institutions:

1. the Assembly of Heads of State and Government;
2. the Council of Ministers;
3. the General Secretariat;
4. the Commission of Mediation, Conciliation and Arbitration.

THE ASSEMBLY OF HEADS OF STATE AND GOVERNMENT

Article VIII

The Assembly of Heads of State and Government shall be the supreme organ of the Organization. It shall, subject to the provisions of this Charter, discuss matters of common concern to Africa with a view to co-ordinating and harmonizing the general policy of the Organization. It may in addition review the structure, functions and acts of all the organs and any specialized agencies which may be created in accordance with the present Charter.

Article IX

The Assembly shall be composed of the Heads of State and Government or their duly accredited representatives and it shall meet at least once a year. At the request of any Member State and on approval by a two-thirds majority of the Member States, the Assembly shall meet in extraordinary session.

Article X

1. Each Member State shall have one vote.

2. All resolutions shall be determined by a two-thirds majority of the Members of the Organization.

3. Questions of procedure shall require a simple majority. Whether or not a question is one of procedure shall be determined by a simple majority of all Member States of the Organization.

4. Two-thirds of the total membership of the Organization shall form a quorum at any meeting of the Assembly.

Article XI

The assembly shall have the power to determine its own rules of procedure.

THE COUNCIL OF MINISTERS

Article XII

1. The Council of Ministers shall consist of Foreign Ministers or such other Ministers as are designated by the Governments of Member States.

2. The Council of Ministers shall meet at least twice a year. When requested by any Member State and approved by two-thirds of all Member States, it shall meet in extraordinary session.

Article XIII

1. The Council of Ministers shall be responsible to the Assembly of Heads of State and Government. It shall be entrusted with the responsibility of preparing conferences of the Assembly.

2. It shall take cognizance of any matter referred to it by the Assembly. It shall be entrusted with the implementation of the decision of the Assembly of Heads of State and Government. It shall co-ordinate inter-African co-operation in accordance with the instructions of the Assembly and in conformity with Article II (2) of the present Charter.

Article XIV

1. Each Member State shall have one vote.

2. All resolutions shall be determined by a simple majority of the members of the Council of Ministers.

3. Two-thirds of the total membership of the Council of Ministers shall form a quorum for any meeting of the Council.

Article XV

The Council shall have the power to determine its own rules of procedure.

GENERAL SECRETARIAT

Article XVI

There shall be an Administrative Secretary-General of the Organization, who shall be appointed by the Assembly of Heads of State and Government. The Administrative Secretary-General shall direct the affairs of the Secretariat.

Article XVII

There shall be one or more Assistant Secretaries-General of the Organization, who shall be appointed by the Assembly of Heads of State and Government.

Article XVIII

The functions and conditions of services of the Secretary-General, of the Assistant Secretaries-General and other employees of the Secretariat shall be governed by the provisions of this Charter and the regulations approved by the Assembly of Heads of State and Government.

1. In the performance of their duties the Administrative Secretary-General and the staff shall not seek or receive instructions from any government or from any other authority external to the Organization. They shall refrain from any action which might reflect on their position as international officials responsible only to the Organization.
2. Each member of the Organization undertakes to respect the exclusive character of the responsibilities of the Administrative Secretary-General and the staff and not to seek to influence them in the discharge of their responsibilities.

COMMISSION OF MEDIATION, CONCILIATION AND ARBITRATION

Article XIX

Member States pledge to settle all disputes among themselves by peaceful means and, to this end decide to establish a Commission of Mediation, Conciliation and Arbitration, the composition of which and conditions of service shall be defined by a separate Protocol to be approved by the Assembly of Heads of State and Government. Said Protocol shall be regarded as forming an integral part of the present Charter.

SPECIALIZED COMMISSIONS

Article XX

The Assembly shall establish such Specialized Commissions as it may deem necessary, including the following:

1. Economic and Social Commission;
2. Educational and Cultural Commission;
3. Health, Sanitation and Nutrition Commission;
4. Defence Commission;
5. Scientific, Technical and Research Commission.

Article XXI

Each Specialized Commission referred to in Article XX shall be composed of the Ministers concerned or other Ministers or Plenipotentiaries designated by the Governments of the Member States.

Article XXII

The functions of the Specialized Commissions shall be carried out in accordance with the provisions of the present Charter and of the regulations approved by the Council of Ministers.

THE BUDGET

Article XXIII

The budget of the Organization prepared by the Administrative Secretary-General shall be approved by the Council of

Ministers. The budget shall be provided by contributions from Member States in accordance with the scale of assessment of the United Nations; provided, however, that no Member State shall be assessed an amount exceeding twenty per cent of the yearly regular budget of the Organization. The Member States agree to pay their respective contributions regularly.

SIGNATURE AND RATIFICATION OF CHARTER

Article XXIV

1. This Charter shall be open for signature to all independent sovereign African States and shall be ratified by the signatory States in accordance with their respective constitutional processes.

2. The original instrument, done, if possible in African languages, in English and French, all texts being equally authentic, shall be deposited with the Government of Ethiopia which shall transmit certified copies thereof to all independent sovereign African States.

3. Instruments of ratification shall be deposited with the Government of Ethiopia, which shall notify all signatories of each such deposit.

ENTRY INTO FORCE

Article XXV

This Charter shall enter into force immediately upon receipt by the Government of Ethiopia of the instruments of ratification from two-thirds of the signatory States.

REGISTRATION OF THE CHARTER

Article XXVI

This Charter shall, after due ratification, be registered with the Secretariat of the United Nations through the Government of Ethiopia in conformity with Article 102 of the Charter of the United Nations.

INTERPRETATION OF THE CHARTER

Article XXVII

Any question which may arise concerning the interpretation of this Charter shall be decided by a vote of two-thirds of the Assembly of Heads of State and Government of the Organization.

ADHESION AND ACCESSION

Article XXVIII

1. Any independent sovereign African State may at any time notify the Administrative Secretary-General of its intention to adhere or accede to this Charter.
2. The Administrative Secretary-General shall, on receipt of such notification, communicate a copy of it to all the Member States. Admission shall be decided by a simple majority of the Member States. The decision of each Member State shall be transmitted to the Administrative Secretary-General, who shall, upon receipt of the required number of votes, communicate the decision to the State concerned.

MISCELLANEOUS

Article XXIX

The working languages of the Organization and all its institutions shall be, if possible, African languages, English and French.

Article XXX

The Administrative Secretary-General may accept on behalf of the Organization gifts, bequests and other donations made to the Organization, provided that this is approved by the Council of Ministers.

Article XXXI

The Council of Ministers shall decide on the privileges and immunities to be accorded to the personnel of the Secretariat in the respective territories of the Member States.

CESSATION OF MEMBERSHIP

Article XXXII

Any State which desires to renounce its membership shall forward a written notification to the Administrative Secretary-General. At the end of one year from the date of such notification, if not withdrawn, the Charter shall cease to apply with respect to the renouncing State, which shall thereby cease to belong to the Organization.

AMENDMENT OF THE CHARTER

Article XXXIII

This Charter may be amended or revised if any Member State makes a written request to the Administrative Secretary-General to that effect; provided, however, that the proposed amendment is not submitted to the Assembly for consideration until all the Member States have been duly notified of it and a period of one year has elapsed. Such an amendment shall not be effective unless approved by at least two-thirds of all the Member States.

IN FAITH WHEREOF, We, the Heads of African State and Government have signed this Charter.

Done in the City of Addis Ababa, Ethiopia this 25th day of May, 1963.

ALGERIA	GUINEA
BURUNDI	IVORY COAST
CAMEROUN	LIBERIA
CENTRAL AFRICAN REPUBLIC	LIBYA
CHAD	MADAGASCAR
CONGO (Brazzaville)	MALI
CONGO (Leopoldville)	MAURITANIA
DAHOMEY	MOROCCO
ETHIOPIA	NIGER
GABON	NIGERIA
GHANA	RWANDA

SENEGAL

SIERRA LEONE

SOMALIA

SUDAN

TANGANYIKA

TOGO

TUNISIA

UGANDA

UNITED ARAB REPUBLIC

UPPER VOLTA

THE FIRST OAU RESOLUTIONS

(Final Version, 25 May 1963)

A

Agenda Item I: DECOLONIZATION

The Summit Conference of Independent African States meeting in Addis Ababa, Ethiopia, from 22 May to 25 May 1963;

Having considered all aspects of the questions of decolonization;

Unanimously convinced of the imperious and urgent necessity of co-ordinating and intensifying their efforts to accelerate the unconditional attainment of national independence by all African territories still under foreign domination;

Reaffirming that it is the duty of all African Independent States to support dependent peoples in Africa in their struggle for freedom and independence;

Noting with deep concern that most of the remaining dependent territories in Africa are dominated by foreign settlers;

Convinced that the colonial powers, by their forcible imposition of the settlers to control the governments and administrations of those territories, are thus establishing colonial bases in the heart of Africa;

Have agreed unanimously to concert and co-ordinate their efforts and actions in this field, and to this end have decided on the following measures:

1. *Declares* that the forcible imposition by the colonial powers of the settlers to control the governments and administrations of the dependent territories is a flagrant violation of the inalienable rights of the legitimate inhabitants of the territories concerned;

2. *Invites* the colonial powers to take the necessary measures for the immediate application of the Declaration on the Granting of Independence to Colonial Countries and Peoples; and *insists* that their determination to maintain colonies or semi-colonies in Africa constitutes a menace to the peace of the continent;

3. *Invites*, further, the colonial powers, particularly the United Kingdom with regard to Southern Rhodesia, not to transfer the powers and attributes of sovereignty to foreign minority governments imposed on African peoples by the use of force and under cover of racial legislation; and the transfer of power to settler minorities would amount to a violation of the provision of United Nations Resolution 1514 (XV) on Independence;

4. *Reaffirms* its support of African nationalists of Southern Rhodesia and solemnly declares that if power in Southern Rhodesia were to be usurped by a racial white majority government, State Members of the Conference would lend their effective moral and practical support to any legitimate measures which the African nationalist leaders may devise for the purpose of recovering such power and restoring it to the African majority: the Conference also *undertakes* henceforth to concert the efforts of its Members to take such measures as the situation demands against any State according recognition to the minority government;

5. *Reaffirms*, further, that the territory of South-West Africa is an African territory under international mandate and that any attempt by the Republic of South Africa to annex it would be regarded as an act of aggression; *Reaffirms* also its determination to render all necessary support to the second phase of the South-West Africa case before the International Court of Justice; *Reaffirms* still further, the inalienable right of the people of South-West Africa to self-determination and independence;

6. *Intervenes* expressly with the Great Powers so that they cease, without exception, to lend direct or indirect support or assistance to all those colonialist governments which might use such assistance to suppress national liberation movements, particularly the Portuguese Government which is conducting a real war of genocide in Africa; *informs* the

allies of colonial powers that they must choose between their friendship for the African peoples and their support of powers that oppress African peoples;

7. *Decides* to send a delegation of Ministers of Foreign Affairs to speak on behalf of all African States in the meetings of the Security Council which will be called to examine the report of the United Nations Committee of 24 on the situation in African territories under Portuguese domination: (The Conference has decided the members of the Delegation to be: Liberia, Tunisia, Madagascar and Sierra Leone);

8. *Decides* further the breaking off of diplomatic and consular relations between all African States and the Governments of Portugal and South Africa so long as they persist in their present attitude towards decolonization;

9. *Asks for an effective boycott* of the foreign trade of Portugal and South Africa by:
   (a) prohibiting the import of goods from those two countries;
   (b) closing African ports and airports to their ships and planes;
   (c) forbidding the planes of those two countries to overfly the territories of all African States.

10. *Earnestly invites* all national liberation movements to co-ordinate their efforts by establishing common action fronts wherever necessary so as to strengthen the effectiveness of their struggle and the rational use of the concerted assistance given them;

11. *Establishes* a Co-ordinating Committee consisting of Algeria, Ethiopia, Guinea, Congo (Leopoldville), Nigeria, Senegal, Tanganyika, United Arab Republic and Uganda, with Headquarters in Dar-es-Salaam, Tanganyika, responsible for harmonizing the assistance from African States and for managing the Special Fund to be set up for that purpose.

12. *Establishes* a Special Fund to be raised by voluntary contribution of Member States for the current year, the deadline for such contribution being 15 July 1963; *Requests* the Co-ordinating Committee to propose the necessary fund and the apportionment among Member States to the

Council of Ministers so as to supply the necessary practical and financial aid to the various African national liberation movements;

13. *Appoints* the day of 25 May as African Liberation Day so as to organize popular demonstrations on that day to disseminate the recommendations of the Summit Conference and to collect sums over and above the national contributions for the Special Fund; (The Conference has decided that this year it will be the opening day of the 18th Session of the General Assembly of the United Nations);

14. *Decides* to receive on the territories of independent African States nationalists from liberation movements in order to give them training in all sectors and afford young people all the assistance they need for their education and vocational training;

15. *Decides* further to promote, in each State, the transit of all material aid and the establishment of a body of volunteers in various fields, with a view to providing the various African national liberation movements with the assistance they need in the various sectors.

B

Agenda Item II: APARTHEID AND RACIAL DISCRIMINATION

The Summit Conference of Independent African States meeting in Addis Ababa, Ethiopia, from 22 May to 25 May 1963;
Having considered all aspects of the questions of apartheid and racial discriminations;
Unanimously convinced of the imperious and urgent necessity of co-ordinating and intensifying their efforts to put an end to the South African Government's criminal policy of apartheid and wipe out racial discrimination in all its forms;
Have agreed unanimously to concert and co-ordinate their efforts and actions in this field, and to this end have decided on the following measures;

(a) To grant scholarships, educational facilities and possibilities of employment in African government services to refugees from South Africa;

(b) To support the recommendations presented to the Security Council and the General Assembly by the Special Committee of the United Nations on the apartheid policies of the South African Government;

(c) To despatch a delegation of Foreign Ministers to inform the Security Council of the explosive situation existing in South Africa: (The Conference has decided the members of the Delegation to be: Liberia, Tunisia, Madagascar and Sierra Leone);

(d) To co-ordinate concerted measures of sanction against the Government of South Africa;

1. *Appeals* to all States, and more particularly to those which have traditional relations and co-operate with the Government of South Africa, to apply strictly UN resolution 1761 (XVII) of 6 November 1962 concerning apartheid;

2. *Appeals* to all governments who still have diplomatic, consular and economic relations with the Government of South Africa to break off those relations and to cease any other form of encouragement for the policy of apartheid;

3. *Stresses* the great responsibility incurred by the colonial authorities administering territories neighbouring South Africa in the pursuit of the policy of apartheid;

4. *Condemns* racial discrimination in all its forms in Africa and all over the world;

5. *Expresses* the deep concern aroused in all African peoples and governments by the measures of racial discrimination taken against communities of African origin living outside the continent and particularly in the United States of America; *Expresses* appreciation for the efforts of the Federal Government of the United States of America to put an end to these intolerable mal-practices which are likely seriously to deteriorate relations between the African peoples and governments on the one hand and the people and Government of the United States of America on the other.

C

Agenda Item III: AFRICA AND THE UNITED NATIONS

The Summit Conference of Independent African States

meeting in Addis Ababa, Ethiopia, from 22 May to 25 May 1963;

Believing that the United Nations is an important instrument for the maintenance of peace and security among nations and for the promotion of the economic and social advancement of all peoples;

Reiterating its desire to strengthen and support the United Nations;

Noting with regret that Africa as a region is not equitably represented in the principal organs of the United Nations;

Convinced of the need for closer co-operation and co-ordination among the African Member states of the United Nations:

1. *Reaffirms* its dedication to the purposes and principles of the United Nations Charter and its acceptance of all obligations contained in the Charter, including financial obligations;

2. *Insists* that Africa as a geographical region should have equitable representation in the principal organs of the United Nations, particularly the Security Council and the Economic and Social Council and its Specialized Agencies;

3. *Invites* African Governments to instruct their representatives in the United Nations to take all possible steps to achieve a more equitable representation of the African region;

4. *Further invites* African Governments to instruct their representatives in the United Nations, without prejudice to their membership in and collaboration with the African-Asian Group, to constitute a more effective African Group with a permanent secretariat so as to bring about closer cooperation and better co-ordination in matters of common concern.

D

Agenda Item IV: GENERAL DISARMAMENT

The Summit Conference of Independent African States meeting in Addis Ababa, Ethiopia, from 22 May to 25 May 1963;

Having considered all aspects of the questions of general disarmament;

Unanimously convinced of the imperious and urgent necessity of co-ordinating and intensifying their efforts to contribute to the achievement of a realistic disarmament programme through the signing, by all States concerned, of a treaty on general and complete disarmament under strict and effective international control;

Have agreed unanimously to concert and co-ordinate their efforts and actions in this field, and to this end have decided on the following measures:

1. To affirm and respect the principle of declaring Africa a Denuclearized Zone; to oppose all nuclear and thermonuclear tests, as well as the manufacture of nuclear weapons; and to promote the peaceful uses of nuclear energy;
2. The destruction of existing nuclear weapons;
3. To undertake to bring about, by means of negotiation, the end of military occupation of the African continent and the elimination of military bases and nuclear tests, which elimination constitutes a basic element of African Independence and Unity;
4. To appeal to the Great Powers to:
   (a) reduce conventional weapons;
   (b) put an end to the arms race; and
   (c) sign a general and complete disarmament agreement under strict and effective international control;
5. To appeal to the Great Powers, in particular to the Soviet Union and the United States of America, to use their best endeavours to secure the objectives stated above.

E

Agenda Item V:

AREAS OF CO-OPERATION IN ECONOMIC PROBLEMS

The Summit Conference of Independent African States meeting in Addis Ababa, Ethiopia, from 22 May to 25 May 1963;

Concerned with the active share of the developing countries in world trade and at the persistent deterioration of the terms of trade in their external commercial relationships;

Conscious of the fact that owing to its extreme dependence on the export of primary products, Africa, more than any other developing region, is adversely affected by persistant deteriorations in export earnings;

Convinced of the necessity for concerted action by the African countries in order to ensure a much more remunerative price from the sale of their primary products;

Mindful of the need to eliminate the barriers to trade among the African countries and thereby to strengthen their economies;

Considering that economic development, including the expansion of trade on the basis of fair and remunerative prices, should tend to eliminate the need for external economic aid and that such external economic aid should be unconditional and should not prejudice the independence of African States;

Considering the imperative necessity for African countries to pool their resources and harmonize their activities in the economic field;

Aware of the necessity for the joint utilization of river basin resources, the study of the use of Sahara Zones, the co-ordination of means of transport and communication systems, and the provision of research facilities, all of which serve to stimulate economic growth and expansion of trade, both regionally and inter-regionally;

Convinced that the acceleration of the rate of economic and social development of the various African countries lies in the industrialization of these countries and the diversification of their production;

Considering the serious problems arising from the great shortage of trained and skilled personnel, the lack of qualified staff, scarce capital resources, grossly inadequate infrastructure, limited outlines for industrial products and the far too inadequate participation of Africans in the economic construction of their countries;

Desiring to explore the effects of regional economic groupings on the African economy;

Noting with satisfaction that the Executive Secretary of the Economic Commission for Africa has decided to convene a Conference of African Ministers of Finance, to be held in Khartoum (Sudan) in July 1963, with a view to setting up an African Development Bank;

Resolves to:

1. *Appoint*, pending the establishment of the Economic Commission of the Organization, a preparatory economic committee to study, in collaboration with governments and in consultation with the Economic Commission for Africa, *inter alia*, the following questions and submit their findings to Member States:

   (a) the possibility of establishing a free trade area between the various African countries;

   (b) the establishment of a common external tariff to protect the emergent industries and the setting up of a raw material price stabilization fund;

   (c) the restructuralization of international trade;

   (d) the means for developing trade among African countries by the organization and participation in African trade fairs and exhibitions and by the granting of transport and transit facilities;

   (e) the co-ordination of means of transport and the establishment of road, air and maritime companies;

   (f) the establishment of an African Payments and Clearing Union;

   (g) a progressive freeing of national currencies from all non-technical external attachments and the establishment of a Pan-African monetary zone; and

   (h) the ways and means of effecting the harmonization of existing and future national development plans.

2. *Invite* ECA to request its Executive Secretary to give the Commission of Experts all the necessary support and assistance which it may require in the fulfilment of its assignment;

3. *Welcome* the forthcoming Conference of African Ministers of Finance and give the respective Ministers of Finance instructions to take the necessary measures for the rapid establishment of the African Development Bank;

4. *Note* with satisfaction the progress achieved by the Economic Commission for Africa in establishing the Dakar Institute of Economic Development and Planning and to affirm their profound interest in that institute and their intention of giving it appropriate financial and other support;

5. *Welcome* the forthcoming World Conference on Trade and

Development which is to examine international trade problems in relation to the economic development of emerging countries;

6. *Urge* all States concerned to conduct negotiations, in concert, with a view to obtaining from the consumer countries real price stabilization and guaranteed outlets on the world market so that the developing countries may derive considerably greater revenue from international trade.

F

Agenda Item VI:

AREAS OF CO-OPERATION – THE FUTURE OF THE CCTA

The Summit Conference of Independent African States meeting in Addis Ababa, Ethiopia, from 22 May to 25 May 1963;

Considering that at the last CCTA Session in Dar-es-Salaam in January to February 1963, the final adoption of the new CCTA convention was deferred until the Heads of African States had had an opportunity to consider the role and direction of the CCTA within the overall context of Pan-African Co-operation,

And in view of the fact that Article 23 of this new convention lays down as follows:

'Pending the signature and the ratification of this convention as provided in Article 16, the Parties having initialled this convention agree to apply it provisionally as if it had entered into force as from the date of initialling, subject to any decision which may be taken by the Heads of African and Malagasy States at the Conference at Addis Ababa or at any subsequent conference on the role of the CCTA within the overall context of Pan-African Co-operation.'

Decides to maintain CCTA and to reconsider its role in order to bring it eventually within the scope of the Organization of African States which will have, as one of its arms, an organ for technical, scientific and cultural co-operation.

. . . . .

Supplementary Resolutions adopted by the Summit Conference of the Independent African States on the proposal of the delegation of the Kingdom of Libya and to be presented to the appropriate institutions provided for under Article X of the Charter of the Organization of African Unity.

A

SOCIAL AND LABOUR MATTERS

The Summit Conference of Independent African States meeting in Addis Ababa, Ethiopia, from 22 to 25 May 1963;

Realizing the importance of social standard for the African peoples and the urgent need for raising such standard;

Considering that co-operation amongst the African States in the social and labour fields is vital and will contribute to the realization of a sound solidarity amongst their peoples;

Believing that the coming together of youth from African States will create better understanding and contribute to the realization of the desired African unity;

Believing further that co-operation in the labour field amongst African States is vital for our continent;

Decides that a Committee of Experts be called to convene within three months, pending the setting up of the Economic and Social Commission provided for in Article XX of the Charter of the Organization of African Unity, to submit a report to the above Commission:

With regard to social and labour matters:

1. To conduct extensive studies on social and labour problems in the continent;
2. To lay down detailed programmes with a view to raising the social standard and to strengthen inter-African co-operation through:
   (a) The exchange of social and labour legislations;
   (b) The establishment of African Youth Organization;
   (c) The organization of African Scouts Union and an annual continental jamboree;
   (d) The organization of an annual African Sport Games;

(e) The organization of vocational training courses in which African workers will participate;

(f) The establishment of an African Trade Union.

B

EDUCATION AND CULTURE

The Summit Conference of Independent African States meeting in Addis Ababa, Ethiopia, from 22 to 25 May 1963;

Desirous of strengthening educational and cultural ties amongst the peoples of Africa;

Considering that the educational and cultural co-operation amongst African States will break down linguistic barriers and promote understanding amongst the peoples of the continent;

Believing that once this co-operation in the educational and cultural fields amongst African States has been organized, co-ordinated and harmonized and fully implemented, it will pave the way to the final goal, namely African Unity;

Realizing the lack of information media in various parts of the African continent and the necessity of strengthening exchange of information amongst African States in order to promote better understanding amongst their peoples;

1. *Decides* that a Committee of Experts be called to convene within three months, pending the setting up of the Educational and Cultural Commission provided for in Article XX of the Charter of the Organization of African Unity, to submit a report to the above Commission on educational and cultural matters by taking into account the resolutions which have been adopted by the Conferences of Casablanca and Lagos;

2. *Proposes*:

(a) the establishment of an institute of African Studies to be a department of the African University proposed by Ethiopia;

(b) the introduction, as soon as possible, of programmes in the major African languages in the Broadcasting Stations of the various African States and the exchanges of radio and television programmes;

(c) the establishment of an African News Agency.

C

HEALTH, SANITATION AND NUTRITION

The Summit Conference of Independent African States meeting in Addis Ababa, Ethiopia, from 22 to 25 May 1963;

Realizing the importance of health standard for the African peoples and the urgent need for raising such standard and improving sanitation and nutrition amongst the peoples;

Considering that the co-operation amongst the African States in health, sanitation and nutrition fields is vital and will contribute to the realization of stronger solidarity amongst their peoples;

Decides that a Committee of Experts be called to convene within three months, pending the setting up of the Commission on Health, Sanitation and Nutrition provided for in Article XX of the Charter of the Organization of African Unity, to submit a report to the above Commission;

With regard to health:

1. To conduct extensive studies on health problems facing the continent;
2. To lay down detailed programmes with a view to raising health standards among the peoples and to strengthen inter-African co-operation through:
   (a) The exchange of information about endemic and epidemic diseases and the means to control them;
   (b) The exchange of health legislations;
   (c) The exchange of doctors, technicians and nurses;
   (d) The reciprocal offer of scholarships for medical students and the establishment of training courses on health, sanitation and nutrition;
3. To conduct research in all African States on sanitation and nutrition and to study ways and means to improve them.

NOTES

Chapter One

[1] It was West Indians and American Negroes like Marcus Garvey and W.E.B.Dubois who launched Pan-Negroism on to a world stage. The first Pan-African conferences were primarily conferences of Afro-Americans. It was, as we shall later discuss, at the fifth Pan-African conference in Manchester in 1945 that Africans became prominent in the movement. Among those who took part in this fifth conference were Jomo Kenyatta and Kwame Nkrumah. In 1958 Pan-Negroism at last became essentially Pan-Africanism – it was in that year that the Accra conference of independent African states and the first All-African People's conference were held in independent Ghana. George Padmore, the West Indian founding father of black nationalism, discusses the American beginnings of Pan-Negroism in his book *Pan-Africanism or Communism? The Coming Struggle for Africa* (London: Dobson 1956. esp. chapters V to X). A more recent account of the movements is Colin Legum's *Pan-Africanism, A Short Political Guide* (Praeger, 1962 and 1965). See also the articles in *African Forum* Vol. I, No. 2, Fall 1965.

[2] British West Indians – though under imperial rule – were more like American Negroes in their quest for Negro dignity than like African nationalists passionately hating 'colonialism'.

[3] It ought to be noted here that, at least in the early stages, a desire for self-government was more evident among English-speaking Africans than among French-speakers. Yet, curiously enough, most of the English-speaking African countries won their independence *after* the French-speakers had won theirs.

[4] See, for example, J.H.Price's comment on Kenneth Little's paper on 'Parliamentary Government and Social Change in West Africa' in *What are the Problems of Parliamentary Government in West Africa?*, Report of Conference held by Hansard Society in Oxford in September 1957 (London: Hansard Society for Parliamentary Government, 1958), p. 48.

[5] Hancock, *Colonial Self-Government*, Cust Foundation Lecture, University of Nottingham, 1956, p. 18.

[6] 'Nationalism in Tropical Africa', *The American Political Science Review*, XLVIII, No. 2, June 1954, p. 407.

[7] *Nationalism: A Religion* (New York: Macmillan, 1960), pp. 38–9.

[8] *Idea of Nationalism, A Study of Its Origins and Background* (New York: Macmillan, 1943), pp. 155–83.

[9] —. Kohn, *Prophets and Peoples: Studies in Nineteenth Century Nationalism* (New York: Macmillan, 1957).

[10] On liberal values in the United States see, for example, Louis Hartz, *The Liberal Tradition in America* (New York: Harcourt, Brace, 1955).

[11] *Zik* (Cambridge: Cambridge University Press, 1961), p. 85.

[12] *Ibid.*

[13] *Parliamentary Debates*, House of Commons, 22 April 1959. Hansard, Vol. 604. Cols. 563–4.

[14] *Nationalism in Colonial Africa* (London: Frederick Muller, 1956), p.179.

[15] *The Approach to Self-Government* (Cambridge: Cambridge University Press, 1956), p. 56.

[16] See *Report of the Commission of Rapporteurs*, 16 April 1921. League Council Doc. B.7.21/68/106.

[17] The Prime Minister at the time was Joseph Ileo. See 'News of the Week in Review', *New York Times*, 12 February 1961, p. E.9.

[18] For a discussion of the issue of Katanga in relation to this matter, see Rene Lemarchand, 'The Limits of Self-Determination: The Case of the Katanga Secession', *The American Political Science Review*, Vol. LVI, No. 2, June 1962.

[19] See *The League of Nations Official Journal*, Special Supplement No. 3, October 1920, p. 5.

[20] *Appeal from the New to the Old Whigs, Works*, Vol. 4 (London: World Classics edition, 1907), p. 94.

[21] *From Empire to Nation: The Rise to Self-Assertion of Asian and African Peoples* (Cambridge, Mass: Harvard University Press, 1960), p. 313.

[22] On 21 December 1902 Chamberlain made the following entry into his diary: 'If Dr Herzl were at all inclined to transfer his efforts to East Africa, there would be no difficulty in finding suitable land for Jewish settlers. But I assume that this country is too far removed from Palestine to have any attractions for him.' Dr Theodor Herzl, the founding father of Zionism, later recorded in his own diary that Chamberlain had offered him 'Uganda'. But Herzl had declined, saying: 'Our starting point must be in or near Palestine. Later on we could also colonize Uganda; for we have vast numbers of human beings who are prepared to emigrate. We must, however, build upon a national foundation; that is why the political attraction of El Arish is indispensable to us.' Actually, as Julian Amery has pointed out in his biography of Chamber-

lain, Chamberlain's offer to the Zionists was not of Uganda but of the highlands of Kenya. And according to Amery 'there is no better white-man's country anywhere in the Tropics.' See Amery, *The Life of Joseph Chamberlain*, Vol. IV (London: Macmillan, 1951), esp. pp. 262–5. It should also be noted that Kenya as a territorial entity had not been created at the time, and the boundaries of Uganda were very different from what they are today.

[23] *Pan-African Unity and the N.F.D. Question in Kenya* (May, 1963). I am grateful to Joseph S. Nye, Jr., for giving me access to some of his notes and documents on Pan-Africanism. See also Rupert Emerson, *Self-Determination Revisited in the Era of Decolonization*, Cambridge, Mass: Center for International Affairs, Harvard. Occasional Paper in International Affairs, No. 9, December 1964, esp. pp. 49–53.

[24] *Ibid.* See also Anthony S. Reyner, *Current Boundary Problems in Africa* (Pittsburgh: Duquesne University Institute of African Affairs, 1964).

[25] Speech at a meeting of the United Kenya Club. See *Mombasa Times*, 11 January 1962. The emphasis is mine.

[26] See Mboya, 'Vision of Africa', in *Africa Speaks*, eds. James Duffy and Robert A. Manners, (Princeton: D. Van Nostrand Company, Inc., 1961), pp. 24–5.

[27] Speech to the UN General Assembly, 23 September 1960. Edition of Permanent Mission of Ghana to the UN, p. 10.

[28] *Ibid.*, pp. 9–10.

[29] *The Rise and Fall of Western Colonialism* (New York: Praeger, 1964) p. 123.

[30] Emerson has said: 'Where Wilson himself stood in relation to colonial demands for freedom is somewhat obscure. At home he had earlier denied that the Filipinos had any right to liberty until the United States had brought them maturity and self-mastery, but late in his presidency he urged Philippine Independence. In the Paris peace negotiations colonial issues, save for the Mandates System, played an insignificant role for him. Of the famous Fourteen Points only the fifth made any mention of the colonies, calling for a free and impartial adjustment of colonial claims, based upon the principle that "the interests of the populations concerned must have equal weight with the equitable claims of the government whose title is to be determined." It is symbolic of the times that the man who set out to make the world safe for democracy went no further than to suggest that the interests – not the national desires – for the colonial peoples should be lifted to an equality with the claims of their alien rulers.' See *From Empire to Nation*, p. 25.

[31] Wilson's conversion to the idea of granting independence to the

Philippines seemed to be an *ad hoc* conversion on the specific issue of American colonial rule in those islands.

[32] 'The Atlantic Charter', *United States Executive Agreement Series* No. 236, Department of State Publication No. 1732, Washington, D.C.: US Government Printing Office, 1942.

[33] Speech to House of Commons, 9 September 1941. See Charles Eade (ed.), *War Speeches of Winston Churchill* (London: Cassell, 1952) Vol. 2, pp. 71–2.

[34] See the resolutions cited in Colin Legum, *Pan-Africanism* (New York: Praeger, 1962), Appendix 2.

[35] See Robert A. Goldwin with Ralph Lerner and Gerald Stourzh (eds.), *Readings in World Politics* (New York: Oxford University Press, 1959), p. 539.

[36] In the earlier days Azikiwe used to talk about the 'manifest destiny' of the Ibo nation. Awolowo taunts Azikiwe for this early Ibo militancy. See *Awo* (Cambridge University Press, 1960), p. 172. Borrowing from Marxist-Leninist language is, in recent years, more common.

[37] Lord Hailey said in 1962: 'Communism . . . has waged an unceasing assault on what it stigmatizes as "colonialism". (If you ever want to denigrate something the best way is simply to add "–ism" to the end of it!).' Hailey also said that Margery Perham spoilt her 'otherwise admirable Reith Lectures' by seeming to apologize for British colonial rule. See *African Affairs* (London) Vol. 61, No. 243, April 1962. Margery Perham has said: ' "Colonialism". . . is generally used in contexts which do not leave us in much doubt that it is a word of abuse.' *The Colonial Reckoning* (London: Collins, 1961), p. 9.

[38] *Ibid.*

[39] ' "Colonialism" and the Transfer of Power', Inaugural Address to the Royal Empire Society Summer School at Oxford. Printed in *United Empire*, Vol. XLVII, No. 5, September–October 1956. Oxford University Institute of Commonwealth Studies Reprint Series No. 16, p. 1.

[40] *Ibid.*, p. 3.

[41] *The Idea of Responsible Government*, University of Hull Publications, 1962, p. 11.

Chapter Two

[1] This Jeffersonian dictum was cited by President Nkrumah in a speech to the resumed session of the United Nations General Assembly on 7 March 1961. See the edition of this issued by the Ghana Ministry of Information, p. 8.

[2] See NBC script of 'The Nation's Future', NBC Television Debates, 3 December 1960, p. 3.

[3] *Ibid.*

[4] The *New York Times*, 29 November 1960. The emphasis is mine.

[5] The *New York Times*, 11 October 1960.

[6] *On Alien Rule and Self-Government* (London: Longmans, 1960) pp. 22–3.

[7] See 'News of the Week in Review', The *New York Times*, 18 December 1960.

[8] *On Alien Rule and Self-Government, op. cit.*, p. 23.

[9] Paul Hoffman, writing for the *New York Times*, argued that the Belgians themselves were not unduly concerned about such distinctions – 'after building the Congo . . . into what it thought was a model colony, Belgium must feel the right to participate in the affairs of the now sovereign state'. See Hoffman's article 'Congo: Return of the Belgians', The *New York Times*, 6 November 1960.

[10] In regard to the Congo after independence, the description 'troops of aggression' was applied to Belgian troops by, among others, the All-African Conference held in Leopoldville at the behest of Lumumba towards the end of August 1960. The conference passed a resolution commending the United Nations 'for the work it is doing for peace in the Congo by effecting the withdrawal of the Belgian troops of aggression from the entire territory of the Republic of the Congo.' See United Nations Document No. A/PV 860, 18 September 1960, p. 81.

[11] *Africa on the Threshold of 1961*, Tunisian Government Publication, 30 December 1960, pp. 23–4.

[12] 'In what way would a lawful government deriving its power from a constitutional text be legitimate if it is unable to save the country from anarchy and civil war?' (*Ibid.*, pp. 23–4). This was, of course, a reference to the Congo. Algeria at the time had a civil war but had yet to deteriorate into the OAS anarchy.

[13] *Ibid.*, pp. 25–6.

[14] David Apter, *The Political Kingdom in Uganda* (Princeton: Princeton University Press, 1961), p. 481.

[15] J.S.Mill, *Dissertations and Discussions*. See Robert A. Goodwin with Ralph Lerner and Gerald Stourzh (eds.), *Readings in World Politics* (New York: Oxford University Press, 1959), p. 325. Mill, however, does concede that there is a morality between individual men regardless of nationality or social organization. If, for example, an Englishman found an African wounded by a lion in the wilderness, there would be an obligation to help the wounded. As Mill put it, 'The only moral laws for the relation between a civilized and a barbarous government are the universal rules of morality between man and man.'

[16] Starr in the first of his series of articles on the Congo, *Chicago Tribune*, 20 January 1907.

[17] *The Colonization of Africa by Alien Races*, Cambridge Historical Series, 1899, pp. 277–8.

[18] *The Making of Rhodesia* (London, 1926), p. 66.

[19] See David Apter, *op. cit.*, pp. 62–4. The French were, of course, much less impressed by mere 'resemblances' to French ways.

[20] Quoted in a memorandum to Queen Elizabeth II submitted by members of the Lukiko of the kingdom of Buganda. See Appendix in David Apter's book cited above, pp. 480–1.

[21] Quoted by Colin Legum, *Congo Disaster*: Penguin Special, 1961), pp. 38–9.

[22] *Ibid.*, p. 28 – Legum's own description.

[23] See H. F. Indley, *The Acquisition and Government of Backward Territory in International Law* (London: Longmans 1926), p. 46.

[24] Quoted by Harold Cooper, 'Political Preparedness for Self-Government', *The Annals of the American Academy of Political and Social Science*, Vol. 306, July 1956, p. 71. The choice was not really 'Either you are capable of governing yourselves or you must be governed by others.' There was at least one more possible alternative – expressed in the *Accra Evening News* that Africans had a right to 'mismanage our affairs in this country', if need be. See, for example, *Accra Evening News* (Publisher: Kwame Nkrumah), 14 January 1949.

[25] Lord Lugard, *Federation and the Colonies*, Federal Tract No. 7 (London: Macmillan, 1941), pp. 4, 12.

[26] Margery Perham, *Lugard: The Years of Authority*, 1898–1945 (London: Collins, 1960), pp. 148–9.

[27] *Yugoslav Facts and Views*, 2 March 1961 (New York). The emphasis is mine.

[28] Speech at dinner in Accra in honour of Soviet Deputy Premier Mikoyan. See *Ghana Today*, Vol. 5, No. 25, 21 January 1962, p. 1.

[29] Their statement of policy is reproduced in *Great Issues in American History* (R. Hofstadter, ed.) (New York: Vintage Book, 1961), pp. 202–3.

[30] *Ibid.* The League was appealing to the American Government to uphold the tradition of 'government by consent' as a criterion of legitimate sovereignty.

[31] W. E. Abraham, *Mind of Africa* (London: Weidenfeld, 1962), p. 152.

[32] For a brief description of the positions taken see 'Question of Defining Aggression', *United Nations Review*, Vol. 9, No. 5, May 1962, pp. 14–16.

[33] '[The General Assembly] calls upon the Government of Belgium

to withdraw and evacuate its forces still remaining in Rwanda and Burundi, and that, as of 1 July 1962, the Belgian troops in process of evacuation will no longer have any role to play and that the evacuation must be completed by 1 August 1962, without prejudice to the sovereign rights of Rwanda and Burundi.' This resolution was passed on 27 June 1962.

[34] *On Alien Rule and Self-Government*, *op. cit.*, p. 40.

[35] Amsterdam: Djambatan, 1960.

[36] See *Ghana Today*, Vol. 5, No. 25, 31 January 1962, p. 7.

[37] Address to Fifteenth Session of the General Assembly, 23 September 1960. The argument occurs on pp. 1–2 of the reproduction of the speech in the edition of the Permanent Mission of Ghana to the United Nations.

[38] Statement of Ghana's policy on the Congo sent to Patrice Lumumba on 13 July 1960. See Ghana Government's W.P. No. 6/60, p. 4. Nkrumah found United Nations' intervention legitimate on the ground that it had been invited by a 'legitimate' government of the Congo.

[39] Reproduced in Ghana Government's W.P. No. 6/60, p. 8.

[40] Speech to Fifteenth Session of General Assembly, 23 September 1960. Publication of Ghana's Permanent Mission to the UN, p. 5.

[41] *Voice of Africa*, Vol. 1, No. 4, Accra, April 1961.

[42] *Peace Through Justice*, Pastoral Instruction of the Catholic Bishops of Southern Rhodesia. Gwelo, Rhodesia: Catholic Mission Press. Pentecost 1961, pp. 27–8. The emphasis is mine.

[43] See *The Times* (London), 12 November 1965.

Chapter Three

[1] An earlier version of this chapter was published as an article under the same heading in *The American Political Science Review*, Vol. LVII, No. 1, March 1963.

[2] See, for instance, Nkrumah, *I Speak of Freedom: A Statement of African Ideology* (New York: Praeger, 1961), p. 133.

[3] *The Emergence of Modern Turkey* (Oxford University Press, 1961). See especially his Introduction: The Sources of Turkish Civilization, pp. 1–17.

[4] Melville J. Herskovits, 'Does "Africa" Exist?' Wellesley College *Symposium on Africa* (Wellesley, Mass., 1960), p. 15.

[5] Speech to the 15th Session of the United Nations General Assembly, 23 September 1960. Publication of the Permanent Mission of Ghana to the United Nations, p. 9.

[6] See NBC Script of 'The Nation's Future', 3 December, 1960, *NBC Television Debates, op. cit.*

[7] Wellesley College, *Symposium, op. cit.*, p. 16.

[8] *Ibid.*

[9] Speech to 15th Session of the UN General Assembly, *op. cit.*, p. 9.

[10] 'The Prospects for Atlantic Union', *The Times* (London), 2 February 1962.

[11] Preface, *I Speak of Freedom*, p. xi.

[12] A distinguished African philosopher argued at a meeting in Oxford once that a state of independence was a state of nature – and one to be 'gained' only because it had been lost, certainly not as something new.

[13] *The Times* (London), 19 January 1962.

[14] 'Africa's Place in the World', Wellesley College *Symposium, op. cit.*, p. 149. For brief analysis of his argument see my article 'Why does an African Feel African?', *The Times* (London), 17 February 1962, reproduced in Canada in *The Globe and Mail*, 22 February 1962.

[15] Gamal Abdul Nasser, *The Philosophy of the Revolution* (Economica English edition, Buffalo, 1959), p. 74. A discussion of the limits of Nasser's role in Africa occurs in my article in *African Affairs* (Journal of the Royal Institute of African Affairs), entitled 'Africa and the Egyptian's Four Circles', Vol. 63, No. 251, April 1964.

[16] Indeed, that the Indians considered one another 'fellow Indians' at all was, to a great extent, an outcome of their shared colonial experience too. But fellow *Asians* was much too sophisticated. As Iain Lang observed in a review in the *Sunday Times* (London, 25 February 1962), 'If you were to tell a Punjabi peasant or a Malay fisherman that he was an Asian he would be most unlikely to know what you were talking about.' Roy Sherwood (*Peace News*, London, March 1962) even moralizes on the subject, saying: 'A regrettable survival of colonialist thinking is the lumping together of all the non-white peoples of the Indian and Pacific Oceans under the comprehensive term "Asians".' The phenomenon is discussed in Michael Edwardes' *Asia in the Balance* (Baltimore: A Penguin Special, 1962), esp. pp. 11–14. No less significant, however, was the phenomenon of 'Asian' jubilation over the 1905 Japanese victory over Russia.

[17] *An African Survey, Revised* 1956 (Oxford University Press, 1957), p. 252.

[18] Such clubs or hotels could, of course, carry either the double-negative sign of 'No non-Europeans admitted' or the sign 'Europeans only'. But a country like South Africa would present complications since Japanese, though geographically 'non-Europeans', were legally 'white'. Official South African terminology prefers to call their black citizens 'Bantu', but Albert Luthuli, in his Nobel Prize lecture, asserted

his own preference for the term 'African'. Kenya certainly needed also a proper name for the 'blacks' more acceptable than 'natives'. Nor was the stratification in Kenya simply between 'White' and 'non-White'. For example, three scales of pay used to prevail – 'European', 'Asian' and 'African' – just as three types of lavatories, schools and the like were provided. Even further sub-divisions were observed in some instances, but these are less relevant to this discussion.

[19] Wellesley College *Symposium, op. cit.*, p. 149.

[20] *An African Survey, op. cit.*, p. 255. The small High Commission territories are indeed extreme examples of this, but this only puts them at one end of the scale.

[21] Frank Johnson, 'United States of Africa', *Pan-Africa*, Vol. 1, No. 6 (June 1947). See esp. pp. 3-4. The journal included at the time among its 'Associate and Contributing Editors' Kwame Nkrumah and Jomo Kenyatta.

[22] *Op. cit.* The article is reproduced in *Voice of Africa*, Vol. 1, No. 4 (Accra, April 1961).

[23] *Education in African Society*, Colonial No. 186, 1944, p. 55.

[24] A strong, radically nationalist trend has existed within at least the younger generation of Nigerians. Following the 1962 Commonwealth Prime Ministers' Conference speculation in Britain started as to why the Nigerian Government, with all its pragmatism, rejected out of hand a proposal for associate membership in the EEC. Walter Schwarz, speaking on the European Service of the British Broadcasting Corporation in October 1962, suggested that 'Nigeria's Government, always open to attack from its own youth for being too lukewarm about its nationalism, simply finds it politically impossible to lag behind Ghana on this issue.' See also my article, 'African Attitudes to the EEC', *International Affairs* (London), Vol. 38 No. 1 (January 1963). Visiting newsmen to Nigeria once discovered at a special meeting with young Nigerians at Nsukka that most of the youth were strongly in favour of Nkrumah's brand of militant African nationalism, without by any means necessarily coupling it with hero-worship for Nkrumah. One reference to this meeting appeared in the *New York Times*, 3 March 1962. Of course, the radicalism of youth is not peculiar to African countries; but young people are a stronger pressure group in the new states than in some of the older ones.

[25] Speech to 15th Session of General Assembly, *op. cit.*

[26] See my article 'Edmund Burke and Reflections on the Revolution in the Congo', *Comparative Studies in Society and History*, Vol. 5, No. 2 (January 1963).

[27] *Commonwealth Journal* (London, Royal Commonwealth Society), Vol. 4, No. 6 (November-December 1961), p. 254.

[28] There is some ambivalence about this. It is permissible, at least as an ideal, to unite two *complete* countries. But a change of frontiers that would, say, make Ghana bigger and Togo smaller, and still leave two countries independent, is unacceptable to most Africans. In such a case, most Africans would agree with the UN representative of the Ivory Coast who put forward the policy of accepting the territorial limits obtaining at the time of independence at least 'in order to avoid internecine wars which might jeopardize the independence just acquired with such difficulty'. (UN Document A/PV.1043, 27 October 1961). The Brazzaville group is clearly unenthusiastic about any radical or immediate unification measures; but this distinction between changing colonial frontiers by complete integration and changing them by partial annexation would be accepted by many of even the most radical Pan-Africanists.

[29] Edwin S. Morisby, 'Politics of African Unity: No Longer Tail to the Asian Dog?', *Manchester Guardian*, 2 January 1959.

[30] 'Africa's Destiny', *Africa Speaks, op. cit.*, p. 35.

[31] '. . . the idea of government as an institution began to take hold of some African "agitators" such as myself, who had been reading Abraham Lincoln and John Stuart Mill . . .' – Nyerere, 'The African and Democracy', *Africa Speaks, op. cit.*, p. 33.

[32] Saul K. Padover makes a somewhat different claim – that a great interest in Jefferson had emerged abroad after a long period of ignorance. See his 'Jefferson Still Survives . . .,' *New York Times Magazine*, 8 April 1962, p. 28.

[33] 'We hold with Abraham Lincoln, that ". . . When the white man governs himself, that is self-government, but when he governs himself and also governs another man, that is more than self-government – that is despotism. . . . Those who deny freedom to others deserve it not for themselves, and under a just God cannot long retain it." ' – Platform of the American Anti-Imperialist League, 17 October 1899, reprinted in *Great Issues in American History*, ed. Richard Hofstadter, Vol. II, p. 203.

[34] Zik's speech to graduates of Storer College, Harpers Ferry, West Virginia, on the occasion of his receiving the honorary degree of Doctor of Literature, 2 June 1947. See *Zik, op. cit.*, p. 83.

[35] 'Africa Struggles with Democracy', *New York Times Magazine*, 21 January 1962, p. 10.

[36] Elspeth Huxley's correspondence with Margery Perham was published as a book, *Race and Politics in Kenya* (London: Faber, 1944), with an introduction by Lord Lugard. Eighteen years later, when it was a question of white settlers' rights as against the British Government rather than of their rights as against the Africans, the two women were at last in agreement. 'Having often disagreed over Kenya's affairs', they said in their joint letter to *The Times* (London, 5 July 1962), 'we now

find ourselves in harmony about one issue – the claims of the European farmers for compensation' – from the British Government.

[37] *Nationality in History and Politics* (New York: Oxford University Press, 1944), pp. 12–13.

[38] *Representative Government*, ed. R. B. McCallum (Oxford: Blackwell, 1946), p. 291.

[39] Thomas Hodgkin and Ruth Schachter, 'French-Speaking West Africa in Transition', *International Conciliation*, No. 528 (May 1960), p. 387.

[40] 'West Africa in Evolution', *Foreign Affairs*, Vol. 39, No. 2 (January 1961), p. 244.

[41] See *Africa 1962*, No. 15, 27 July 1962, p. 4.

[42] 'West Africa in Evolution', *op. cit.*, p. 243.

[43] *Contrat Social* (1st version). See C. E. Vaughan *The Political Writings of J. J. Rousseau* (Cambridge, 1915), Vol. 1, p. 453.

[44] *Pan-Africa*, Vol. 1, No. 6, June 1947, p. 7. *White Man's Country* is the title of a famous book by Elspeth Huxley about Lord Delamere's Kenya (London and New York: Macmillan, 1935). At the time Mrs Huxley was convinced that there was not even such a thing as an 'African', and she was therefore something of a precursor of Herskovits. As late as 1950 she was being taken to task by an 'African' in these terms: 'On the evidence of the many varied ethnic groups which exist in Africa, she (Mrs Huxley) asserted that there was no such thing as an African. This assertion was made during a radio debate with Leonard Woolf. One wonders why an entity that did not exist had to be debated.' Dr S. D. Cudjoe, *Aids to African Autonomy* (London: The College Press, 1950), p. 23.

[45] Reported in *Mombasa Times* (Kenya), 11 January 1962.

[46] The phrase is from Dr Azikiwe's message to President Nkrumah on the occasion of Ghana's fifth anniversary as an independent state. See *The Times* (London), 7 March 1962.

[47] *Nationalism in Colonial Africa, op. cit.*, p. 172.

[48] *Ibid.*

[49] Obote's stand on the Federation of Rhodesia and Nyasaland was the more interesting because, while he refused to recognize the *present* government of the Federation, he was nevertheless against the Federation's dissolution – a stand which put him almost in a class by himself among African nationalists.

[50] This means more than 'Mr African'; it has deeper connotations of respect. On its own the Swahili word *Bwana* can loosely be translated as 'Sir'. On 14 October 1961, Jomo Kenyatta said: 'Non-Africans who still want to be called "Bwana" should pack up and go, but others who are prepared to live under our flag are invited to remain.' On 28 January

1962, the price of being welcome in Kenya was raised a little higher. It was no longer enough that the immigrant should cease to expect 'Bwana' for *himself*: 'I want Europeans, Asians and Arabs to learn to call Africans "Bwana". Those who agree to do so are free to stay,' said Kenyatta. *The Times* (London) aired a controversy – with distinguished Africanists taking part – on what Kenyatta really meant by his demand. The *Sunday Times* (London) carried a controversial article by Tom Stacey on 3 June 1962, on the subject. By that time Kenyatta himself had explained that he was demanding respect rather than servility from the Kenya European. The quest for this 'respected image of *Bwana Mwafrika*' can conflict with 'freedom' in some sense. See my article 'Consent, Colonialism and Sovereignty', *Political Studies*, Vol. II, No. 1 (February 1963).

[51] In his address to his compatriots on the occasion of the Congo's independence. Like many another African nationalist, he would have addressed the rest of the continent in similar terms. A translation of the speech is reproduced under the title 'The Independence of the Congo' in *Africa Speaks, op. cit*. The phrase occurs on p. 93.

Chapter Four

[1] See Nkrumah's *Autobiography, op. cit.*, p. 45.

[2] Nkrumah, *I Speak of Freedom, op. cit.*, p. 107. Joseph Caseley Hayford, one of the founding fathers of Gold Coast nationalism, was also a defender of and expert on Gold Coast traditional ways. See his *Gold Coast Native Institution* (London, 1903) and *The Truth about the West African Land Question* (London, 1913).

[3] *I Speak of Freedom, ibid.*, p. 96.

[4] *Ibid.*, p. 135.

[5] *Ibid.*, p. 147.

[6] I was present at the rally.

[7] See Nkrumah, 'Positive Action in Africa', *Africa Speaks, op. cit.*, p. 56. See also Nkrumah's speech 'Africa for Africans' at the All African Peoples Conference on 8 December 1958. Reproduced in *Hands Off Africa!!!* (Accra: Ministry of Local Government, 1960), pp. 25–33.

[8] *I Speak of Freedom, op. cit.*, p. 125. The emphasis is mine.

[9] *Ibid.*, p. 131. At the final session of the conference Nkrumah returned to the theme. He said: 'The former imperialist powers were fond of talking about "Arab Africa" and "black Africa"; and "Islamic Africa" and "Non-Islamic Africa".... These were all artificial descriptions which tended to divide us. . . . Today the *Sahara is a bridge uniting us.*' See *Hands Off Africa!!!, op. cit.*, p. 23. The emphasis is original.

[10] *I Speak of Freedom, op. cit.*, p. 140.

[11] *Ibid.*, p. 241. Nkrumah linked this tribute with a tribute to 'the victims of apartheid in South Africa'. See also the Resolution on the war in Algeria, Proceedings, *Positive Action Conference for Peace and Security in Africa* (Accra, 7 to 10 April 1960), Accra: Community Center, 1960, p. 13.

[12] See, for example, Nkrumah's opening address at the Conference on Positive Action and Security in Africa, *ibid.*, p. 3. The emphasis is mine.

[13] Speech to the General Assembly on 23 September 1960.

[14] For the Brazzaville Declaration, 19 December 1960, see Colin Legum, *Pan-Africanism, op. cit.*, Appendix 13.

[15] *Ibid.*, p. 180.

[16] French anti-Egyptianism culminated in the triple invasion of Egypt in 1956, but it has taken other forms as well. No major Western power has been as uninhibited in its friendship with Israel as France has been in the last ten years.

[17] See *West African Pilot*, 21 January to 28 January 1962. See also *West Africa*, No. 2329 of 20 January; No. 2330 of 27 January; and No. 2332 of 10 February 1962. See also leading article 'Divided Africa', *The Times* (London), 31 January 1962.

[18] In fact, Mali and Guinea had other reasons apart from religious partiality for their support of the Algerians. They might even have regarded the Algerians as 'fellow revolutionaries'. In any case, Algeria was a fellow member of the Casablanca group of African states – of which the other members were Ghana, Morocco and the United Arab Republic. It should also be noted that Mali does have citizens who are virtually of the same 'racial stock' as some North Africans.

[19] See Legum, *Pan-Africanism, op. cit.*, Appendix 15, p. 188. It is true that Israel's friendship with France tended to make her support the French position on Algeria whenever the subject came up in the UN.

[20] See *West African Pilot*, 18 May 1961. See also *West Africa* (London, 6 May 1961).

[21] See *Africa 1964*, No. 6, 20 March 1964. See also 'No More Politics for the UAM,' *Sunday News* (Dar-es-Salaam), 15 March 1964. See also Victor T. Le Vine, 'New Directions for French-speaking Africa?' *Africa Report*, Vol. 10, No. 3, March 1965; *West Africa*, 13 February 1965 and 20 February 1965.

[22] See his later formulation in *Africa Must Unite* (New York: Praeger, 1963), pp. 171–87. On some occasions he has also been dubious about Sierra Leone's capacity for independence. See *I Speak of Freedom, op. cit.*, p. 253.

[23] Address to Ghana National Assembly, 30 May 1961.

24 Records of Topical Talks, European Service, British Broadcasting Corporation, October 1962.

25 See Le Vine, 'New Directions for French-speaking Africa?', *Africa Report, op. cit.* For Nkrumah's letter to President Hamani Diori of Niger denying any link with the attempt to assassinate Diori see *Ghanaian Times*, 27 April 1965. See also *Africa Diary*, Vol. 5, No. 24, and Vol. 5, No. 26, June 1965. Consult also *Africa* 1965, No. 8, 23 April 1965 and No. 12, 18 June 1965.

26 Among such radicals is the group which Wallerstein calls 'the ultra-modernists, the proponents of the internal class struggle'. See Immanuel Wallerstein, 'Elites in French-speaking West Africa', *Journal of Modern African Studies*, Vol. 3, No. 1, May 1965, esp. pp. 31–2.

27 Robert W. July, 'Nineteenth-Century Negritude: Edward W. Blyden', *Journal of African History*, Vol. V, No. 1, 1964.

28 *I Speak of Freedom, op. cit.*, p. 125.

29 *Ibid.*, p. 81.

30 'The new nations with political religion regard themselves as being without sin. This stems from the notion of rebirth, that is, the rise of the new political units from colonial status, with all the purity of the newly born.' Apter, 'Political Religion in the New Nations', in *Old Societies and New States*, ed. by Clifford Geertz (New York: Free Press of Glencoe, 1963), p. 79. See also Apter, Introduction, *Ideology and Discontent* (New York: Free Press of Glencoe, 1964), pp. 18–21, 28–30.

31 *I Speak of Freedom, op. cit.*, p. 96.

32 See, for example, Tom Mboya, 'Vision of Africa', *Africa Speaks*, eds. James Duffy and Robert A. Manners, *op. cit.*, p. 15.

33 This union was later joined by Mali – and showed even less life as a result. For the declarations of the two unions see Legum, *Pan-Africanism, op. cit.*, Appendices 6 and 12.

34 I am grateful to Professor Arthur Macmahon for stimulation on this line of interpretation.

35 *Africa Must Unite, op. cit.*, pp. 214–15.

36 Cited by Richard Cox, *Pan-Africanism in Practice, an East African Study* (London: Oxford University Press, 1964), p. 77.

37 This was the Declaration signed by Jomo Kenyatta, Milton Obote and Julius Nyerere in Nairobi in June 1963 announcing their intention at the time to form a federation before the end of the year. The text of the declaration is now an Appendix A. J. Hughes' *East Africa: The Search for Unity*, London, Penguin African Library, 1963.

38 See my article, 'Tanzania versus East Africa: A Case of Unwitting Federal Sabotage', *The Journal of Commonwealth Political Studies*, Vol. III, No. 3, November 1965.

[39] *I Speak of Freedom, op. cit.*, p. 144.

[40] For the texts of Nkrumah's letters see *Ghana Today*, 7 November 1962. This exchange between Macmillan and Nkrumah will be discussed more fully when we come to analyse the residuum of *Pax Britannica*.

[41] See Nkrumah's account of the purposes of the conference in *Africa Must Unite*, p. 199.

[42] See *Ghana Today*, Vol. 8, No. 21, 16 December 1964.

[43] Quaison-Sackey was elected to the Presidency when the General Assembly met on 1 December 1964. He regarded his election not only as the fulfilment of the African personality, but also as 'a tribute to Africa, and to Ghana in particular and to millions of people of African descent everywhere.' See *Ghanaian Times*, 2 and 3 December 1964. In his book Quaison-Sackey devotes a chapter to a discussion of 'the African personality'. See his *Africa Unbound* (New York: Praeger, 1963), pp. 35–58.

Chapter Five

[1] For the relevant resolutions of the All-African People's Conference in Cairo (23–31 March 1961) see Colin Legum, *Pan-Africanism, A Short Political Guide*, esp. pp. 254–7. See also H. A. Philby, 'Africans Switch Attack to Neo-Colonialism', the *Observer* (London), 2 April 1961.

[2] See *The Times* (London), 2 October 1962.

[3] Nkrumah, *Address to the National Assembly on African Affairs* (Accra), 8 August 1960. (Ghana Government Publication GP/A283/20,000/8/60–61), p. 9.

[4] Cited by Margery Perham, *Lugard: The Years of Authority, 1898–1945* (London: Collins, 1960), p. 567.

[5] *The Dual Mandate in British Tropical Africa* (Edinburgh and London: W. Blackwood, 2nd ed., 1923, pp. 60–2.

[6] *Address to the National Assembly . . .*, 8 August 1960, *op. cit.*

[7] Lugard's Inaugural Speech at the Oxford University Summer School in *Colonial Administration* (Second Session, 27 June–8 July 1938). Proceedings printed for Oxford University Press by John Honson, 1938.

[8] Perham, *op. cit.*, pp. 148–9.

[9] See the *New York Times*, 19 December 1961.

[10] 'A Revolution Intended for All Mankind', the *New York Times Magazine*, 10 December 1961.

[11] *A History of the Colonization of Africa by Alien Races, op. cit.*, p. 279.

[12] *Ibid.*, p. 280.

[13] Starr and his articles are singled out for two primary reasons – firstly, because he was addressing a traditionally 'anti-imperialist' people and yet could still speak of his 'anti-exploitation' views as heretical. And secondly, because views frankly expressed in newspapers are a better guide to the accepted norms of an age than a confidential dispatch about where British interests lie on a colonial issue. The tone of Starr's articles was, in fact, in partial defence of how Leopold ruled the Congo – at a time when even those who approved of colonization in principle were critical of the Belgian. Starr virtually says that he is against exploitation, but if it has to be done the way in which it was done in the Congo was not unduly bad. *Chicago Tribune*, 20 January 1907.

[14] See *The Times* (London), 18 July 1962.

[15] 'Achievements of 1961', the President's Christmas broadcast to his nation, 22 December 1961. Text used is that of the Supplement to *Ghana Today*, 3 January 1962.

[16] *Peace Through Justice, op. cit.*, pp. 27–8. It must be pointed out that the bishops went on to say that the exploitation of these resources must take into account the rights of the indigenous people, though what these rights were was not clearly defined.

[17] This particular example of the businessman's reasoning is drawn from Herbert Solow, 'The Congo is in Business', *Fortune*, November 1952, p. 106. A glance at more recent issues of business publications of this kind will show that there has not been much change in attitude by and large.

[18] *Address to National Assembly on African Affairs*, 8 August 1960, *op. cit.*, p. 14.

[19] See *Ghana Today*, 11 April 1962.

[20] This is from the Nigerian Governor-General's address to the Committee of African Organizations in London on 12 August 1961. See also Alhaji Sir Abubakar Tafawa Balewa, *Nigeria Speaks* (Speeches selected by Sam Epelle) (Lagos: Longmans, 1964), esp. p. 107.

[21] For an analysis of these three stands see my article 'African Attitudes to the European Economic Community', *International Affairs* (London), Vol. 38, No. 1, January 1963.

[22] Barclays (DCO) *Overseas Review*, 1961. See *Africa Digest*, Vol. IX, No. 6, June 1962, pp. 207–8.

[23] Quoted by Nora Beloff in her 'Why the Six Fell Out with the Africans', the *Observer*, 7 July 1962.

[24] Barclays *Review, op. cit.*

[25] See his 'Africa and the Common Market', *The Listener*, 10 August 1961.

²⁶ *Ibid.* As for the Aga Khan's version of the argument, this was 'I do feel very strongly that – economically speaking – Western Europe and Africa are largely complementary and each would benefit enormously from a free expansion of trade and mutual aid. . . . And if this means a transformation – and close co-operation, leading perhaps even to the amalgamation of the British Commonwealth and the French Community – then I believe the price is worth paying, because it will be an association based not on common ideals (for those will take time to evolve) but on solid mutual interest.' See H.H. the Aga Khan, 'The Great Gamble – in Africa', *Commonwealth Journal* (Journal of the Royal Commonwealth Society), Vol. V, No. 4, July-August 1962, p. 187.

²⁷ Part One of the Treaty, Principles, Article 3 (f).

²⁸ 'The problem of Africa, looked at as a whole, is a wide and diversified one. But its true solution lies in the application of one principle, namely, the right of a people to rule themselves.' Nkrumah to the Fifteenth Session of the General Assembly, New York, 23 September 1960. See the edition of the Ghana UN Mission, *op. cit.*, p. 10.

²⁹ *The African Nations and World Solidarity* (Translated from the French by Mercer Cook) (London: Thames & Hudson, 1962), p. 3.

³⁰ This rendering is from *Africa Digest*, Vol. IX, No. 6, June 1962, p. 205.

³¹ See p. 6 of the Policy Paper.

³² 'Caretaker', the *Sunday Post* (Nairobi), 4 March 1962.

³³ Address to the United Kenya Club, Mombasa, Kenya, 10 January 1962. See *Mombasa Times*, 11 January 1962.

³⁴ Action Group Policy Paper on the West African Union, *op. cit.*, p. 1.

³⁵ Action Group Policy Paper on the Scientific and Cultural Development of Nigeria, 1960(?), pp. 1–2.

³⁶ Policy Paper on the West African Union, *op. cit.*, p. 1.

³⁷ Barbara Ward attributes the actual authorship of this now famous phrase to Stevenson. See her *The Rich Nations and the Poor Nations* (New York: Norton, 1962), p. 23. Nkrumah in his speech to the Resumed Session of the Fifteenth General Assembly, on 7 March 1961, referred approvingly to an article by Stevenson in the *Sunday Times* (London) in which Stevenson 'pointed out the absolute madness of partitioning Africa economically along the pattern established in Europe'.

³⁸ 'The Problem of Race in World Politics', 15 December 1961.

³⁹ Speech at luncheon of the New York Liberal Party, 18 February 1962. See 'Danger of EEC "nationalism",' news report in the *Guardian* (Manchester), 19 February 1962.

⁴⁰ See 'The Impact of Western European Integration on African

Trade and Development', UN Economic and Social Council document E/CN.14/72, 7 December 1960.

⁴¹ See *Ghana Today*, 28 February 1962.

⁴² 'Africa and the Common Market', *op. cit.*

⁴³ *The National and Grindlays Review*, 1961. See *Africa Digest*, June 1962, pp. 206–7.

⁴⁴ The Aga Khan in his address at Cambridge (*Commonwealth Journal*, *op. cit.*) argued that Africa needed a market like the European Common Market for its primary products and yet conceded that 'it is an alarming but salutary thought that a fall in the world prices of coffee, cocoa, sisal, copper or vegetable oils can wipe out almost overnight the gains achieved by millions of pounds worth of direct economic aid.' In view of the vulnerability of the prices of these products, delay in diversifying Africa's economies could hardly be deemed to be in Africa's interests, economic or political.

⁴⁵ UN Document on EEC, *op. cit.*

⁴⁶ *The Rich Nations and the Poor Nations*, *op. cit.*, pp. 31–4.

⁴⁷ See *Ghana Today*, 28 February 1962. There would, of course, be some tropical products that the Western world could not produce itself. But if the West really needed them, they would presumably seek to buy them whether Africa *as a whole* was in associate membership with Europe or not. Africa would then be in competition with other tropical countries. And a united Africa – not desperately dependent on the sale of the agricultural produce – should be in a better position to compete with other tropical countries.

⁴⁸ 'Africa's Destiny', *Africa Speaks*, *op. cit.*, p. 37. At the Cairo Conference of the Casablanca Group of African States Touré argued that in his mind there was no basic difference between themselves and the Monrovia Group of African States – all Africans were at least united in their common plight of underdevelopment and poverty. They should therefore have a common policy of inter-African aid and understanding. Touré was particularly concerned about the need for a common economic policy.

⁴⁹ Address to Ghana National Assembly, 30 May 1961, *op. cit.*

⁵⁰ 'Atlantic Pact and European Unity', *Foreign Affairs*, Vol. 40, No. 4, July 1962, pp. 543–4. Altiero Spinelli was at the time Delegate General of the Congress of the European People and Secretary General of the Italian branch of the Movement of European Federation.

⁵¹ 'The Atlantic Pact is a defensive alliance among sovereign states, but is fundamentally different from the traditional alliance common in European history. The latter remained dormant, as it were, until the common enemy had committed an act of aggression. In the meantime each ally carried out its own foreign and military policies, free from any

specific commitment toward its partners. In letter, the Atlantic Pact conforms to this conception, but in reality it has rapidly gone beyond it. ... NATO is not a classical alliance but rather a true military confederation – an association of states that have decided on common defence of particular territories, for which purpose they have created representative bodies, as well as various common military services and a common strategy. As with other confederations which have meant something in history, this one is viable only because it contains one member "more equal than others"– indeed, a super-power.' *Ibid.*, pp. 542–3.

[52] *Ibid.*, p. 544.

[53] *Ibid.*, p. 545.

[54] David Thompson discussed this French desire to 'assert independence abroad' in, among other places, his article 'De Gaulle's Wider Aims in Europe', *The Times* (London), 12 September 1962.

[55] See the EEC *Bulletin*, No. 5, May 1962, p. 6.

Chapter Six

[1] See A. Creech Jones, 'The Labour Party and Colonial Policy' in *New Fabian Colonial Essays* (London: Hogarth, 1959), pp. 21–3.

[2] See William H. Friedland and Carl G. Rosberg, Jr. (eds.), *African Socialism* (Stanford: Stanford University Press, 1964); Kenneth W. Grundy, 'Marxism-Leninism: The Mali Approach', *International Journal*, Vol. XVII, No. 3, Summer 1962; L. Gray Cowan, 'Guinea' in Gwendolen M. Carter (ed.), *African One-Party States* (Ithaca, N.Y.: Cornell University Press, 1962); Kenneth W. Grundy, 'Nkrumah's Theory of Underdevelopment: An Analysis of Recurrent Themes', *World Politics*, Vol. XV, No. 3, April 1963; Kenya Government Paper, *African Socialism and its Application to Planning in Kenya*, 1965; *Africa Report*, Special issue on African Socialism, VIII, May 1963.

[3] It is true that from the beginning socialists like Saint-Simon and Owen were as struck by the wastefulness of capitalism as by its injustice. But there is a difference between viewing socialism as a method of avoiding waste and viewing it as a positive instrument for accelerating *growth*.

[4] See, for example, Charles F. Andrain, 'Democracy and Socialism: Ideologies of African Leaders', in David E. Apter (ed.), *Ideology and Discontent*.

[5] J. A. Hobson, *Imperialism: A Study* (London, 1902). V. I. Lenin, *Imperialism, the Highest Stage of Capitalism*. See, for example, International Publishers Revised Translation (New York: International Publishers, 1933).

[6] Nkrumah wrote his little book *Towards Colonial Freedom, Africa in*

the Struggle Against World Imperialism almost exactly a decade before his own country attained 'colonial freedom'. At the time of writing he himself was as yet to become an active politician in the Gold Coast. The preface to his book is datelined 'London, October 1947'. This book was reissued by Heinemann in 1960. Nkrumah's interpretation of imperialism in this instance was based on Lenin and Rosa Luxembourg. For a later interpretation see Nkrumah, *Consciencism* (London: Heinemann, 1964), esp. pp. 98–106, and *Neo-Colonialism: The Last Stage of Imperialism* (London: Nelson, 1965).

[7] Henry L. Bretton suggested in 1958 that the dialogue between British socialists and Gold Coast nationalists had not resulted in an ideological influence. Whatever socialism was at the time discernible in Gold Coast nationalism probably came directly from Marxism and not from British socialism. See his article 'Current Political Thought and Practice in Ghana', *American Political Science Review*, Vol. LII, No. 1, March 1958.

[8] J. P. Plamenatz has argued that Marx took it too readily for granted that class differences necessarily meant inequalities. (Plamenatz, *Man and Society*, Vol. 2 (New York: McGraw-Hill, 1963)), esp. pp. 294–8. We might therefore say that what Marxism was after was not equality between classes but the abolition of classes altogether. Yet when the intellectuals are conceded a place in a dictatorship of the proletariat, or when the whole socialist venture came to be regarded as an alliance between the peasants, the proletariat and the intellectuals, these three classes were deemed to be distinct and yet on a basis of equality.

[9] See Dia, *The African Nations and World Solidarity, op. cit.* Ardant is quoted on p. 19.

[10] Cited by Immanuel Wallerstein, 'The Political Ideology of the PDG', *Présence Africaine*, Vol. 12, First Quarter 1962, p. 32.

[11] From a speech opening the World Assembly of Youth Seminar in Dar-es-Salaam in 1961. See *The Second Scramble* (Dar-es-Salaam: *Tanganyika Standard*, 1962).

[12] Mboya, *Freedom and After, op. cit.*, p. 163.

[13] *Ibid.*

[14] See Nyerere, *Ujamaa: The Basis of African Socialism*, reprinted in William H. Friedland, and Carl G. Rosberg, Jr., *African Socialism, op. cit.*, Appendix II, p. 246.

[15] *Ibid.*

[16] See *Transition* (Kampala), Vol. 3, No. 11, November 1963, p. 6. Mboya's critic was also an East African – C. N. Omondi by name. The critic's letter first appeared in *Kenya Weekly News*, 2 August 1963. The Swahili word 'Ujamaa' has a strong suggestion of ethnicity as the basis of the fellowship.

[17] Apter, Introduction, *Ideology and Discontent*, *op. cit.*, pp. 26–8.

[18] Mboya, 'African Socialism', *Transition*, Vol. 3, No. 8, March 1963, p. 17.

[19] *Ibid.*

[20] It was felt that the trade imbalance between Tanzania and Kenya could be eased by enabling Tanzania to have one or two industrial monopolies. The Kampala agreement was supposed to become a legal convention soon after a meeting in Mbale, Uganda, by the three Heads of Governments in January 1965. The Kenya Minister for Commerce and Industry released a summary of the Agreement on 21 January 1965. See *East African Standard*, 22 January 1965. The full agreement is now available in *East Africa Journal*, April 1965, pp. 24–32. For a brief analysis of the risks of the quota restrictions in inter-territorial trade in East Africa see Philip Ndegwa, 'Development Effects of the East African Common Market', Proceedings of the East African Institute of Social Research Conference, December 1964.

[21] See *The Times* (London), 11 and 14 June 1965. In August 1965 John Hatch put it in this way: 'Without federation Tanzania felt that free trade prejudiced her own progress. The immediate crisis was resolved by an agreement in Kampala. . . . But last year Kenya's exports to Tanzania rose again by 30 per cent and the trade deficit increased. So two months ago Tanzania took the drastic action of establishing her own currency and restricting imports from Kenya and Uganda.' See Hatch, 'The Kaunda-Nyerere Axis', *New Statesman*, 20 August 1965, p. 244.

[22] Ernst B. Haas and Philippe C. Schmitter, 'Economics and Differential Patterns of Political Integration: Projections about Unity in Latin America', *International Organization*, Vol. XVIII, No. 4, Autumn 1964, p. 706.

[23] Julius K. Nyerere, *Democracy and the Party System* (Dar-es-Salaam: *Tanganyika Standard*, 1963[?]), pp. 14–15.

[24] *Ujamaa*, *op. cit.*, p. 245.

[25] *Democracy and the Party System*, *op. cit.*, p. 1.

[26] But a Nigerian writer has provided a contrary interpretation of traditional life. Writing under the pen-name of Frank Niger the writer has argued along the following lines: 'Sitting in a legislative assembly of two or more organized parties with paid Head of Government and Leader of the Opposition is certainly foreign to Africa. But not the idea of parties representing different viewpoints on the one hand, and *organized* as pressure groups on the other. The different clans and families within the traditional system were in fact embryonic groups of dissent, in character with the limited field of activity of traditional society.' – See Niger, 'The New African Myths', *Transition*, Vol. 4, No. 16, 1964, p. 17.

[27] Nyerere sees the two levels of unity from a slightly different perspective. He sees his Tanganyika African National Union as a movement for integrating the nation state – and 'the African national state is an instrument for the unification of Africa'. See his 'Scramble for Africa', *Spearhead*, 1 February 1962, p. 16.

[28] *Africa Must Unite, op. cit.*, p. 76.

[29] *Federal Government* (first published 1946); London: Oxford University Press, 1962, reprint, p. 46.

[30] A. H. Birch discusses similar problems of trying to combine federalism with a one-party structure in his paper 'Opportunities and Problems of Federation', Proceedings of the University of East Africa and Ford Foundation Conference on Public Policy, Nairobi, 24 to 30 November 1963. See pp. 3–5 of Birch's paper. See also paper presented at the same conference, by Arthur W. Macmahon, entitled 'The Opportunities of Federation: Some Structural Problems', esp. pp. 7–11.

[31] Wheare, *op. cit.*

Chapter Seven

[1] *Awo, The Autobiography of Chief Obafemi Awolowo, op. cit.*, p. 312. But Awolowo went on to be less than relevant on this issue when he gave vent to his anti-Nasserism – 'With his undisguised totalitarianism, and his territorial ambitions in Africa and the Moslem world, effective co-operation with Nasser, in any field at all, would be possible only if the black races of Africa were prepared to remain as satellites in Egypt's orbit, as Syria now is.'

[2] Cited by L. Carl Brown, 'Colour in Northern Africa', Proceedings of the Conference on Race and Colour (sponsored by the American Academy of Arts and Sciences and the Congress for Cultural Freedom), Copenhagen, September 1965, p. 6 of Brown's paper.

[3] *Philosophy of the Revolution, loc. cit.*

[4] 'Colour in Northern Africa', *loc. cit.*

[5] See Boutros Boutros-Ghali, 'The Foreign Policy of Egypt' in Joseph E. Black and Kenneth W. Thompson, *Foreign Policies in a World of Change* (New York: Harper and Row, 1963); Jacques Baulin, *Arab Role in Africa* (London: Penguin African Library, 1962); Ibrahim Abu-Lughod, 'The Islamic Factor in African Politics', *Orbis*, Vol. VIII, No. 2, Summer, 1964; Vernon McKay, 'The Impact of Islam on Relations among the New African States', in J. Harris Proctor (ed.) *Islam and International Relations* (New York: Praeger, 1964); Ali A. Mazrui, 'Africa and the Egyptian's Four Circles', *African Affairs*, Vol. 63, No. 251, April 1964.

[6] *Addis Ababa Summit*, 1963, Collection of Speeches and other Documents, Addis Ababa: Ministry of Information, 1963(?), p. 29.

[7] 'Colour in Northern Africa', *op. cit.*, p. 10.

[8] This sort of answer was given by a Nigerian and by an Afro-American resident in Ghana in discussions in September 1964.

[9] Awolowo has claimed, however, that class distinctions in Egypt coincide with shades of colour. See his 'Statement on African Affairs', issued as a Press statement in Lagos on 28 June 1961. An extensive summary of the statement is given as Appendix 24, Legum, *Pan-Africanism, op. cit.*, pp. 266–71. Awolowo's accusation does not, however, assert that the fairer Egyptians are 'intruders' in the land or less 'native' to Egypt. On the contrary, Awolowo talks in terms of Egyptians discriminating against 'fellow Egyptians'.

[10] Some French geographers sometimes refer to North Africa as *l'Afrique blanche*. In his paper on this issue L. Carl Brown deliberately decides to use the labels 'black' and 'white' in what he calls 'a loose, non-technical sense'. He says: 'Black' as used here is not synonymous with Negro. It might well indicate Nubian, Ethiopian or Fula, just as 'white' might refer to Berber, Arab, or Egyptian Copt'. See his 'Colour in Northern Africa', *op. cit.*, p. 1.

[11] *Christianity, Islam and the Negro Race* (London, 1888), pp. 24–5.

[12] Herbert Aptheker (ed.), *One Continual Cry: David Walker's Appeal to the Colored Citizens of the World* 1829–1830 (New York: Humanities Press, 1965), p. 41.

[13] *Black Reconstruction in America* 1860–1880 (first published 1935) (Cleveland and New York: The World Publishing Company, 1962, reprint), p. 35.

[14] *The World and Africa* (first published 1946; New York: International Publishers, 1965, enlarged edition), p. 184.

[15] *Autobiography, op. cit.*, p. 312.

[16] Speech to fifteenth session of the UN General Assembly, *op. cit.*, p. 10.

[17] The best literary expression of this danger is perhaps Bernard Shaw's *The Apple Cart*. The United States' Ambassador applied to England's King Magnus for permission to join the Commonwealth on her credentials as a former imperial possession. King Magnus saw the danger to his Kingdom involved in such an eventuality.

[18] 'The Foreign Policy of Egypt', Black and Thompson, *Foreign Policies in a World of Chance, op. cit.*, p. 328.

[19] 'Statement on African Affairs', Appendix 24, Legum, *Pan-Africanism, op. cit.*, p. 269.

[20] *Autobiography*, p. 312.

[21] Australia and the Americas might have been pigmentationally

homogeneous before they were populated by Europeans. But that is now a matter of historical interest. Australia, in her white Australian policy, is trying to save that continent from the fate of having more than one colour. But until the last aboriginal Australian dies, that continent is not yet *uni*-pigmentational in Europe's sense.

[22] W. E. B. Dubois, 'The Truth is Winning', *Voice of Africa*, Vol. I, No. 3, March 1961.

[23] In this context we might perhaps safely exclude from our data the relatively small number of non-white immigrants into Europe. As for the white people who now inhabit lands outside Europe, they are overwhelmingly of European extraction. In any case, the claim here is not that all white people are Europeans but that all Europeans are, in fact, white. It should also be noted that just as there are white people outside Europe, so, of course, are there black people outside Africa.

[24] Speech at the final session of the Conference of Independent African States, 22 April 1958. The emphasis is Nkrumah's. See *Hands Off Africa!!!*, p. 24. The countries represented at the conference were, as we indicated, Tunisia, Morocco, Egypt, the Sudan, Libya, Ethiopia and Liberia.

[25] Second Pan-American Scientific Congress, *Proceedings*, VII (Washington, D.C.: 1917), pp. 687–92.

[26] *Ibid.*

[27] Speech to the Belgrade conference, 1961. See the collection of documents entitled *The Conference of Heads of State or Government of Non-Aligned Countries, September 1–6, 1961* (Belgrade: Publicistico-Izdavacki Zavod 'Jugoslavia', 1961).

[28] Consult Edmund Burke, *Remarks on the Policies of the Allies* (1793), *Works*, Beaconsfield Edition, New York: J. F. Taylor, 1801, pp. 433–4.

[29] See *Tanganyika Standard* (Dar-es-Salaam). 26 January 1963.

[30] The Congo became a member of the Afro-Malagasy Common Organization (OCAM) after a meeting of the organization in Abidjan on 27 May 1965. See 'Congo in OCAM', *West Africa*, No. 2505, 5 June 1965. See also 'Ghana and the OAU' and 'OCAM in Abidjan' in *West Africa*, No. 2504, 29 May 1965. Not all the thirteen members of the OCAM were enthusiastic about the Congo's admission. President Ahmadou Ahidjo of Cameroun did not attend the Abidjan meeting partly because the issue of the Congo's admission was coming up. In July 1965 President Ahidjo was quoted as saying that the Congo problem had divided Africa and it was therefore inopportune for the time being to admit the Congo into the OCAM. See *Presse du Cameroun* (Yaounde), 11 July 1965.

[31] *The Western Hemisphere Idea: Its Rise and Decline* (Ithaca, New York: Cornell University Press, 1954), p. 30.

Chapter Eight

[1] Speech of the Rt Hon. Oliver Stanley to the American Outpost, London, on 19 March 1945. See *British Speeches of the Day* (London: British Information Services, 1945), pp. 318–20. This quotation, and much of the material for the rest of this chapter, is drawn from my article 'The United Nations and Some African Political Attitudes', *International Organization*, Vol. XVIII, No. 3, Summer 1964.

[2] E.H. Carr, *The Twenty Years' Crisis* (London: Macmillan, 1948), p. 86.

[3] Stanley, *loc. cit.*

[4] Carr, *loc. cit.*

[5] *Ibid.* I have not overlooked the fact that internationalist values are sometimes invoked for tactical reasons rather than out of genuine conviction.

[6] Taken from the opening lines of reaffirmation of the United Nations Charter.

[7] Text given in Robert A. Goldwin with Ralph Lerner and Gerald Stourzh (ed.), *Readings in World Politics*, p. 539. The interpretation of the Charter in moral terms is by no means peculiar to 'the Bandung spirit'. At the time of the Suez crisis Mr Rodriguez-Fabreget of Uruguay described the Charter as 'the deepest expression of human conscience'. (General Assembly *Official Records* [first special session], p. 55, paragraph 115.) But what 'the Bandung spirit' best illustrates is the emphasis on the proposition that colonial rule itself offended 'human conscience' and was not adequately consistent with the Charter.

[8] See, for example, Clyde Eagleton, 'Excesses of Self-determination', *Foreign Affairs*, July 1953 (Vol. 31, No. 4), pp. 592–604. He said, 'If the decision on such a claim is made by the United Nations, it is no longer correct to speak of self-determination.' He was sorry to see the United Nations becoming 'the midwife of all groups desiring to be politically born'. Up to 1964, however, it was possible for an article in an African newspaper to start with the words: 'The United Nations is preparing to renew its annual campaign to end colonial rule throughout the world.' See Gerald Ratzin, 'The U.N. Fights Colonialism', *Uganda Argus*, 25 January 1964.

[9] See my observations in the *Sunday News* (Dar-es-Salaam), 24 November 1963.

[10] This is quite apart from trying to deter others from doing the same.

[11] From the lines of reaffirmation opening the Charter.

[12] Hans Morgenthau has argued in these terms: 'Our foreign policy

since the end of the two World Wars has had the overall objective to prevent a change in the territorial status quo. The rationale for this policy is sound: a change in the status quo by force or likely to lead to the use of force can no longer be tolerated in the atomic age. The flaw which invalidates the policy is the refusal to recognize that not every status quo is inherently unstable, and that it is the task of foreign policy to create a status quo which is defensible because the nations directly concerned with it consider it worth defending.' (Hans J. Morgenthau, *The Impasse of American Foreign Policy* [Vol. 2 of his *Politics in the Twentieth Century*; Chicago: The University of Chicago Press, 1962], p. 69.)

[13] Even such a militantly anti-*apartheid* country as Ghana under Nkrumah was once accused of not practising the sermon of boycotting South Africa. South Africa's Eric Louw had claimed that Ghana still traded with South Africa. Ghana's Ministry of Trade issued a statement recalling that on 16 February 1961, a ban was imposed on the import of South African goods by the Ghanaian government, and in October of the same year the open licence for imports from South Africa was revoked. The statement continued: 'The effect of these two measures was immediately reflected in the trade returns.' The statistics showed that in 1960 Ghana imported goods valued at £1,300,000. In 1961 the balance of trade fell to £10,000 for imports and £228,000 for exports. In 1962 the position changed 'out of all proportion' – Ghana's imports from South Africa totalled only £33 and her exports to South Africa amounted to £50. The statement explained that the figures for 1962 comprised 'personal effects of South African citizens resident in Ghana as well as the return to South Africa of spare parts previously bought'. (*Ghana Today*, 18 December 1963 [Vol. 7, No. 21], p. 2).

[14] Cited in Julius Stone, *Aggression and World Order* (London: Stevens, under the auspices of the London Institute of World Affairs, 1958), p. 165, footnote 29.

[15] But for a more thorough discussion of this and of what reforms are needed, see Grenville Clark and Louis B. Sohn, *World Peace Through World Law* (Cambridge, Mass.: Harvard University Press, 2nd ed. (Revised) 1960, especially pp. xx-xxii; 20–34).

[16] Home was probably worried not only about relations between the new and old states in the United Nations but also about those relations in other areas of international life. I related Home's fear to the African relations with the European Economic Community (EEC) in my article 'African Attitudes to the European Economic Community', *International Affairs* (London), *op. cit.*

[17] Carr, *op. cit.*, p. 13.

[18] Quoted in Stone, *loc. cit.*

[19] Hugh Foot said this in, among other places, a BBC overseas programme called 'African Forum'. I was present when the programme was recorded on 14 December 1962, in the BBC London Studios.

[20] For the text of Dr Nkrumah's letters to Mr Macmillan on the subject, see *Ghana Today*, 7 November 1962 (Vol. 6, No. 18).

[21] See 'The Stress is Now on Dignity', *Sunday News* (Dar-es-Salaam), 8 September 1963, p. 9.

[22] Speech at the opening of the World Assembly of Youth Seminar in Dar-es-Salaam in August 1961. See *The Second Scramble, op. cit.*

[23] Cited in *Manchester Guardian Weekly*, 1 July 1965, p. 5.

[24] Hans J. Morgenthau, *Politics Among Nations: The Struggle for Power and Peace* (2nd ed., revised and enlarged, New York: Alfred A. Knopf, 1956), esp. pp. 35–40.

[25] Edgar Snow, *China, Russia and the U.S.A., Changing Relations in a Changing World* (New York: Marzan and Munsell, 1962), p. 632.

Chapter Nine

[1] This rendering is from Hans Kohn, *World Order in Historical Perspective* (Cambridge, Mass.: Harvard University Press, 1942), pp. 141–2.

[2] See George Bennett (ed.), *The Concept of Empire: Burke to Attlee, 1774–1947* (London: Black, 1953), p. 138. Lord Milner put it thus: 'Pax Britannica is essential to the maintenance of civilised conditions of existence among one-fifth of the human race', cited by Margery Perham, *Colonial Reckoning, op. cit.*, p. 19.

[3] *The Concept of Empire, ibid.*, p. 316.

[4] See Margery Perham, *Lugard: The Years of Authority*, 1898–1945, *op. cit.*, p. 566.

[5] Lugard, *The Dual Mandate in British Tropical Africa, op. cit.*, p. 62.

[6] Speech at Guildhall, London, on receiving the Freedom of the City, 30 June 1943. See *British Speeches of the Day*, Vol. I, No. 5, 1943 (New York: British Information Service), p. 8.

[7] Lugard, *Federation and the Colonies*, Federal Tract No. 7, *op. cit.*, p. 5.

[8] Speech at Guildhall, *op. cit.*

[9] For the full texts of Nkrumah's letters see *Ghana Today*, 7 November 1962. For a brief statement of Nkrumah's neutralist position generally see 'Dr. Nkrumah States the Neutralist Case', *Africa Report*, Vol. 7, No. 8, August 1962.

[10] *Ghana Today, ibid.*

[11] *The Times* (London) important editorials during this period included 'China's Gain and Loss', 22 November 1962; 'India's Eddies',

1 November 1962, and 'Wooing the Neutrals', 1 December 1962. Refer also to the article by *The Times*' Delhi correspondent entitled 'India After the Fighting; 1: Need to Reconsider Non-Alignment', 31 December 1962.

[12] *East African Standard*, 13 February 1964

[13] *Ibid.*

[14] Reported in the *East African Standard*, 7 February 1964

[15] In his speech to his National Assembly asking for ratification of the merger between Zanzibar and Tanganyika, President Nyerere denied that there was any connection between the decision to unite the two countries and any threat of commitment to communism in Zanzibar. See *Sunday News* (Dar-es-Salaam) 26 April 1964. President Karume a day earlier had, however, found it relevant to stress that Zanzibar's union with Tanganyika would be 'long-lasting and non-aligned'. (*Uganda Argus*, 25 April 1964.) In Kenya the Leader of the Opposition at the time, Mr Ronald Ngala, received the news of the proposed merger with the comment: 'I hope . . . that the overseas influence infiltrated into Zanzibar will not spread to Tanganyika in any malicious way.' (*Uganda Argus*, 25 April 1964).

[16] See editorial in *East African Standard*, 5 March 1964. The emphasis is mine. The Fabian Commonwealth Bureau had had a different conception of the Commonwealth in this regard. 'For us the Commonwealth is not primarily a mutual defence pact, nor even an association of exactly like-minded states. It is, or should be, a weapon in the war against war.' See 'Commonwealth and Neutralism', *Venture*, Journal of the Fabian Commonwealth Bureau, Vol. 13, No. 9, October 1961. This was a month following the Belgrade Conference of the Non-aligned that year.

[17] *East African Standard*, 8 February 1964.

[18] Henry Tanner's dispatch, *New York Times*, 25 March 1962. A revealing foil is perhaps the Guinean army. See Victor D. DuBois, 'The Role of the Army in Guinea', *Africa Report*, Vol. 8, No. 1, January 1963. A year later the journal published a useful survey of the state of the military in the continent as a whole. See George Weeks, 'The Armies of Africa', *Africa Report*, Vol. 9, No. 1, January 1964.

[19] See dispatch from Peter Mansfield, *Sunday Times* (London), 6 January 1963.

[20] See *The Arab Review*, Vol. II, No. 16, 1961.

[21] The two levels of sovereignty are discussed more fully in Chapter V and in my article 'Consent, Colonialism and Sovereignty', *Political Studies*, Vol. II, No. 1, February 1963.

[22] See 'Soldiers Outside Politics?' *West Africa*, No. 2494, 20 March, 1965.

[23] Speech on Imperial Defence, 30 June 1897. Printed in Imperial Federation (Defence) Committee pamphlet (1897): *The Colonies and the Navy*, p. 20. See Bennett, *Concept of Empire, op. cit.*, pp. 322–3.

[24] Cited by the Lukiiko of Buganda in their 1960 memorandum to the British Queen seeking independence. See David E. Apter, *The Political Kingdom in Uganda, op. cit.*, Appendix, pp. 480–1.

[25] We discussed this point more fully in the chapter on racial sovereignty. 'Abyssinia – for many reasons connected with its history ... and its sturdy assertion of independence, deserves more than any other state to preserve her independence. . . .' Sir Harry Johnston, *The Colonization of Africa by Alien Races, op. cit.*, pp. 277–8. We might also remind ourselves that Frederick Starr, in the first of his articles on the Congo for the *Chicago Tribune* in 1907, talked about the imperial assumption that 'civilized folk have a perfect right to interfere with any native tribe too weak to resist encroachment.' See *Chicago Tribune*, 20 January 1907, *op. cit.*

[26] Reported in the *Mombasa Times* (Kenya), 22 February 1964.

[27] *East African Standard*, 27 January 1964.

[28] See *Mass Education in African Society, op. cit.*

[29] *Nationalism in Colonial Africa, op. cit.*, p. 142.

[30] *West Africa and the Commonwealth* (London: Penguin African Series, 1957), p. 14.

[31] *The Colonial Reckoning*, p. 49. Also see Walter Wallbank, *Contemporary Africa*, Anvil Original No. 15 (Princeton, New Jersey: van Nostrand, 1956), p. 52.

Chapter Ten

[1] See *Uganda Argus*, 27 June 1964.

[2] Although the significance of the Security Council has not formed a part of this analysis, there are important implications in African demands for effective representation on that body. For one thing, the military insecurity sensed by individual African countries often arises out of relations with other African countries: Morocco and Algeria; Ethiopia and Somalia; Kenya and Somalia; Rwanda and Burundi. The Security Council can thus assume an intra-African significance when a crisis arises. Emperor Haile Selassie once said in Addis Ababa that Africans were now prepared and able to settle African quarrels – but then went on to add that 'the United Nations represents the best and perhaps the last hope for peace in the modern world.' (*Uganda Argus* [Kampala], 22 November 1963).

[3] K. C. Wheare, *Federal Government* (3rd ed.: London: Oxford University Press [under the auspices of the Royal Institute of International Affairs], 1962), p. 37.

[4] Spaak complained at the United Nations about the lack of a clear-cut definition of 'neo-colonialism'. His intention was apparently to suggest that the term was meaningless, *The Times* (London), 2 October 1962. See 'Neo-Dependency and Africa's Fragmentation', pp. 74–77 above.

[5] Wheare, *loc. cit.* Author's italics.

[6] E. H. Carr, *Conditions of Peace* (London: Macmillan, 1942), p. 56. These points are also discussed in my article 'The United Nations and Some African Political Attitudes', *op. cit.*

[7] *Ibid.*, p. 60.

[8] A discussion of the distinction occurs in Tom Soper, *Commonwealth and Common Market: Economic Implications* (London: Fabian Commonwealth Bureau, September 1962), pp. 12–13.

[9] See Thomas Balogh, 'Africa and the Common Market', *Journal of Common Market Studies*, Vol. I, No. 1, Summer 1962, p. 101.

[10] See *The Times* (London), 24 November 1962.

[11] Aaron Segal has argued, however, that the new Convention of Association provides no incentive for the expansion of inter-African trade. On the contrary, 'in some instances it provides a disincentive in the expansion of inter-African trade by impeding regional industrialization.' See his 'Africa Newly Divided?', *Journal of Modern African Studies*, Vol. 2, No. 1, March 1964, esp. pp. 87–9. For an earlier view of the *unifying* potential of African association with the EEC see Tom Soper, 'Africa and the Common Market', *The Listener*. See also his *Commonwealth and Common Market, loc. cit.*

[12] See Aaron Segal, 'East Africa and the EEC', *Kenya Weekly News*, 13 November 1964.

[13] See the collection of documents entitled *The Conference of Heads of State or Government of Non-Aligned Countries, September 1–6, 1961, op. cit.*, p. 256.

[14] *Ibid.*, p. 255.

Chapter Eleven

[1] George Padmore discusses communism and Pan-Negroism in his book *Pan-Africanism or Communism? The Coming Struggle for Africa.* Consult also Colin Legum, *Pan-Africanism. A short Political Guide*; and Wilson Record, *Race and Radicalism: The NAACP and the Communist Party in Conflict* (Ithaca, N.Y.: Cornell University Press, 1964). For

useful background see also G. Hall, *Marxism and Negro Liberation* (New York: New Century Publishers, 1951) and *The American Negro in the Communist Party*, Committee on Un-American Activities, U.S. House of Representatives, Washington D.C., 1954.

[2] *Stride Toward Freedom* (New York: Ballantine Books, 1958), p. 73.

[3] See Colin Legum, *Pan-Africanism*. See also Padmore's *Pan-Africanism or Communism?*, p. 379. Also Julius Nyerere, 'A United States of Africa', *The Journal of Modern African Studies*, Vol. I, No. 1, March 1963.

[4] Examples of federalist language in African discussions on unity are numerous. These include Nkrumah's *Africa Must Unite*, *op. cit.*; Awolowo, *Awo* (Autobiography), *op. cit.*, esp. chapters 12–16; Nnamdi Azikiwe, 'The Future of Pan-Africanism', *Présence Africaine*, Vol. 12, No. 40, First Quarter 1962.

[5] In French-speaking Africa anti-Americanism is, in some ways, an earlier phenomenon. The earlier institutional connection between the mass party of French-speaking Africa and the Communist Party of France had some anti-American implications. But this aspect was not particularly important to the great majority of African nationalists. Mention must also be made of the significance of racialism in the United States in conditioning African attitudes to the United States. But in the colonial days this was so much a part of white racial arrogance at large in different parts of the world that it was not distinctively 'anti-American'.

[6] See, for example, *Uganda Argus*, 15 February 1965. A month earlier – before the bombing of two Uganda villages by Congolese government forces in American-made planes – Uganda's Minister of State at the time, Mr Grace Ibingira, said: 'The late President Kennedy demanded the Soviet withdrawal from Cuba on the grounds that Cuba was in the American sphere of influence. . . . What is wrong when African states demand to be responsible for the solution of the Congolese problem, since the Congo both geographically and even politically is naturally tied to them?' – *Uganda Argus*, 15 January 1965.

[7] With Dorothy Pizer, Padmore once wrote *How Russia Transformed Her Colonial Empire*. But of greater interest is Padmore's chapter on 'Communism and Black Nationalism' in his *Pan-Africanism or Communism? op. cit.* See also the brief biographical note on Padmore in Franz Ansprenger's 'African Profiles', *Survey*, A Journal of Soviet and East European Affairs, No. 43, August 1962, pp. 84–6.

[8] See chapter on 'Political Parties' in Virginia Thompson and Richard Adloff, *French West Africa* (London: Allen & Unwin, 1958). See also Thomas Hodgkin and Ruth Schachter, 'French-Speaking West Africa in Transition', *International Conciliation*, No. 528 (May 1960). See also

Ruth Schachter Morgenthau, *Political Parties in French-Speaking Africa* (Oxford: The Clarendon Press, 1964).

[9] Virginia Thompson and Richard Adloff, *op. cit.*, chapter 3 and 4. Hodgkin and Schachter, *op. cit.* See especially Chapter III on 'West Africans in the French Parliament', Morgenthau, *op. cit.*, pp. 75–124.

[10] *Pan-Africanism or Communism?*, *op. cit.*, p. 379.

[11] Cited by Mary Holdsworth, 'Soviet Writings on Africa–II', *Contact*, Summer 1961, pp. 15–17.

[12] Cited by Edgar Snow, *The Other Side of the River: Red China Today* (New York: Random House, 1962), p. 646.

[13] See *Uganda Argus*, 29 May 1964.

[14] See *Reporter*, East Africa's Fortnightly Magazine, 11 September 1964, p. 13.

[15] *Ibid.* Also see *East African Standard*, 23 October 1964.

[16] The author had a brief discussion with the late Malcolm X in Harlem in 1961 on the subject of Islamic solidarity. Malcolm, who was later assassinated, was in 1961 second in command in the 'Black Muslim' movement.

[17] Nkrumah, *Autobiography*, *op. cit.*, pp. 53–4. The italics are Nkrumah's.

[18] *New World A-Coming* (Dutton), p. 76. Cited by George Padmore, *Pan-Africanism or Communism?*, p. 95.

[19] See the general conclusion in W. E. B. Dubois, *Black Reconstruction in America* 1860–1880, p. 728.

[20] Padmore, *Pan-Africanism or Communism?*, p. 295.

[21] Sir Frederick D. Lugard, 'The White Man's Task in Tropical Africa', *Foreign Affairs*, October 1926. Reprinted in Philip W. Quigg (ed.), *Africa: A Foreign Affairs Reader*, pp. 9–10.

[22] See Paul-Marc Henry's comment on these remarks by DuBois in Henry's 'Pan-Africanism: A Dream Come True', *Foreign Affairs*, October 1959. Quigg, *op. cit.*, p. 161.

[23] See Leon M. S. Slawecki, 'The Two Chinas in Africa', *Foreign Affairs*, Vol. 41, No. 2, January 1963.

[24] See Walter Z. Laqueur, 'Communism and Nationalism in Tropical Africa', *Foreign Affairs*, July 1961. Quigg, *op. cit.*, pp. 189–190. Colin Legum observed more recently 'The Chinese are liberal in the payments to individuals selected by them as useful allies. . . . Large sums have been paid to individual politicians in Zanzibar.' See 'Peking's Strategic Priorities', *Africa Report*, Vol. 10, No. 1, January 1965, p. 21.

[25] The statement was issued on 10 September 1964.

[26] This statement was issued on 8 September 1964, and reported in East Africa.

²⁷ Robert A. Scalapino, *On the Trail of Chou En-lai in Africa* (Santa Monica, California: The Rand Corporation, 1964), p. v.

²⁸ See Fellows' dispatch 'Chou's Visit Perils East Africa Unity', *New York Times*, 8 June 1965.

²⁹ 'Peking's Strategic Priorities', *loc. cit.*

³⁰ The other sensitive subject was the 'hospitality' extended by Nkrumah's Ghana to rebels from her neighbours. See Victor T. Le Vine, 'New Directions for French-speaking Africa?', *Africa Report*, *op. cit.* For the more purely Pan-African implications of the conference see also 'UAMCE back to UAM?' *West Africa*, 13 February 1965, p. 175, and 'UAMCE into OCAM' 20 February 1965, p. 203.

³¹ See *Manchester Guardian Weekly*, 1 July 1965.

Chapter Twelve

¹ See the collection of speeches and other conference documents, *Addis Ababa Summit*, 1963, *op. cit.*, p. 102.

² Jomo Kenyatta, *Facing Mount Kenya* (first published 1938) (London: Secker and Warburg, 1959), p. 199. The initiation ceremonies have been simplified since then.

³ *Ibid.*, p. 212.

⁴ See George Padmore (ed.), *History of the Pan-African Congress*, *op. cit.*, pp. 22–3.

⁵ See Max Weber, 'Politics as a Vocation', H. H. Gerth and C. Wright Mills (eds.), *From Max Weber: Essays in Sociology* (New York: Oxford University Press [Galaxy Book] 1958), pp. 77–8. Gabriel A. Almond has broadened Weber's definition in order to include types of political organization other than the state. See Almond's 'Introduction' to Gabriel A. Almond and James S. Coleman (eds.), *The Politics of the Developing Areas* (Princeton: Princeton University Press, 1960), pp. 6–7.

⁶ See Eric Stokes, *The Political Ideas of English Imperialism*, an Inaugural Lecture given at the University College in Salisbury, Rhodesia (Oxford University Press, 1960), esp. pp. 21–33. See also Ernest Barker, *Ideas and Ideals of the British Empire* (Cambridge: Cambridge University Press, 1941), esp. pp. 61–70; 139–64.

⁷ *Harijan* (Ahmedabad), 30 June 1946. See also Haridas T. Muzumdar (ed.), *Sermon on the Sea* (Chicago: Universal Publishing Co., 1924).

⁸ See Speeches, *Positive Action Conference on Peace and Security in Africa*, *op. cit.*, p. 4. Other African leaders who have paid tribute to Gandhi include Jomo Kenyatta, Tom Mboya, Rashidi Kawawa and Kenneth Kaunda. See *Africa Quarterly* (New Delhi), Vol. II, No. 2,

July–September 1962. See also Gandhi, *Satyagraha in South Africa*, translated from the Gujarati by Valji Govindji Desai (Madras: S. Ganesan, 1926).

[9] Kenyatta has felt that the entire interpretation of the Bible as propagated by Europeans was calculated to vindicate the superiority of whiteness over blackness. The forces of evil were 'black', the angels 'white'. In January 1962 Kenyatta called for a reinterpretation of Christianity and for a reversal of symbolism as between those two colours. See *The Guardian* (Manchester), 30 January 1962.

[10] Quoted in the *New York Times*, 19 March 1961. See my article, 'Africa and the Egyptians' Four Circles', *African Affairs, op. cit.*

[11] E. H. Carr, *The Twenty-Years Crisis, op. cit.*

[12] *Stride Towards Freedom, op. cit.*, pp. 76–7.

[13] *Ibid.*

[14] *Young India*, 1924–1926 (Madras: S. Ganesan, 1927), pp. 839–40. Consult also Pyarelal, 'Gandhiji and the African Question', *Africa Quarterly*, Vol. II, No. 2, July–September 1962. See as well the selection from Gandhi entitled 'Mahatma Gandhi on Freedom in Africa', *Africa Quarterly*, Vol. 1, No. 2, July–September 1961. For a more extensive discussion by Gandhi on non-violence consult Gandhi, *Non-Violence in Peace and War* (2nd ed.) (Ahmedabad: Navajivan Publishing House, 1944).

[15] Jawaharlal Nehru, 'Portuguese Colonialism: An Anachronism', *Africa Quarterly*, Vol. 1, No. 3, October–December, 1961, p. 9. See also Nehru, 'Emergent Africa', *Africa Quarterly*, Vol. 1, No. 1, April–June, 1961, pp. 7–9.

[16] *Harijan*, 14 March 1936.

[17] See *Black Government*, Lusaka: United Society for Christian Literature, 1960.

[18] *Autobiography, op. cit.*, p. 92.

[19] The *Morning Telegraph*, 27 June 1949.

[20] See *Uganda Argus*, 29 May 1964.

[21] *Harijan*, 14 October 1939.

[22] Tanganyika *Assembly Debates*, Thirty-Sixth Session (sixth meeting), 30 November 1961. Cols. 18, 20.

[23] See *The Second Scramble, op. cit.*, p. 7.

[24] This point is discussed in a different context in my article 'Tanzania Versus East Africa: A Case of Unwitting Federal Sabotage', *The Journal of Commonwealth Political Studies, op. cit.*

[25] *The Second Scramble, op. cit.*

[26] M. Janowitz, *The Military in the Political Development of New Nations* (Chicago: Chicago University Press, 1964), p. 100.

[27] Reported in the *Mombasa Times* (Kenya), 22 February 1964.

[28] For Nyerere's sense of 'national humiliation' at having had to use non-African troops consult his opening speech to the OAU meeting he had called. For the text of the speech see *East African Standard*, 13 February 1964.

[29] See UN Document No. A/PV 860, 18 September 1960, p. 81.

[30] Address to the resumed session of the United Nations General Assembly, 7 March 1961. See the edition issued by the Ghana Ministry of Information, p. 8.

[31] *Ibid.*

[32] In Europe, of course, employing soldiers of fortune used to be a long-established tradition in warfare. One of its remnants today is the idea of Swiss Guards for the Pope. A more operative survival is the French Foreign Legion. A reviewer of Patrick Turnbull's *The Foreign Legion* (London: Heinemann, 1964) said in the East African news magazine, *Reporter*, in January 1965, 'The French Foreign Legion, which is now a dwindling force, is basically an army of mercenaries. This is, of course, a dirty word today, although why it should be worse to kill one's fellow men for money than to kill them for nothing is never clearly explained.' (*Reporter*, 29 January 1965, p. 7.)

[33] All this is *assuming* that the mercenaries would have been no more ruthless in their treatment of their opponents than native troops would have been.

[34] Reproduced in Ghana Government's W.P. No. 6/60, p. 8.

[35] For resolutions of conference see Colin Legum, *Pan-Africanism*, *op. cit.*, Appendix 22.

[36] See Mboya, 'Vision of Africa', in *Africa Speaks*, *op. cit.*, pp. 22–3.

[37] See *Addis Ababa Summit*, 1963, *op. cit.* The emphasis is mine.

[38] The nine members of the Committee appointed were Algeria. Congo (Leopoldville), Ethiopia, Guinea, Nigeria, Senegal, Tanganyika, Uganda and the United Arab Republic. It was decided that the Head-quarters of this Liberation Committee was to be Dar-es-Salaam. *Ibid.*, p. 101.

[39] *Ibid.*, p. 10.

[40] See *Mombasa Times*, 11 January 1962.

[41] Speech by Nkrumah. See *Ghana Today*, 21 January 1962. Refer also to Nehru, 'Portuguese Colonialism: An Anachronism'. Of historical interest also is Gandhi's *Goan Struggle for Freedom* (Ahmedabad: Navajivan Publishing House, 1954, reprint).

[42] Radio Tanzania, 31 May 1965. See BBC Monitoring Records, ME/1874/B/3.

[43] Radio Tanzania, 11 June 1965. See BBC Monitoring Records, ME/1883/B/2.

INDEX

References in the Notes (bibliographical references excepted) have
been indexed with the page numbers in *italics*.